ROMAN
HOLIDAY

ROMAN HOLIDAY

THE SECRET LIFE OF HOLLYWOOD IN ROME

CAROLINE YOUNG

The
History
Press

Cover illustrations: *Front*: Photo 12/Alamy Stock Photo. *Back*: Anita Ekberg. (Author's collection)

First published 2018

The History Press
The Mill, Brimscombe Port
Stroud, Gloucestershire, GL5 2QG
www.thehistorypress.co.uk

British Library Cataloguing in Publication Data.
A catalogue record for this book is available from the British Library.

ISBN 978 0 7509 8278 8

Typesetting and origination by The History Press
Printed and bound in Great Britain by TJ International Ltd

CONTENTS

PROLOGUE

The outdoor cafés of the Via Veneto, one of the most exclusive streets in Rome, filled up early as well-dressed society people, starlets and tourists sipped on a Bellini or a Negroni beside the potted azaleas and tightly parked scooters that lined the pavement. By 7 p.m. the city was soaked in the last of the day's sunlight, its golden domes glowing beneath the sunset as the scent of Coco Chanel and cigarette smoke drifted amongst the tree-shaded tables. Well-known faces were commonplace, and the chatter grew louder as the evening progressed, trying to be heard over the roar of traffic. The word on everyone's lips in 1962 was the affair between Elizabeth Taylor and Richard Burton on the set of *Cleopatra*. Despite both being married, they flaunted their affair on the Via Veneto, the beating heart of Rome's celebrity culture, in the elegant white tableclothed restaurants on colourful, lively Piazza Navona, looking out onto the fountain with its Egyptian obelisk, or they indulged in secret kisses in their dressing gowns on the Cinecittà backlot. All the while the relentless, cunning paparazzi came up with even more inventive ways of capturing the romance.

Movie stars like Elizabeth Taylor or Ava Gardner, beautiful, impulsive and living the good life, were easy targets for the press in Italy when away from the protective grip of Hollywood, and Rome had become a free-for-all. Back in the States, the studios could build their own myths around their stars which the American movie magazines would happily support, whilst press agents were used to being able to suppress the bad publicity. But in Rome the new wave of independent press photographers, ambitious self-starters who had no such loyalties and needed only a light 35mm camera, a Vespa and a good eye for a story, could sell the most scandalous photos to the highest-bidding publication. Suddenly, the stars of the screen seemed a little more human.

The photographers in their crumpled suits were stereotypically aggressive and rude and whilst it wasn't until 1960, with the release of Federico Fellini's *La Dolce Vita*, that they would collectively be known as 'paparazzi', they were a common and feared sight for celebrities around Rome. Tazio Secchiaroli, Velio Cioni, Elio Sorci, Marcello Geppetti – these were some of the photographers who 'must be seen in action to be believed', as an American journalist in the late 1950s noted. Using twin-lens Rolliflexes with a hand-held flash, they had to get as close to their subjects as possible, and this created the startled shots that were so typical of the era. After they had taken snatch shots, the photographers would go to the telephoto window at the central post office in Piazza San Silvestro and they would pay $20 to develop their film and send the images to Fleet Street in London as exclusives.

The happenings of Rome could be relied upon to fill the papers in every country on every day of the week, whether it was fights, secret weddings, public break-ups, or even murder trials, like that of Wilma Montesi. She was a young woman whose body was found on a beach near Rome in April 1953. Her death was linked to the upper echelons of society, and the secretive drugs and sex parties of society people and politicians. Life in Rome seemed more dramatic than the movies themselves.

La dolce vita grew out of the ruins of post-war Italy, where the glamour of celebrity offered a much needed escape from the memories of the bombings, the food shortages and of a country very much at breaking point. And it was Italian actresses, as well as Hollywood stars, who would be at the vanguard. Producers Carlo Ponti and

Dino De Laurentiis invested in Italian cinema and multinational productions, pushing up the reputation of Italian-made film.

In the 1950s, Rome had become a place where people could finally celebrate the good times following the Second World War, and when the international film studios began to use Cinecittà for their sword and sandal epics, along came the Hollywood stars to enjoy their drinks on piazzas, the sun sparkling on the water as it splashed from ancient fountains surrounded by ancient symbols of its former empire. Parties took place across Rome in penthouse hotel rooms, rooftop terraces with views of terracotta tiles and shimmering renaissance domes, ivy-covered villas along the Appian Way and artist's studios in the bohemian Via Margutta. But the centre of celebrity life was the Via Veneto, which since the end of the Second World War had become Rome's fashionable street, defined by new notions of fame as cinema stars, tourists and the press collided. People spilled out into the street and rested under the parasols of the outdoor tables, almost like it was a 'seaside resort', as Ennio Flaiano observed in 1958.

By the mid 1950s the three blocks of Via Veneto situated between the Aurelian Wall and US Embassy had become an exclusive strip of luxury hotels, clubs and cafés populated by the rich, the famous and the fame-hungry. The notable sights included the Hotel Excelsior, the Café de Paris, the Bar Rosati, Harry's Bar and the all-night drugstore L'Alka Seltzer. Bricktop, owned by the legend of 1920s Paris, Ada 'Bricktop' Smith, was fashioned like a prohibition-era drinking den, creating a sense of the illicit with jazz music and cigarette smoke seeping out of it, its glamorous aura drifting out into the street.

If Italian cities like Milan and Rome were gradually embracing the economic boom of the 1950s, then the Via Veneto was the heightened symbol of the new affluence. Traffic clogged the streets as Fiats, horse-drawn carriages, Vespa scooters, taxis and buses all travelled up and down this half-mile stretch. It was here that you could see Clint Eastwood skateboarding down the road, Anita Ekberg drunk and barefoot, Jayne Mansfield eating spaghetti, or the early sixties chi-chis with their animal-print coats or their tamed leopards on a lead. It was the glittering, hedonistic heart of Italy, where the wealthy and connected could congregate before heading off for romantic weekends in a smart hotel on the Amalfi coast or to find some respite on a yacht moored off the Isle of Capri.

The 1940s and 1950s was considered 'the Flash Age' of agency photographers whose close-up images created a sense of reality, a moment captured in time, rather than the atificiality of posed photos. However it was in the 1960s, the Richard Burton and Elizabeth Taylor era, where the telephoto became more common. Taylor and Burton marked the modern era of celebrity, of packs of paparazzi, long-lens snatch shots on the front pages of tabloids and illicit love affairs. Their extravagant lifestyle was firmly played out in public, travelling the world with an entourage and where Rome served as a base for their fast, expensive life. Elizabeth collected expensive jewels, they holidayed on yachts with Onassis and held Paris dinners with the Windsors and Rothschilds. The grainy photos taken from the shoreline while the rich and famous frolicked and sunbathed on the deck of their yachts became a mainstay for photographers of that era.

But what really defined the paparazzi was the way they created the story by triggering their subjects. Photographers realised that an action photo of a celebrity under attack or being chased made a more valuable picture than those posed photos outside cafés. It became a game, of provoking the stars to react – of sneaking into Cinecittà and hiding in boxes or under cars, of climbing into the trees around Elizabeth Taylor's pool to find that lucrative shot. The photographers were mostly poor young men who found a way to make money and to feed their family, and their subjects were the rich and famous – illustrating the gap in wealth of the era. And with a never-ending stream of famous faces drifting into view, Rome was ripe with opportunities.

In the 1950s, it was advantageous for Hollywood to film overseas, where they could access their frozen profits in local currency, and where they could fully promote exotic scenery with widescreen and Technicolor formats. At the time, anyone living out of the States for eighteen months at a time would also avoid paying tax. So here you would find Ingrid Bergman, under self-imposed exile after coming to Rome for love; Audrey Hepburn, who represented joyful holidays in the city in the early 1950s; Ava Gardner, whose tempestuous love life and appreciation of the nightlife always served for a good photo; Elizabeth Taylor, the queen of Hollywood excess and jet-set lifestyle; and Anita Ekberg, the face and body of *la dolce vita*. Sophia Loren was the home-grown star who captivated Hollywood and who represented the struggles and dream of young girls who survived the Second World War and lived through Rome's 1950s recovery, and Anna Magnani, the icon of Italian neorealism and one of the most admired, revered women in the country.

1

ROMILDA

Like many young girls growing up after the First World War, Romilda Villani dreamt of experiencing the glamour and excitement of the movies. She was from the small fishing village of Pozzuoli, 25km along the coast from Naples and built on the volcanic rock of the mighty Vesuvius. It was a place of myth, the location of the entrance to Dante's inferno, where the sea crashed against the rocky cliffs during stormy winters and where residents could feel the shuddering movement under their feet from the magma flowing beneath them.

Romilda had the enigmatic beauty of Greta Garbo, the most popular movie star in the early 1930s. She plucked her eyebrows into Garbo's crescent shape, wore her hair shoulder length and with a side parting just like Garbo, and owned a camel-coloured coat that she could wear the Garbo way, with the collar turned up. Such was the similarity that people even stopped her on the street to ask for her autograph. Romilda was also a talented pianist, having studied piano at Naples's conservatoire San Pietro a Maiella, and she could dance, which surely put her in a good standing for going into show business.

When the American film studio MGM held a contest in 1932 to find the Italian Garbo, 17-year-old Romilda jumped at the chance to enter, and she won the prize – a ticket to Hollywood to take a screen test at MGM. It may have been her dream come true, but her mother refused to let her daughter go overseas. America was too far away and too dangerous, and Romilda was too young.

Despondent at not being able to go to Hollywood, she walked along the waterfront of the town she had grown up in, dreaming of her escape to Rome, the next best place to go to after America. Romilda had heard that aspiring actresses could be discovered in the capital. At this time, in the early 1930s, the cinema was one of the few ways for finding fame and fortune. Once Romilda had saved enough money from playing and teaching piano, she bought a train ticket and headed for the eternal city. The Rome she arrived in was under the leadership of Benito Mussolini, who had ambitions to create a new Italian empire.

Mussolini and around 30,000 of his Blackshirts marched into Rome in 1922 and he was quickly given power by King Victor Emmanuel III to form part of a new coalition government. His promises were as authoritarian as the manner of his arrival, with emphasis on law and order, the promise of more rights for war veterans and above all the burning desire to create a stronger nation. He was a ruthless man, and by 1925 he had seized complete power, creating a police state and purging the country of all opposition. As part of Mussolini's new plans, Rome would be a beacon that shone across Italy.

But an awe-inspiring city needed a large population, and from 1920 to the mid 1930s the population of Rome doubled to over 1 million people as he encouraged citizens from across the nation to migrate to the city. With the huge increase in population came domestic challenges, and there was a housing shortage as families were crammed into apartments. When Mussolini's plans for fascist Rome were officially adopted in 1931, they involved measures to address the population swell: the creation of new expansion zones and a modern rail network, hospitals, schools and covered markets. New housing projects sprung up during the 1930s, creating communities in apartment blocks on the outskirts of town, which lost a degree of connection with the historic past of the city. The implementation of the new Roman city plan was considered by Mussolini to be a 'bloodless battle' which would start 'the fatherland towards a brighter future'.

Il Duce ordered ground to be cleared to create a highway through the ancient city, linking it to the Piazza Venezia where he could stand high on his balcony, delivering his speeches to the crowds below.

Mussolini also had a keen interest in cinema. Italy in the thirties was the world's third largest exporter of films despite the dominance of American studios and the challenges that came with the introduction of sound, as new technology had to be developed accordingly. When Mussolini came to power, his plan was to completely reinvigorate film-making as a tool for propaganda. 'Cinema is the most powerful weapon' was Mussolini's slogan as he pushed ahead for an Italian film centre. He saw film-making's power to influence the population, as Hitler and Goebbels had managed to formidable effect in Germany.

He introduced the first Venice Film Festival in 1932, founded the Centro Sperimentale film school in 1935 and his next plan was to create a studio centre in Rome which could compete with Hollywood. Cinecittà, or 'cinema city', was officially opened to great fanfare by Mussolini in 1937. Despite its later reputation as a propaganda machine, Cinecittà churned out 279 films from 1937 to its temporary closure in 1943. Out of this number were 142 historical films, 120 comedies and 17 propaganda films such as *Scipio L'Africano*, which justified Mussolini's invasion of Ethiopia. Just like in Hollywood films of the same era, there was a fashion for movies showing the dreams of the poor, with lonely shop girls finding love and rising up the ranks, or epic historic dramas that told tales of ancient Rome. Popular 'Telefoni Bianchi' films were light-hearted comedies set in lavish drawing rooms and with conservative values to appease government control. In 1941 alone, 424 million cinema tickets were sold in Italy.

But in 1933, when Romilda was looking for work, Cinecittà Studios was still to be built. She found a job at a variety show at the Adriano theatre, and where she dressed in a costume like that of Garbo in *Queen Christina*, the sixteenth-century Swedish queen. In her free time, she strolled in her camel coat, turning heads with her movie-star appearance as she browsed the shop windows in the elegant Prati district. One evening in the autumn of 1933 Romilda was walking on Via Coli di Rienzo when a handsome, charming and aristocratic-looking man called Riccardo Scicolone sparked up a conversation and told her he was in the film business. He asked her out on a date, and Romilda was pleased that she not only had someone she could spend time with in the city, but who had promised to help champion her career. In reality Riccardo was poor and unemployed despite having claim to an aristocratic title, and was more suited to ingratiating himself in the world of show business and meeting young and beautiful starlets like Romilda. As was the fate of many girls at the time, she was seduced and then abandoned. A month after their first meeting, she broke the news to him that

> ... according to the woman she would become, 'frail and not particularly pretty'.

she was pregnant, and he wasn't quite so keen anymore. The heartbroken Romilda gave birth in the ward for unwed mothers at Rome's Santa Margherita hospital on 20 September 1934, putting an end to her dream of stardom.

Romilda's baby was named Sofia, and was, according to the woman she would become, 'frail and not particularly pretty'. Nevertheless, she would grow into the icon Sophia Loren – with the spelling of her name slightly changed – and while her birth put an end to her mother's dreams of stardom, Romilda would later dedicate herself to her daughter's career.

Riccardo had no intention of marrying Romilda – he was a lothario with his sights set on many other women – but he visited his baby in the hospital and gave her his surname, Scicolone, which made a big difference to Sofia's legitimacy. It was better an absent father than no father at all on the birth certificate.

Romilda moved into a little *pensione* in Rome, occasionally leaving Sofia in the care of her landlady while pounding the pavements looking for work. As she was living in Rome on her own, she didn't have older family members to advise her on how to care for the child. When Sofia became sick with enterocolitis, a doctor advised her that a warmer climate would be beneficial. It was now December and Rome's warm autumn had given way to a cold winter.

Romilda returned to Pozzuoli, despite the shame of being an unwed mother and the guilt of ruining her family's reputation; Sofia was so sick that she was close to death, and Romilda needed her family's help. She and Sofia were back in time for Christmas, and as soon as she arrived at the doorstep her parents, Luisa and Domenico, welcomed her with an embrace, and the local wet nurse was sent to feed up the baby. With eight people crammed into 5 Via Solfatara it was a full house, but it had a view of Pozzuoli's Roman amphitheatre from the kitchen window, while a balcony looked out over the gulf of Naples.

Grandma Luisa cared for Sofia while Romilda played piano in the cafés and trattorias of Pozzuoli and Naples. Sometimes she would visit Rome to meet up with Riccardo in the hope that she could persuade him to marry her. Following one trip to Rome in 1937, she came back pregnant by him once again – yet still she remained unmarried.

As Sofia grew older and went to school she began to feel embarrassed about not having a real father; even though her grandfather Domenico had taken on the role, everyone knew the reality. Sofia had big dark eyes and a shy smile, and she was given the nickname Toothpick because she was so skinny. Her thin arms and legs were made all the more so by the lack of food during the war, which broke out when Sofia was 6 years old.

The threat of war had been bubbling under the surface of Europe throughout the 1930s as the fascist governments of both Germany and Italy had ambitions to create their own empires through aggressive foreign policy. By 1936 Mussolini had fought and gained controlled of Ethiopia during the Second Italo-Ethiopian War, and he had his sights on spreading out the empire across the Mediterranean and North Africa.

Germany and Italy, with their shared ideology, signed a Berlin–Rome axis treaty and Italy exited the League of Nations. With this formation of an alliance with Hitler, war in Europe was inevitable for Italy. Mussolini thought the war would be over quickly and believed that once the Allies were defeated he would be able to move in on French and British colonies in Africa.

What had been promised by Mussolini before entering into the war on the side of Germany failed to come true, and his plans to create a proud new section of the city – EUR – which harked back to ancient Rome fell to ruin at the start of the war.

Italy was a country with an economy still based on agriculture, and it was quite unprepared for the requirements of battle on multiple fronts. The 1939 invasion of Albania had weakened the Italian army and their artillery and tanks had not advanced in technology since the First World War. Mussolini pushed forward in North Africa with plans to invade Egypt, but the British held their ground and pushed them back into Libya. When Italy invaded Greece from Albania, they were supported by German troops to hold off the British. Winston Churchill warned that if Athens or Cairo were damaged by Axis powers then Italy would face strong retaliation on Rome despite its ancient treasures and sanctity of the Vatican.

For Romilda and Sofia the war first seemed far away, with the first effects a trickle-down of food shortages and gradually-growing austerity measures. But then the bombing came to Pozzuoli as the Allies targeted the Port of Naples from 1940. With the sound of the air raid siren Romilda and her family would rush out of their house to find cover in the cavernous railway tunnel on the Pozzuoli to Naples line, which was also a target for the Allies. They placed their mattresses down on the gravel next to the railway tracks, and would spend hours in the dark tunnels listening to the scuttling of mice and cockroaches, the sound of airplanes roaring in the sky and the falling bombs. They had to be out of the tunnel before the first train of the day at 4.10 a.m. and during one of these scrambles Sophia tripped and fell and hit her chin on rocks, leaving a scar.

It was cold and draughty in the tunnel and the girls didn't have coats, so Romilda sacrificed one of her prize possessions, her camel coat, cutting it up and making it into two little coats for her daughters. Romilda would also take her girls to visit a friend of one of her brothers, a goat-herder who lit a fire in one of the volcanic caves along the coastline and who would give the girls a cup of nourishing goat's milk, so fresh it was still warm.

As the bombing intensified across the country transport links and water mains were destroyed, resulting in a shortage of food and water. By 1942 popular support of the war was declining. With the country close to breaking point, the Allies invading former Italian territories in North Africa and the potential invasion of Sicily, Mussolini was forced to resign by King Victor Emmanuel in 1943, and went into hiding before being shot by Partisan rebels. Desperate for an exit strategy, the new Italian government held talks with President Eisenhower and an armistice was signed with the Allies on 9 September 1943. As soon as Italy effectively switched sides, the Germans tightened their grips on the population.

Sofia saw the Germans in Pozzuoli as they marched in unison through the town. They seemed harmless to her eyes, but then she would overhear her grandparents discussing the deportations of Jews, the torture and the fears they had of what happens next, and she knew that these soldiers weren't as harmless as they seemed. In the summer of 1943 Pozzuoli was evacuated and residents were transported by train to Naples. The Villanis stayed with friends in Naples, but there were even more food shortages and limited water supplies. Sometimes Romilda would take water from the car radiator to give to her daughters, or she would beg for pieces of bread. Maria caught measles and typhus fever.

By September 1943, the Germans had marched into Rome, which fell without a struggle and was declared an Open City. For the next nine months Nazi soldiers terrorised and intimidated Rome's citizens, setting up a command centre near the Villa Borghese and at the Excelsior Hotel, on the Via Veneto, where the top officers, led by General Kurt Malzer, stayed. They held grand luncheons while 1000 Roman Jews were deported to Auschwitz over the 270 days of occupation.

The Allies fought their way up from southern Italy and swept into Naples in October 1943, and Rome was liberated in June 1944 – the first of the three Axis capitals to be taken, marking a significant victory in the war. The first to march into Naples were the Scottish regiments in their kilts, followed by the American GIs, who paraded down Via Toledo, and the crowds cheered for they knew that with the soldiers came powdered milk, coffee and white bread. The GIs gave out chocolates and chewing gum to the children as they swept into town. 'The Allies handed out real food – even white bread, which was a real luxury for us – and the farmers, little by little, began to cultivate the land again,' remembered Sophia Loren. 'But when winter came, the cold took our breath away … we'd all stay close together in the kitchen, the warmest room in the house. But outside, the world was still a daunting place.'

The Second World War had turned out to be more desolate and destructive than people could ever have imagined and as the capital, Rome was particularly dazed by war for years afterwards. 'The Rome of today is much changed from its pre-war self and the returning tourist – if such there were – would find many surprises,' *The Times* reported in February 1946. 'It is a city degraded and demoralised by the stress of war and defeat and foreign occupation, in which the stately beauty of its monuments and palaces tend to become obscured by an oppressive consciousness of the hard facts of life.'

Rome was a shell of what it had been before, its bombed-out streets filled with rubble. Instead of a carpet of wish-making coins, empty ration tins littered the basin of the Trevi Fountain, which had been turned off for the duration of the conflict. Under the threat of air raids, the city's historic sites, including Trajan's column, had been protected through the war years by bricks and concrete, which had been built up about them and were now slowly being taken down. Gas and electricity were in short supply, so cooking was carried out on charcoal or with cast-iron grates for cooking stoves, and candles and lamps used for lighting when the electricity failed. It was a tough existence, where even an apartment's water supply had to be carried up the stairs in buckets.

The hardships of the war resulted in a new type of film-making known as neorealism. The gritty genre was born from necessity due to the closure of Cinecittà after it was stripped of all its equipment by the Germans, and then turned into a centre for refugees and displaced people. Director Roberto Rossellini had begun preparing *Rome, Open City* shortly after the liberation of Rome in June 1944, but with no film industry left, everything had to be improvised and self-funded. The film was written in a week, and had a documentary style due to the shortage of film stock. People living in the poorer sections of the city were hired as actors, or lent their homes for interiors and helped behind the scenes. It was this authenticity that made the film such a success, with *The Times* hailing its depiction of Rome. 'The people are so tired, the tenements are so crowded, the children are so unruly; nerves are frayed, and the shadow of Germany is everywhere, but out of their last reserves of courage and strength men and women find enough courage to comfort one another and confound the Nazi-Fascist enemy.'

Roman actress Anna Magnani was named Best International Actress at the Venice film festival in 1947 for the role of Pina in *Open City*. Magnani's powerful scene as she runs after the truck taking away her partner, only to be shot dead by Nazi officers, stayed with the audience long after the film finished. Magnani recalled how the famous scene was filmed with real German prisoners of war playing the guards, with their own machine guns over their shoulders and wearing their own boots that crunched into the ground as they walked. It was as intense as could be without being a documentary.

Following *Rome, Open City's* success, Vittorio De Sica's 1948 film *The Bicycle Thief* was also filmed on the streets of Rome and was similarly peopled with a cast of non-professionals. It showed a city that was not only physically damaged by war, but emotionally damaged too. It was something of a paradox that, whilst Italy as the subject of neorealist film was exhausted and broken, the films themselves were rapturously received, bringing Italian cinema into a recovery period.

Sofia was 11 years old when the war ended, haunted by the horrors and still the little toothpick from the lack of food during the conflict. Romilda began playing piano again in a Naples trattoria filled with American soldiers, with Sofia's sister Maria belting out songs as accompaniment. Because the GIs enjoyed the performance so much, they were invited to their home on Sundays to sing along to Romilda playing Frank Sinatra and Ella Fitzgerald while they were served home-made cherry brandy.

At the end of the war the cinemas reopened and 11-year-old Sophia would go to the theatre to watch American films like *Duel in the Sun* with Gregory Peck or *Blood and Sand* with Rita Hayworth and Tyrone Power, one of the most handsome of on-screen lovers. In cities like Naples and Rome, suffering from food and clothing shortages, the cinema and the dance hall offered an escape from the drudgery of life.

By the spring of 1947 Sofia was maturing and her appearance had started to change: she seemed to grow into her large brown eyes, wide mouth and high cheek bones. She found herself the object of sometimes unwanted attention when she walked down the street – like for many girls, it was a shock to be suddenly stared and whistled at in the street while still very much feeling like a child. Even more of a shock was when one of her young teachers asked Sofia's family if he could marry his pupil.

Once a month Sofia would be treated to a trip to Naples for a chocolate drink with whipped cream and a sweet, doughy sfogliatella pastry at a famous chocolatier called Caflish. It was here that Sofia saw Rome's iconic actress Anna Magnani for the first time – broodingly staring down from a poster at a theatre where she was performing. She would have a huge effect on the young toothpick. For Sofia, the Rome of Anna Magnani and the movies would be a place she would soon be heading for herself, a fatherless child trying to make it as an actress and a star, who would be one of the central stars of a new age of celebrity journalism and paparazzi. Soon, Romilda and Sofia would travel to Rome together themselves, in order to help Sofia build her career.

2

TENNESSEE

Gradually sloping downhill from the gardens of the Villa Borghese to the Piazza Barberini, the tree-lined Via Veneto was built on the grounds of the Villa Ludovisi – an eighteenth-century park decorated with statues and fountains, flowered fields and pine trees, which had inconceivably been flattened in 1887 in order to create the solid stone apartment blocks of the Ludovisi neighbourhood and to build a palace for Princess Margherita of Savoy, King Victor Emmanuel's mother. The palace became the American Embassy after the fall of the Royal Family in 1946, and was used as a centre for the Allied forces as a new Italian government was formed.

In the first decades of the twentieth century, the Via Veneto was occupied by popular trattorias and shops, which drew in an eclectic crowd to its bookshops and cafés. It was where you could play a leisurely game of boules in the afternoon, browse Libreria Rossetti, the city's most prestigious bookshop and discuss politics with the intellectuals at Caffe Rosati, opened in 1911. But it was the fascists themselves who helped designate the Via Veneto as the place to be seen, with the construction of large marble buildings for government offices and hotels that were in easy reach of the outdoor cafés. In the 1920s and 1930s Mussolini's son-in-law Galeazzo Ciano enjoyed an aperitif or two at the bar of the Hotel Ambasciatori, while the Grand

Hotel was built in 1927 by Mussolini's favourite architect, Marcello Piacentini. As the Via Veneto gained a reputation as the voguish street, the 'gaga', or Italian dandy, would come there for drinks after the horse racing where they could mix with Italy's movie stars like Alida Valli and Clara Calamai.

After Italy declared war, the Via Veneto became more of a practical base. Farmers planted cabbages, tomatoes and onions in its flowerbeds, as part of Italy's 'grow more food' campaign, and then the luxury hotels became the headquarters for the Axis powers. After Rome was freed and the Germans driven out, the US army moved into the hotels instead. The Hotel Excelsior, which was nicknamed Rest Camp, was where many GIs took their first bath in years in the hotel's plush marble bathrooms. General Mark Clark still had his office there when the first tourists arrived again.

With American GIs inhabiting the post-war city, a new economy developed around their large pay packets and expendable income. Not only did they discover the joys of pizzerias, but a red-light district sprung up around the Spanish Steps. Italian women went crazy for the Americans, many leaving the country to go over to the states as post-war brides. Some poor young Italian men found work as *scattini*, or street photographers, who lingered around train stations and tourist sites looking for American soldiers or tourists to take a snapshot of. After posing for a photo, the GIs were given a card with details of where they could pick up their photo. The *scattini* would then develop their rolls of film in improvised darkrooms set up in old apartments in the historic quarter with the hope that their subject would turn up to pay for the photo. Over time there were fewer and fewer American GIs on the streets, as the city opened to tourists fascinated to see the ancient treasures and charms of a city that was recovering after having been brought to its knees. The street photographers now used their tricks on the tourists, and they could earn just about enough to live by taking their photos by the Colosseum or at the Pantheon. Some of these *scattini* would later use their skills as photo-reporters, and would find celebrity photos to be particularly lucrative.

Gathered again on the Via Veneto was a group of liberal Italian writers and journalists, including Ennio Flaiano, a friend of director Federico Fellini, who met up at the cafés of the Via Veneto, where they would discuss politics, films and books into the early hours. Flaiano remembered the smell of warm brioche in the air, how they could bicycle on the street on warm days, the breeze rustling through the plane trees that lined the street.

In Italy in the early 1950s less than 8 per cent of homes had electricity, drinking water and indoor plumbing, and more people worked in agriculture than any other sectors. Only a few years before sheep would still graze around the Pantheon, as shepherds moved their flock from the hills to the warmer lowlands. But Rome was changing. There was a sense of hope in the air as Italy tried to forget the pain and the humiliation of Mussolini's broken promises. An increased number of cars were one of the first signs of this new prosperity as they travelled out of the city at the weekends, but the city was becoming infiltrated by scooters – lightweight Vespas and Lambrettas that made it easy to travel between neighbourhoods. Young people took their holidays at the beaches of Ostia and Fregene, travelling there by tram or car and bringing paninis for their snacks, or they could enjoy seafood being caught at the beach and brought straight to their table. At weekends the *scattini* would also travel by scooter to Ostia to sell photos to the families and couples enjoying a break by the sea, eating watermelon or ice cream from one of the beach vendors.

Many young girls lived in a half-fantasy life. They admired the window displays of the elegant shops on the Via Condotti, or they could go dancing at one of the floating piers along the Tiber with their coloured lights and straw roofs. They dreamt of the magical existence they saw on screen or in magazines and, like Romilda more than a decade before, hoped they could be discovered by the film industry.

In Vittorio de Sica's 1948 film *The Bicycle Thief*, the lead character, Antonio, is putting up a poster of Rita Hayworth in *Gilda* the moment his bicycle is stolen. It was De Sica's comment on the gulf between neorealism and Hollywood, but soon the two industries would blend together. As Italy's post-war film industry flourished, Hollywood lured

Italian stars to Los Angeles, where they swapped war-torn Rome for a home with a pool in the Hollywood hills as the countries began to combine their film-making talents. Alida Valli was signed by David O. Selznick and starred in Hitchcock's *The Paradine Case* in 1946, while Valentina Cortesi and handsome Rossano Brazzi, who would play the lead in 1954's *Three Coins in the Fountain*, also tried their luck in Hollywood. And in return, the reputation of Rome's new studio facilities began attracting more and more Hollywood people to the city. Production companies could reclaim their funds that had been blocked from leaving the country before the war and take advantage of favourable exchange rates by working at the recently re-opened Cinecittà Studios.

In September 1949, the *New York Times* announced:

Postwar Italy is playing 'Hollywood' to more American film notables than ever before. Movie-makers or stars, they are finding Italy and her sun both a stimulating workshop and a pleasant vacation spot. For producers, part of Italy's lure has been the unblocking of frozen Hollywood funds. But part, too, has been Italy's own resurgence in film production. With such films as *Open City*, *Paisan*, *To Live in Peace* and *Shoeshine* having received world-wide acclaim. Whatever the reasons, Rome is today being referred to as Hollywood on the Tiber.

By 1948 Hollywood stars like Tyrone Power gathered at the tables on the Via Veneto if they were in town to work on a movie. Power flew into Rome on a goodwill trip in his own plane after being hailed as a hero during the war, and he really captured the imagination of the Italian public. Riding his big American open-top car along the Appian Way and past the Roman Forum he drew gasps from glamour-starved Roman girls, anxious to glimpse this handsome and toned star on the Via Veneto.

It was here that Tyrone met actress Linda Christian and they married in early 1949 – the first fairytale wedding after the war, which received front-page news and magazine spreads dedicated to capturing all the details for their readers. They married at the tenth-century Church of

Santa Francesca Romana overlooking the Roman Forum, which was filled with a sea of white roses. Riot police were drafted in to hold back the screaming fans. Images of Linda Christian in her Fontana-designed wedding gown emerging from the chapel were syndicated around the world, with the ancient city in all its resplendent glory. In the words of photographer Jean Howard who covered the event for *Look* magazine, it was 'the international social event of its time'. The wedding marked a new, more relaxed way of life in Rome after the hardships of war, creating an atmosphere in which the whole city could celebrate together.

The Hotel Excelsior rebuilt an annex and opened the Doney café, with its sidewalk area seating up to 400 people, which became a popular meeting place for Americans in Rome. Little round tables and chairs were lined up at the side of the building and out onto the pavement, and where the smart set would enjoy a ringside seat to see and be seen. Indeed, in 1948 Tennessee Williams described the Doney as 'the fashionable sidewalk café in front of the fashionable hotel Excelsior'. Inside the Excelsior, the American bar was nicknamed The Snake Pit as it was where many movie deals were signed.

Aldo Fabrizzi, from *Open City*, met actress Jennifer Jones on holiday during a dance in Rome. Greta Garbo was spotted on a sightseeing tour, with plans to appear in a film called *Love and Friend* – which would have been her first in eight years if she had decided to return to the screen. Garbo was reported to have tried three hotels in five days in Rome, with none pleasing her, until she settled on the Hassler, where she was spotted emerging from its revolving doors in sunglasses and a large floppy hat. Montgomery Clift was photographed in Rome during a tour of Italy in 1950. He played with children in the garden of the Villa Borghese, wandered the streets with his camera around his neck, sunbathed on a parkbench, and in Milan he met director Vittorio De Sica, who had made such a big impression with *The Bicycle Thief*.

Count Giorgio Cini, president of the company that owned the Excelsior Hotel and the Lido in Venice, fell in love with Hollywood beauty Merle Oberon. The two carried out a whirlwind European romance in Rome, Venice and the French Riviera, and created a stir because he was still married, and she was twice divorced and seven years older than him. In September 1949 the 31-year-old Count boarded his private plane in Cannes, saying goodbye to Merle as he went to Venice for a trip. But as the plane circled low so he could wave farewell to her once again, the wing suddenly dipped and it crashed to the ground, killing him on impact. Merle, who fainted on witnessing the tragedy, was said to be inconsolable.

Betty Eisner, a Red Cross nurse during the war, and later a pioneering psychologist, travelled across Europe to document its recovery through the eyes of a tourist for the *Los Angeles Times*. In Rome in April 1949, she observed that the Via Veneto was 'the winter capital of Hollywood. I can't tell you how many American, Americo-Italian and Italian films are being made here just now, and the Excelsior Hotel looks like a combination of Mike Romanoff's and the Bel Air.' She observed the city full of students, reporters and tourists, those who at first were taken aback by the late serving time of dinner, the way one had to haggle at markets and the contrast between great wealth and abject poverty. They were charmed by the groups of nuns, priests and monks gathered on the streets, the stray cats mewing for scraps of food, the quaint horse carriages carrying tourists around Rome and on the Island of Capri.

In contrast to the poverty of many Romans, the Hollywood stars at the Excelsior could enjoy imported smoked salmon and antipasto Italian style for starters, spaghetti arrabiata with clams, golden fried brains and artichokes, or calf-liver and bacon. And for dessert, crêpes Suzette and peaches cardinal. It was a tradition for Hollywood stars to go to Alfredo's for his famous fettucine and for the guest of honour to be presented with a gold fork and spoon, or to try Sicilian cassata at Café El Greco.

The *New York Times* in 1950 advised American tourists not to follow the guidebook or hotel concierge recommendations as they are 'liable to recommend establishment with about as much Italian food and Roman atmosphere as Schrafft's'. Instead they recommended the Taverna Margutta, on enchanting Via Margutta, where 'there are always people sitting there twirling spaghetti on their forks and enjoying a bottle of Chianti,' or a coffee shop 'where young people stand around the counter, talking, gesticulating, flirting and sipping thick caffe espresso'.

One of Hollywood's top gossip columnists, the indomitable Hedda Hopper, said she fell in love with Rome during the war, despite the hardships, and she made sure she planted herself at the Excelsior Hotel whenever she was in Rome, where she could wire back to the States the latest gossip.

Gladys Lloyd, wife of actor Edward G. Robinson, wrote to Hedda Hopper on 29 June 1949 that Rome 'is swarming with our "own",' and that she was staying on the same floor of the Excelsior with Joan Perry, wife of Columbia Pictures boss Harry Cohn:

> Elia Kazan and Arthur Miller have been at several wonderful dinners given by producers Liper and De Sica who made *Shoe Shine* and a new heartbreaker I have just seen called *The Bicycle Thief*. Wow! What a town ... The cafés and outdoor nightlife generally are just what makes the weary ones gay and you sleep beneath warm blankets every night.

A large cocktail party at the Casina Valadier on the Pincio hill was given in honour of Lloyd and Robinson's arrival in Rome. The actor was hired to judge an Italian beauty contest, Miss Cinema 1949, at open-air nightclub La Lucciola in Villa Borghese. He told the cheering crowd, in Italian, 'having me here tonight instead of a Clark Gable is like asking for caviar and receiving baked beans.'

He thanked Hedda for her support over 'the malicious damage' that could be done to a reputation.

Another reason for the embracing of Rome for many figures in Hollywood was the communist witch-hunt in America at that time. Edward G. Robinson had been a victim of rumour after making an appearance before the Un-American Activities Committee. He thanked Hedda for her support over 'the malicious damage' that could be done to a reputation. However, he knew fine well that it was Hedda who could make or break a career, and was particularly vicious to those she suspected of communist leanings.

September Affair, starring Joan Fontaine and Joseph Cotten, was the first Hollywood production to be filmed entirely in Italy, with locations shot in Rome, Venice, Florence and Capri. Joan Fontaine was given two first-class air tickets with her choice of who she could bring with her. She chose Hedda Hopper, a good friend in Hollywood. That is until they arrived in Naples and met *Life* photographer Slim Aarons. He had been hired to do the still photography for the film and had agreed to photograph Joan and Hedda's arrival at the airport.

As their plane made the approach to Rome, Joan told Hedda, 'Do you realise we're nearing the scene of the crimes – Ingrid Bergman and Rossellini, Linda and Ty Power, Merle Oberon and Count Cini? … and you, you lucky stiff, will probably be the first one to get an interview with Ingrid.' Ingrid Bergman, saint of the cinema screen, was about to be involved in one of the biggest celebrity scandals the world had seen, and Hedda would make sure she was first with the news …

Slim worked as a military photographer during the Second World War, eager to place himself in the action. He followed the invasion of Anzio, Italy, without the proper accreditation, taking control of a jeep to get there. He suffered a head injury when a bomb landed by the press corps, was awarded a Purple Heart for bravery, and was honourably discharged. After the war, he vowed to make the most of his life. 'What the hell did we fight in the war for if it wasn't to make the world a better place to live in and even occasionally enjoy,' he told a friend, Frank Zachary. 'From now on I'm going to walk on the sunny side of the street. I'm going to have fun photographing attractive people doing attractive things in attractive places, and maybe take some attractive photographs as well.' *Life* magazine opened a bureau in Rome as the city made its recovery, and Slim took up a job there in 1948. At the Hotel Excelsior he stayed in room 648, his balcony looking onto Via Veneto, and which cost $150 a month. 'The best part was that you could fill a girl's room with flowers for a hundred lire, fifty cents in those days,' he said. He lived the high life for cheap – he ordering Brioni suits, drank fine wine, and mingled with café society on the Via Veneto. Arons photographed the wedding party of Tyrone Power and Linda Christian, and snapped the happy couple at the Trevi Fountain. As well as the movie stars, his beat involved the gangsters in Italy and the Vatican, and was memorably invited to photograph Lucky Luciano on a visit to Sicily, who had been a neighbour at the Hotel Excelsior.

Joan was instantly attracted to the handsome photographer, and the two drove off together in his convertible, leaving Hedda with *September Affair*'s producer Hal Wallis to go to the Excelsior together. Hedda, who expected to be treated with complete respect, was furious. 'I've never seen such rage,' said Wallis. 'I did everything in my power to appease her, giving her a larger suite at the hotel, besieging her with champagne and flowers, but she refused to melt until Joan apologised.' Joan disappeared for two days with Slim, and when she returned, Hal pressured her to apologise to Hedda, 'who threatened to fly back to Hollywood and destroy our picture in print. Joan finally did so, and a truce was called.'

Fontaine moved into Slim's suite at the Excelsior and she was glowing with happiness as he took her on sightseeing trips in his convertible, or moonlight carriage rides. However Joan had a habit of disappearing from set with Slim without letting anyone know where she had gone, particularly tricky when it was just herself and Joe Cotten who were in most of the scenes together.

Thirty-seven-year-old Tennessee Williams, the American playwright, first arrived in Rome in late January 1948, having shot from obscurity to adoration and critical acclaim following the success of his plays *The Glass Menagerie* and *A Streetcar Named Desire*. Riding on the wave of his sudden success, he left New York for Europe. His first stop was Paris, but the city turned out to be disappointing to him but for 'the quality of the whores'. However, when he arrived in Rome to work on an Italian version of *Streetcar*, the Eternal City captured his heart immediately – the imperial domes, spires and obelisks pushing up through the cityscape. He took advantage of a strong American dollar and low prices, and where 'an Americano could get away with a whole lot'.

Tennessee immediately placed himself in the glamorous heart of the city, taking a penthouse room at the Ambasciatori Palace for the first couple of nights, before finding a furnished apartment on Via Aurora, just off the Via Veneto. It was a 'tawny old high-ceilinged building', only a block from Villa Borghese. His apartment had two rooms – a comfortable living room with huge windows looking out onto the sun-drenched street and old walls of Rome. The bedroom, with its heavy shutters, was almost taken up entirely by a huge double bed.

He found that as a gay man he had some freedom that he couldn't find at home, as he believed the Italians were 'raised without any of our puritanical reserves about sex'. Many evenings would be spent cruising on the Appian Way, where he could park up his car beside the old tombs, listening to the sound of crickets in the air, and then 'a figure appears among them which is not a ghost but a Roman boy in the flesh!' Before he made his name as a playwright, Tennessee cruised Times Square with another young writer, picking up GIs and sailors, soliciting them to come back to their Village apartment. He observed in Rome that prostitution was evident on the streets and in the cafés of the Via Veneto, and where secluded corners of the Villa Borghese offered shelter for illicit trysts for lonely foreigners. 'I was late coming out, and when I did it was with one hell of a bang,' Tennessee wrote in his memoirs.

In Rome in the winter of 1948 there were very few private vehicles on the street and soon after settling into his apartment on Via Aurora he purchased an old jeep from a GI being sent back to the States. It had a defective muffler and as he raced it up the Via Veneto, it made an enormous racket, causing heads on the street to turn. On summer nights when he was very drunk, he would race his jeep through the fountains at St Peter's to cool off.

It was hard to escape from the parties and the drink, particularly the mellow Frascati wine which swept through him like a new blood washing away 'all anxiety and all tensions for a while. Italians take a long three or four hour lunches, and then follow it with a siesta.' He told his agent Audrey Wood that 'the American colony is desperately gregarious and you can only work by bolting doors and shutters. Yes, some of them even climb in the window if they suspect you have a little cognac in the place!' In summer the heat from the *solleone*, or the 'lion sun', dazzling against the the white marble buildings and making the interiors of apartments stifling, combined with the drinking and the partying, made it difficult for him to write. There was also the infrastructure and bureaucracy of Italy, which could be challenging. As he wrote to his friend Maria St Just, 'The complications of sending telegraph messages from Italy seem so enormous, and the hours they're open and the location of the offices are so inconvenient. Even mailing a letter seems a monumental undertaking in this Roman lassitude that I'm falling into.'

He was deeply contented in Rome. Tennessee found Italy restorative and relaxing, particularly his strolls through the Villa Borghese with its pine tree walks, the needles lying soft under foot, its fountains and classical statues. While he thought the closest beaches to Rome not so attractive compared to the golden sands of St Tropez, he soon discovered the Foro Italico, Mussolini's sports complex masterpiece, with its faux classical statues and fascist symbols, and he tried to swim there every day.

The late 1940s tourism of Rome helped inspire him to pen a novella. *The Roman Spring of Mrs Stone* concerned a widow losing herself in the city and struggling to hold on to her youth, and where she would visit these hotspots of a newly reinvigorated Rome. He described Rome at five o'clock, with 'domes of ancient churches, swelling above the angular roofs like the breasts of recumbent giant women, still bathed in gold light', and the 'urchin vendors of false American cigarettes who found the Spanish stairs a convenient place to skip out of sight' and who headed towards the Via Veneto, 'where the American tourists thronged'.

Evenings were spent with his expanding circle of gay expats, who had begun arriving on the scene throughout 1948 and 1949, including Truman Capote and Gore Vidal. He and Vidal went on trips in his jeep to Sorrento and Amalfi, and in Sicily he spent time with director Luchino Visconti and his friend and assistant Franco Zefferelli, also a gay man. On his return trip to Rome in 1949, after having gone back to the States for work, Tennessee shared his apartment on Via Aurora 45 with his new partner Frank Merlo, who was given the official title of 'secretary'.

They would enjoy cream and parmesan fettuccini at Alfredo's, drinks at the Café de Paris or the Rosati – its pristinely clothed outdoor tables standing proud against the cobbles of the Piazza del Popolo – and he talked of 'sunning ourselves like a bunch of lizards on the walk in front of Doney's'. Orson Welles, recently separated from Rita Hayworth, stayed at the Hotel Excelsior while preparing *Macbeth*, and he was spotted by Tennessee at the tables of the Doney, 'reading a book called *Decadence*'. Often Tennessee would fall into the nightclub Chez Bricktop on Via Veneto, and he would always ask Ada Bricktop, the legendary owner, to sing 'Quiéreme Mucho' for him.

But his real desire was to meet the magnetic Anna Magnani, who transfixed him as much as she transfixed a young Sophia Loren. He had said in 1947 that it was, 'not often I am profoundly moved by a performance on the screen, but this woman, Anna Magnani, has sunken the claws into my heart. I feel inspired, perhaps compelled, to write a play for her.'

3

ANNA

Anna Magnani was a regular sight on the Via Veneto, speeding along in her green Fiat station wagon, hopping into the bars dressed casually in black slacks, with uncombed hair and accompanied by her white poodle, Pipo, and black German Shepherd, Micia. She was well known as an animal lover who rescued scrawny Roman street kittens and picked the fleas out of their fur, and who drove around Rome's tourist sites most nights, feeding the stray cats and dogs. 'Animals are good, better than humans really. Animals do not betray you,' she said. Her homes were filled with rescued animals, and at her beach house in San Felice Circeo, guests would often be greeted with a pack of vicious dogs that she had rescued from somewhere. In 1950 *Life* magazine went so far to compare Anna to Micia, said to be aggressive and mistrustful, snapping at the hands of fans and autograph hunters. 'She habitually dresses in black. Her big, strong teeth seem always about to bite. Emotionally she is never far from eruption. As she hurtles through traffic, she uproariously curses Micia, jaywalkers and the frustrations of life in general.'

Magnani was Italy's most enigmatic movie star, providing hope and inspiration through her strong, heartfelt performances at the tail end of the war. Italians adored her because she represented how they saw themselves in her films like *Rome, Open City* – the daughters who had to ingratiate themselves to German occupiers and Allied liberators to survive, the mothers who were desperate for milk to feed their children, those whose relatives were cruelly taken away.

The *New York Times* in 1949 described her as 'hard-boiled, wisecracking' and 'certainly not the traditional "glamour girl" of the screen who idealises life'. She was earthy rather than beautiful, with an appearance that refused to be tamed by make-up artists and her dark straggly hair becoming her trademark. She was a rarity as a woman who reached the peak of her fame in her 40s, but such was her influence in *Open City* that there were reports of starlets trying to copy the messy hair and low, raspy voice. She had the affectionate nickname of Nannarella, meaning 'little Anna', or sometimes just Magnani – one word that evoked her power and strength of character. She described herself as the type of woman who would say exactly what she thinks and feels when asked to give an opinion. But she could also 'be very tough' on herself, full of drama and self-doubt.

She reflected: 'Nothing has ever happened to me by chance, nothing, except for the success of *Rome, Open City* and the fame that came after that. I was so convinced that to make it in films you had to have a pretty face and big blue eyes ...' She'd been told this on many occasions – that she was too big and her features were too bold.

Some biographies indicate she had been born and raised in Alexandria, Egypt by an Italian mother and Egyptian father, but Anna would speak of her pride that she had been born and raised in Rome: 'They claim that I was born in Egypt to an Egyptian father. I was born in Rome; my mother was from Romagna and my father from Calabria,' she insisted to Italian journalist Oriana Fallaci in 1963.

Anna was born out of wedlock in 1908 to an 18-year-old woman called Marina Magnani, after her father swiftly disappeared. When Anna was 3 years old, her mother followed a new love, a wealthy Austrian, to Alexandria in the hope of starting a new life, and left her young daughter behind with her mother, Giovanna Casadio. 'I am really grateful to Marina; had she been the usual sort of mother, I would probably never have become an actress,' Anna recounted years later. 'But she was violent, willful and romantic – I take after her. Egypt was her escape. Acting is mine.'

Anna was raised by Giovanna in the colourful Porta Pia district of Rome, with *Life* magazine describing 'the racy aromas of the Roman alleys (that) still cling to her speech and manner'. Porta Pia is just inside the ancient Aurelian walls, near to where, in September 1870, a cannonball from Captain Alessandro La Marmora's army broke through, completing the unification of Italy. After this, Porta Pia saw a huge influx of migrants who could now come into the city. Following the merchants and the politicians who came to Rome, rural immigrants set up home in the blocks of flats of Porta Pia, which grew into a bustling area with the sounds and smells of active street life. Anna was a frail, plain child, doted on by her grandparents, who deprived themselves so as to provide the girl with clothes and food. 'I am anti-bourgeois. Give me the life of the streets, of common people,' she said.

At the age of 7 Anna attended a French convent school where she learnt to speak French, learnt the piano and to sing in a contralto voice. This skill would serve her in adult life, as she sang in her sombre tones, strumming a guitar as accompaniment. Her time at the convent was also said to have inspired a passion for acting after the nuns put on a Christmas play one December. Her mother would send back money to support her daughter, and these funds were enough to cover tuition for the prestigious Eleanor Duse Academy, which she attended when she was 17. During her time at the academy, a touring repertory company asked if she would like to be an extra and she jumped at the chance to perform for 25 lire a day. She drifted amongst touring groups living on the poverty line, but slowly earned better parts and would eventually get the opportunity to travel to Argentina for a theatre tour.

It was in 1933, acting in plays in Rome, when she was spotted by Goffredo Alessandrini, a director and producer from a wealthy family, whom she would marry two years later. She gave up acting to devote herself to being the dutiful wife, as she suffered separation anxiety when away from him. But her husband couldn't help himself but spend time with other women, and these liaisons were so painful for Anna that she threw herself back into the theatre playing tragic heroines like Anna Christie and Carmen.

When she conveyed to Goffredo that she would like to act in movies, he told her it was impossible, she didn't have the looks, and instead he encouraged her to sing in American nightclubs where she would be paid well. Despite not thinking her beautiful enough, he cast her as a café singer in Cavalleria in 1935. 'I know I'm ugly, but must movies show only beautiful, well-dressed women? Why not ordinary, down to earth women for a change, women of the people – like me?' she would say.

Anna landed a role in the acclaimed film *A Lamp in the Window* and more film roles followed, slowly building up Anna's career in Italian cinema, even as she raised her young son Luca – who had been stricken with Polio – single-handedly. She truly represented Italian women across the nation: fighting to provide for her family whilst remaining true to herself.

As the country began to heal the wounds of conflict, entering into a new republican era, Anna Magnani provided entertainment to the impoverished, hungry people of Italy playing wild street girls battling for survival, with suffering engrained in each facial expression, and with her coarse Roman street dialect adding to the realism. It was passion in a gloomy landscape and Anna Magnani was that fervent symbol in the desolation of war. William Dieterle, who directed her in *Volcano* in 1948, said that Anna was, 'the last of the great shameless emotionalists. You have to go back to the silent movies for that kind of acting. Most of the modern stars try to cultivate understatement and subtlety, but Magnani pulls out all the stops. The style is so old it looks new.'

As a proud Roman, Anna Magnani refused to make the move to Hollywood, despite the offers coming in after her success in *Open City*. Nevertheless, Anna had grown from relative obscurity to her position by 1947 as an award-winning, nationally acclaimed actress, and she knew her worth. She demanded the largest sum paid to an actress in Europe at that time and this assuredness of her value also stemmed from caring for her sick son Luca. He was her priority and providing for him was what drove her.

She was the type of woman Tennessee Williams admired the most – the women who fought for what they wanted and never let social conventions hold them back. Magnani, according to Williams, was like Tallulah Bankhead, the great southern wit who was a 'tramp, in the elegant sense'. Bankhead was known for carrying on her conversation from the bathroom, and she had no inhibitions, no embarrassment in her actions. 'I often wonder how Anna Magnani managed to live within society and yet to remain so free of its conventions … She never exhibited any lack of self-assurance … she looked absolutely straight into the eyes of whomever she confronted.'

'the very meaning of sex, her eyes and her voice and her style are indescribably compelling'.

After trying on many occasions to meet Magnani, Tennessee would eventually encounter her in November 1950. She kept him waiting for three quarters of an hour before she sent a messenger to inform him she was by the front of the Doney, one of the most crowded of spots to meet on the Via Veneto. When he finally caught sight of Magnani he was taken aback by her 'marvelous' looks and that she had appeared to have shed around 20lb. He wrote in a letter to a friend that her new figure was 'the very meaning of sex, her eyes and her voice and her style are indescribably compelling'.

He felt shy around her at first, but his partner Frank, a first generation Sicilian who had a similar temperament, acted as the intermediary. Tennessee and Frank were invited to her apartment at Palazzo Altieri, a grand penthouse close to the Pantheon, with a balcony offering full views of St Peter's and looking down to the bustling, noisy street below. Her apartment was heavy and ornate in its decoration, with dark velvet curtains and thick carpets and bursting with antiques, books and paintings. A double canopy bed was where she spent many a restless night and was said to have been a gift from Romerto Rossellini, who found spending time in bed helped expand his creativity. Journalist Oriana Fallaci commented that 'a lower-class or vulgar, arrogant woman would live in a villa with swimming pool and a jukebox,' and, she added:

> I fail to understand why she is often described as rude and arrogant, or portrayed as a lower-class person who lives on foul language and beans. I know her as a lady and have always got on very well with her. The fact that she is a lady can also be seen from her home.

These evenings in her apartment often followed a similar pattern. A maid welcomed them into the living room, where on the table would be bowls of pretzels and peanuts, a bowl of ice and a bottle of Johnnie Walker Red Label. Tennessee and Frank would sit and drink as they waited for sometimes up to an hour. They wandered onto the terrace to look out over Vecchia Roma under the dusk light. She would have a young man of the moment who would appear before her, stretching himself out on a chair, while her voice, busy and commanding could be heard from the distance. Eventually Anna burst into the room in high animation.

Her apartment had its own elevator to go down to the courtyard, where her luxury cars were kept. Sometimes she would let her lover drive, mostly she took the wheel herself, and was dexterous of Rome's traffic. She had already decided what place she was taking them for dinner, but, as Tennessee recounted, 'her choice was always perfect. Restaurateurs and waiters received her like a queen: they hovered beaming around the table while she ordered wines, pastas, salads, entrees without consulting the menu.'

After the coffees, Anna would order the leftovers to be packed up, and then would take a late evening trip around Rome to where the stray cats and dogs would be. She would feed the cats at the Forum, the Colosseum, under bridges by the Tiber, in the cobbled, narrow streets of the Trastavere. She would return to the Palazzo to pick up her dog Micia, the large black German Shepherd, put him in the back seat of the car and take him to the Villa Borghese where she would let him run free, following the car along one of the paths. They would drive to Rosati's for a nightcap. Anna didn't drink anything but wine.

Tennessee had a whisky, Frank a caffe espresso and her lover, whom she would look at with both lust and indifference, a liqueur. Even after midnight, the Via Veneto was crowded with walkers, people-watchers and street photographers looking for a celebrity sighting. Anna would tolerate them for a short moment before shooing them away.

Despite her volcanic personality, and her shrewd financial demands, Anna was also known to be spontaneous in her generosity. Maria St Just, a close friend of Tennessee Williams, recalled meeting her one evening in Rome, where she was given her shoes. Maria wrote:

> Anna was dressed in black and wearing some very curious black shoes … for want of anything better to say, I said, 'what lovely shoes you have on!' Anna with a yell of delight, took them off and gave them to me. I took mine off, threw them into the gutter and donned Anna's, who walked barefoot.

The success of *Open City* had other effects on Anna Magnani's life too, which ranged far beyond the professional. She fell in love with her director Roberto Rossellini on the set of the film, despite the fact that he was already married to, but separated from, costume designer Marcella De Marchis and they had two sons. Rossellini's oldest son Romano died in 1946, aged nine, from appendicitis, and this painful time had brought Anna closer to him, particularly as she had a sick child to care for. She said of Rossellini, 'I thought at last I had found the ideal man. He had lost a son of his own and I felt we understood each other. Above all we had the same artistic conceptions.'

Rossellini seemed to reciprocate and dedicated his two-episode film *Love* to Anna and 'her great art'. One of these episodes, written by Jean Cocteau, took place entirely in one room and with Anna acting out a scene on the telephone, as her character pleads with the love of her life after he tells her he is leaving her for another woman.

At the 1948 Venice Film festival, when her part in *Love* lost out to Jean Simmons's Ophelia, Anna was reported to have torn through the Hotel Excelsior screaming of her disappointment at not getting the prize, but this was part of the narrative that followed Magnani, as the temperamental tigress. Her performance had conjured up desperation, anger and sadness, conveying all the emotions of a heartbroken woman, as if she knew she would soon be experiencing this herself. She often showed a bravado that love didn't matter, that 'women like me only submit to men capable of dominating them, and I have never found anyone who was able to dominate me. I have always found men … cute. We even weep over the cute ones, mind you, but they are tears worth only half a lira.'

But in 1948, as she dated Rossellini, she would often fly into rages at his possible infidelities, as she was distressed at the thought of him leaving her for another woman, just as her husband had. Magnani was also deeply superstitious, following horoscopes and fortune tellers, worried that she foresaw a love affair that would take Rossellini, perhaps the great love of her life, away from her.

4

INGRID

O ne sunny afternoon in Los Angeles in early 1947 Ingrid Bergman went to a showing of *Rome, Open City*, hoping that it might be a pleasant enough film to while away her time. But watching Roberto Rossellini's neorealist masterpiece would prove to be life-changing. She was transfixed by the screen for every heart-wrenching moment, and 'came out of the theater another person than the one I was when I went in. I didn't want the film to end. I wanted to go in to it.'

When she saw another of Rossellini's films, *Paisan*, months later in New York, with its six documentary-style episodes depicting the liberation of Rome by Allied troops, she knew that she would have to meet this genius director who had so moved her.

Bergman in 1947 was one of Hollywood's biggest stars. She was considered a natural, wholesome actress, a devoted wife and mother who was married to a Swedish doctor, Petter Lindstrom, and had a young daughter named Pia. In Hollywood she appeared to have it all – wealth, family life, celebrity and the pick of films she wished to do. She had become a star with *Casablanca*, won an Oscar for *Gaslight* (1944), and became a Hitchcock heroine with starring roles in *Spellbound* (1945) and *Notorious* (1946). Despite the praise she received for her range of parts, she had become jaded with the system. She was working on *Joan of Arc* on the studio back lots, where medieval France was painstakingly recreated for Technicolor filming. But she had hoped to go to France to the real locations. Hollywood's style of movie-making was 'too polished, too rehearsed, they were cardboard'. When she saw the realism of Rossellini's work she was deeply moved by it and was inspired to experience this authentic film-making for herself, rather than acting out on the studio lot.

Roberto Rossellini was almost unheard of amongst Hollywood circles, but she managed to track down his address to Minerva film studios in Rome and sent a letter of praise him to him, offering herself up as a possible actress and hoping this note would eventually find its way to him. 'Dear Mr. Rossellini,' she wrote. 'I saw your films *Rome Open City* and *Paisan*, and enjoyed them very much. If you need a Swedish actress who speaks English very well, who has not forgotten her German, who is not very understandable in French, and who in Italian knows only *"ti amo"*, I am ready to come and make a film with you.' The *'ti amo'* could have been perceived as flirtatious, and would later be interpreted that way, but it had only been meant as a cute introduction, and besides, she had shown Petter the letter before she had sent it off. Italy's reputation as a fascist country was still ingrained in the aftermath of the war, despite having switched sides half way through, and for Ingrid to offer herself to an Italian director was a brave move.

While Rossellini had a low opinion of Hollywood and all its artificiality, he recalled Ingrid Bergman from when he had sought refuge in a cinema during a wartime bombing raid. Showing on screen had been the Swedish version of *Intermezzo* – the film that had first brought young Ingrid to the attention of producer David O. Selznick – and her clean, shimmering beauty flickered on screen for the four hours that he was trapped there as bombs rained down. Not only was this wartime memory a sign that he should meet her, but he also proclaimed he had received her letter on his birthday. Technically it was the day after, but this didn't sound quite so miraculous. Rossellini sent a telegram from his office at the Hotel Excelsior in May 1948, gushing that 'I dreamed to make a film with you and from this moment I will do everything possible.'

Rossellini was working on an idea for his next film – the vision of which had been inspired while driving past an Italian refugee camp for displaced eastern Europeans. He observed a woman by the barbed-wire fence, with a look of 'mute intense despair'. He later found out she was Latvian and that she had married a soldier and gone to live with him on the Lipari islands as a way to escape from the camp. This idea inspired a rough storyline of a refugee who marries an Italian fisherman to find stability and a home, and who ends up on a lonely and desolate island. For Rossellini, *Stromboli* was really a metaphor about Europe trying to adjust to peace.

Despite having promised his next role to Anna Magnani, he set about making it possible for Ingrid to do the film instead. Her tall, blonde Nordic looks and pristine beauty would stand in contrast to the bleak, ash-strewn volcanic landscape. Ingrid was filming *Under Capricorn* with Alfred Hitchcock in London in autumn 1948, and so she suggested that she and husband Petter meet Rossellini half way, in Paris, to discuss working together. When Rossellini flew to New York in January 1949 to pick up a New York Film Critics Award for *Paisan*, he took the opportunity to travel to LA to meet and spend some more time with Ingrid. Rossellini initially booked into the Beverly Hills Hotel as it was the place to be seen for those in the film industry. But the Lindstroms invited the Italian director to their Benedict Canyon villa as they were worried the Beverly Hills Hotel might prove too expensive for him. Ingrid showed him around Southern California, introducing him to Billy Wilder, and showcasing his film *Germany Year Zero* to Samuel Goldwyn, in the hope that the producer would finance their project. However this film was too brutal for Goldwyn, and so Ingrid went to Howard Hughes. The eccentric billionaire was enamored with Bergman, and so he agreed that his studio, RKO, would finance their film.

Ingrid had felt trapped in her marriage for some time. Petter was precise and controlling, always watching what she ate. As a food lover, Ingrid would end up smuggling butter cookies into her bedroom for secret snacks. Ingrid later indicated that at this time in her life, if the right man came along and swept her off her feet, she would be willing to go. She had tried to be the good wife and mother, but there was so much more she wanted in her life.

After several years with Anna Magnani, Rossellini had tired of her drama and eruptions, the fights and the throwing of crockery. Her reputation amongst the people of Rome, from taxi drivers to concierge, was that she had the strength of a tiger and was as fiery as Vesuvius. Magnani felt they complimented each other professionally. Rossellini would modify scenes to suit her and indulged her moods if she stormed off set. 'To act I must feel the mood. It cannot be forced. Roberto always understood that,' she said. And she was looking forward to his next project.

When Rossellini arrived back in Rome from his Los Angeles trip, he spent a weekend with Magnani at his favourite hideaway on the Amalfi Coast, the Albergo Luna Conventa, a former Capuchin monastery. He was waiting for news from Los Angeles on Ingrid's arrival but asked for complete discretion from the concierge to not deliver this news while he was with Magnani. As they walked into the dining room, the concierge gave a conspiratorial wink at Rossellini that the news had come, and the director could only hope that Anna hadn't noticed. Bowls of spaghetti and tomato sauce were brought to the table and Magnani quietly prepared the dish just the way he liked it, tossing it with just the right amount of olive oil and tomato sauce, sprinkling on the parmesan to his taste. She then calmly lifted up the bowl and dumped the spaghetti directly over his head, before storming out the room.

Despite this act of calm rage, Magnani was heartbroken at the loss of the man she felt so compatible with. As melancholy as she was normally, she was said to be inconsolable with her grief over Rossellini, threatening that she would break every plate of spaghetti in Rome over his head. Yet she tried to remain dignified when she was asked questions by the press. She was reported to have told a journalist in Paris, 'My relationship with him was always a veritable nightmare. The only thing I regret is that Rossellini dropped me to rush off to America leaving me without a director for my next picture.'

On 20 March 1949, Ingrid boarded a plane to Rome to begin filming *Stromboli*. As her plane took off for Rome, she thought of Petter standing at the airport in Los Angeles, looking 'so lonely and silent', and 'I realised my selfishness.' But she felt drawn to Rossellini from the moment of seeing *Open City*. He was so different from any other man she had met in her life:

> I'd never met anyone with his kind of freedom. He made everything larger than life; life took on new dimensions, new excitement, new horizons. And he gave me courage which I never had before. I was always frightened of everything, and he said, 'Frightened of what? What is there to be frightened about?'

As she stepped off the plane at Ciampino Airport she was greeted by huge numbers of cheering fans and photographers, more than she had ever seen. Roberto was waiting by the steps of the plane to present her with a large bouquet of flowers. He led Ingrid through the crowds of photographers, tearing one snapper's jacket in the process, and whisked her away to the Excelsior Hotel in his red Cisitalia sports car. Ingrid was concerned about the photographer's jacket, as he had looked upset, as if it was the only jacket he owned. Rossellini later told her that he had sent the man a new one the next morning.'

Rossellini kept a small apartment at the Excelsior, and he had gathered a group of Italy's acclaimed filmmakers, including Federico Fellini, for a private party to welcome the actress. Fellini, the scriptwriter for *Rome*, *Open City*, who had arrived in Rome from Rimini as a 19-year-old with a briefcase full of story ideas, was known for his skilful, witty illustrations. He had created little caricatures of Ingrid and Rossellini on the island of Stromboli and posted them up on the wall for the party. Fellini spoke of the spell Bergman's arrival cast over Rome. 'For us in Italy, it was as if the Virgin Mary had just descended upon us from Disneyland,' he said.

A press conference was held the next day at the Excelsior, and it ended in near riot. Two-hundred-and-fifty gatecrashers tried to jam themselves into the conference room, and many more pushed through the door, all hoping to get a glimpse of the star in her long skirt, black sweater and pearls. Rossellini was brushed aside as photographers rushed forward to try to get a photo, but without a single question answered, Ingrid was escorted out by Rossellini. Her reception was compared to that of Tyrone Power and his marriage only the year before.

The people of Rome had endured the war under Mussolini, they had been occupied by the Germans and after being cut off from bombing raids, had been close to starvation. Rossellini had depicted the true feelings in Rome with *Open City* and their celebrated, beloved director had captured America's greatest movie star. No wonder they were excited.

The day after Ingrid's arrival, the Via Veneto was still jam-packed with people celebrating her arrival. She was trapped in her hotel room, unable to even get out of the foyer. With the help of the hotel's manager she and Rossellini were shown the back staircases of the hotel and were able to sneak out into the spring air.

Rome was overwhelming to the senses – the noise, the traffic, the narrow cobbled streets leading onto open squares with fountains against butterscotch walls. Rossellini made sure he was never away from her side, showering her with attention and a whirlwind of parties. Roberto lived his life with passion, a man of a thousand moods and personalities, who treated love without consequence, and now that he wanted Ingrid, he wouldn't let her out of his sight.

Luckily for Rossellini, Anna Magnani was in London when Bergman flew to Rome. Hearing second-hand about their meeting from a mutual friend in Rome, Magnani despaired at the answer to her every question – that Rossellini picked Ingrid up from the airport and drove her to the Excelsior by the romantic Old Appian Way, that they kissed, and that Ingrid was indeed beautiful. As an act of revenge Magnani made plans with Hollywood director William Dieterle to make another film on the island of Vulcano, part of the same group of Aeolian Islands as Stromboli. Both films were neorealist, and with Magnani playing an exiled former prostitute who faces hostility by the islanders, the plots were very similar.

For *Stromboli*, Rossellini still didn't have a script to work on for the planned start date of 1 April. But he reassured Ingrid that he knew exactly what he was doing, and they set off on a road trip together to the island of Stromboli in Rossellini's red sports car, with the crew having gone ahead separately. They sped along quiet, rural roads, over the old cobbles of the Appian Way, past Pagan shrines and little trattorias. The wind blew through her hair and the sun warmed her face as he sped south with the skills of his former career as a racing car driver.

They arrived at the port in Naples and took the ferry over to Capri, with the smell of tobacco and sea air, the blue sea frothing and swirling against the sides of the boat as the seagulls cawed overhead. It was in Capri that they danced together their only time, as Roberto, normally flat-footed and reluctant to dance, was determined to woo her with all the means he had.

From Naples, they drove past Pompeii and along the rugged Amalfi coastline with its quiet winding roads and sharp bends that connected the little villages and sheltered bays, at this time still quiet and untouched by tourists. In place of Magnani, he now brought Ingrid to the Albergo Luna Conventa, situated at the crest of a hill which rises steeply out of the village. Ingrid's bedroom window looked out onto the glistening bay and the rugged hillsides beyond, covered in yellow broom and dotted with monasteries and shrines. Rossellini enjoyed impressing her with stories of the classic Roman myths, of ancient tales of the Trojan wars, and that they were right on the very coastline where Ulysses had been seduced by the Sirens. It was in her room, on the Albergo's writing paper, that she wrote the hardest letter to Petter, telling him that she was in love with Rossellini and wished to stay with him. She said she could understand if Petter could not forgive her, and she signed off her letter with 'poor little Papa, but also poor little Mama'.

Keeping up a public denial of their affair, Rossellini was careful to book separate rooms in their hotels, although these often had connecting doors. But interest was swelling amongst international publications, sending photographers to try to capture Ingrid and

Roberto in a comprising moment. As the secret lovers wandered together on the Amalfi Coast, they knew that photographers were around, but, as she recalled, 'Roberto was so calm and quiet and happy that he didn't even bother to punch them.' It was during an unguarded moment, climbing up to one of the round stone towers on the Amalfi coast, holding each other's hand, that a *Life* magazine photographer successfully immortalised this moment. The picture was splashed all around the world, confirming not only their affair, but that Ingrid Bergman was no longer the saintly mother, but an adulterer.

From Amalfi they drove to Salerno, and Roberto pulled up his car alongside a beach where he had spotted a group of fishermen working. Ingrid at first thought he was joking when he asked her which of these men she would like as her leading man. Rossellini wanted to cast a real fisherman who would have the sunburnt skin, the rough hands, the skills in casting the nets in the right way. It didn't even matter to Rossellini if they could act, as he was willing to feed them the lines. He jumped out the car and selected the one with Marlon Brando good looks, 21-year-old Mario Vitale, and another alternative actor, Mario Sponzo. He placed them on his payroll and gave them the name of the hotel in Salerno where they could join the production crew heading to Stromboli.

The final stretch of the journey was down to the Straights of Messina, cutting through mountains to the black coastline where Sicily stretched out in front. They were taken from Sicily to Stromboli by schooner, which was loaded up with camera equipment, crates of groceries and battered suitcases for the four hour journey across the waters.

Ingrid watched the horizon as Stromboli's foreboding volcanic peak came out of the distance. She saw the black sand beaches of the island as they got closer. The volcano dominated life on the island – it gurgled and rumbled throughout the day giving off a smell of sulphur, and its towering, jagged, smoking 8000 ft peak blocked out the sun at certain times of day. The 400 long-suffering residents, mostly elderly or young, who could be overcome by smoke on a windy day, had built Moorish houses on the lower slopes, where fig trees, flowers, vegetables and bougainvillea could grow on the fertile volcanic soil. Despite this, it was a dark, dramatic and foreboding place with nothing much to offer in home comforts. There was no running water, poor sanitation, no transport, and those who lived there had the worn expressions of a life sacrificed to tough work.

Ingrid stayed in a pink stucco house shared with Roberto, his sister Marcella, and Ingrid's secretary Ellen Neuwald, and because it didn't have a bathroom, Roberto ordered one to be specially built for Ingrid, with a funnel pushed through the roof, so that she could take a shower.

On their road trip they had avoided newspapers and telephone calls, staying oblivious to the brewing of a scandal. But following the publication of the *Life* magazine photo, word was now out about the Rossellini–Bergman affair, and photographers and journalists from Italy, America and Britain soon arrived on the island to make enquiries, with some even disguised as tourists or fishermen to get closer to the story. They asked about the sleeping arrangements, whether Rossellini and Ingrid shared a room, and just to make sure, they got someone to count how many toothbrushes were in Ingrid's bathroom.

With Anna Magnani filming her rival movie only 40km away on Salina island, reporters were accredited to one or the other camp, having to choose sides. It was an atmosphere 'crackling with rivalry,' according to *Life* magazine. The 'battle of the volcanoes' was the talk of the Via Veneto, sometimes it felt as if the patrons of its cafés could speak of nothing else. They picked a team – they declared themselves a 'Magnaniac' or a 'Bergmaniac' – and clashed over which film, and which actress, was superior.

The production of *Stromboli* was a slow process, as Rossellini, with his neorealist mode of film-making, wanted complete naturalism. Just like the fishermen sourced in Salerno, he preferred to pick out his actors from the crowds, no matter if they had any experience. He would not give them dialogue until the last minute, so they had no time to rehearse an artificial performance. Ingrid, as a trained actress in the Hollywood style, grew increasingly frustrated by these non-actors' inability to learn lines, to know where to look or where to stand, as it meant she couldn't anticipate when it was her turn to do her line. 'I'm afraid that on my face there was always a worried expression because I was too concerned about their performance and therefore I couldn't always think of my own,' she said.

Ingrid might have hoped she was protected from the gossip and scandal in America concerning her relationship, but as well as struggling with the island hardships, she contended with tough and insulting letters. Ingrid received a letter on 22 April from Joe Breen of the Production Code of America, who threatened Ingrid's career if the rumours were true. The producer of the yet-to-be-released *Joan of Arc*, Walter Wanger, pleaded with Ingrid that his reputation and career hinged on her, and the Swedish Lutheran Church asked her to denounce the rumours of this affair. People got divorced all the time, she thought, yet the weekly mail boat continued to bring critical letters, taunts, newspaper cuttings. Italian tabloids relished in the gossip – *Travaso* created an image of Ingrid as Joan of Arc, tied to a stake upon piles of flammable film, and with Roberto keeping Magnani from setting it on fire. The name Stromboli came to represent salaciousness and scandal, with many jokes at their expense.

After receiving constant press calls at his home and clinic, Petter flew to Italy where he was met by an unidentified American woman at Ciampino airport. Frustrated reporters could not locate Petter despite their extensive searches of Rome's hotels. The woman turned out to be Kay Brown, a good friend of Ingrid's and advisor to David O Selznick.

'you can't talk to her that way. I love her and forbid your making advances.'

She had been sent to Stromboli to visit Ingrid, arriving on a small fishing boat in mink coat and heels, but feeling like a spare part, she returned to Rome and met Petter, who travelled to Messina in Sicily, with the hope of bringing her back to Hollywood.

During a tense meeting in the Sicilian port town, after Roberto had told Ingrid he would kill himself if she left him, Petter begged her to return. To keep the peace, Ingrid issued a statement that she would finish the film, tentatively known as *God's Earth*, and would then 'meet my husband in Sweden or the United States. After this there will be no further statements about our private lives.' She wished Petter would accept her final decision that she wanted a separation, but he would not make it easy for her to let the marriage go.

American swimming champion Brenda Helser, who had become ensconced in the European jet set, wrote in a letter to Hedda Hopper that she had spoken with Rossellini's press agent during the filming of *Stromboli*, and he had witnessed a confrontation:

> Ingrid was all for the idea of going back to her husband's hotel with him as he suggested, but Rossellini stormed into the room shouting 'you can't talk to her that way. I love her and forbid your making advances.' So Ingrid, who sounds more like the sleepwalker she generally resembles on the screen anyway, went off with the loudest shouter, according to this guy. He says she is sick over the fact things got so serious for apparently she was just playing and things got out of hand.

With all this publicity surrounding Stromboli, the tourists soon invaded. Italian promoters organised boat excursions promising visitors they would get the chance to see Bergman and Rossellini at work. When 800 visitors turned up on the island one day, Rossellini had to stop shooting and usher Ingrid safely through the crowd and back into her house. As well as tourists and journalists, famous faces also paid a visit to the islands. In June 1949 Errol Flynn made a visit to see Ingrid and Roberto on Stromboli and then Anna Magnani and William Dieterle on Salina.

On 2 August Ingrid and Rossellini finally left Stromboli, and never had Ingrid been so relieved to finish a film. Her life had completely changed – her position as number one star was in ruins and she had disappointed those close to her. She told friends she was sick of being scrutinised in the public eye and wanted to lead a private life.

She issued an emotional hand-written statement to the press on 4 August that 'I have instructed my lawyer to start divorce proceedings immediately. Also at the conclusion of my present picture, it is my intention to retire into private life.' She spoke of being a prisoner because of the 'persistent malicious gossip', and while she didn't mention Rossellini, she made clear that *Stromboli* would be her last film as she sought a quiet new life in Rome.

Rossellini and Ingrid moved into a small apartment in Rome on Via Antonelli while the city was suffering a heat wave. The shortage of water and electricity also made it uncomfortable. Ingrid would wake just after midday, visit the studios accompanied by a bodyguard to go through the long dubbing process for *Stromboli* and then spend evenings with Roberto in little trattorias.

Ingrid's body was also giving out signs of an inescapable truth – she was pregnant with Rossellini's child. To have a baby out of wedlock, while still married to other people was the ultimate scandal in 1949. This was when Hedda Hopper, with Joan Fontaine, flew into Rome, placing herself in the Excelsior and requesting an interview. Knowing that turning down Hedda for an interview was a mistake, Ingrid invited her to the apartment she was sharing with Rossellini and greeted the gossip columnist with a warm smile. When Hedda asked about the pregnancy rumours, the actress showed her figure and ambiguously answered, 'Good heavens, Hedda, do I like look it?'

Rossellini had amicably separated from his wife several years before, and Rossellini made clear he was free to marry. Marcella, interviewed by the magazine *Omnibus* in September 1949, said that if it had been Magnani she wouldn't have agreed to a divorce because 'their temperaments are too much alike. But Ingrid Bergman is the ideal wife for him – sweet, restful, an oasis of charm.'

The era of the clashes between celebrities and photographers really began with Rossellini and Bergman in Rome, who were trying to avoid the photographers as much as possible. Ingrid was one of the first modern celebrities to face a barrage of press intrusion. She was held captive in her apartment and the press gathered outside the home or tried to take pictures through the windows. The doorman on their apartment tried to protect them from the newspaper reporters gathered outside. Ingrid didn't leave the house for five weeks, but could go up to the roof terrace with her dog Stromboli, where she would sunbathe and read. She would look down on the road to see the photographers below, and sometimes she would lean over and spit on them.

One evening photographers Ivo Meldolesi and Pierluigi Praturlon were tipped off that the secretive couple were dining at a restaurant near Porta Pinciana. They managed to take a couple of shots until Rossellini noticed and threw a plate of spaghetti at them, and then fled the restaurant. Pierluigi chased after them on his motorbike to their apartment in order to capture them entering the building. However, Rossellini managed to close the entrance gates on Pierluigi, trapping him until another tenant arrived to free him.

Even in December of 1949, Ingrid and Roberto kept their news under wraps, and those who saw Ingrid found it difficult to distinguish whether she was pregnant. Roberto's brother Renzo Rossellini refused to be drawn on the reports when questioned by reporters in December. He said his new wife Anna had been trying on clothes with Ingrid at a dressmaker's, and that Ingrid 'had the appearance of a person physically perfectly normal'.

Helen Tubbs, wife of Bill Tubbs, who worked with Rossellini on *Paisan* and *The Machine that Kills Evil*, recounted to Hedda that her husband had spoken with Rossellini. 'Roberto says that he does not want to make any statement right now, and that his lawyers will prepare something. Rossellini feels that the press has ruined his life, and that he is being prosecuted. He feels very bad about it. He longs for a life of his own.' She added in the letter that 'our mutual friend from the *Rome Daily American* saw Bergman less than two weeks ago and he said that he did not think it possible.'

Bergman was photographed at the end of January 1950 in a rare appearance on the streets of Rome dressed in a fur coat and gloves to cover her bump. At a cocktail party for reporters, Rossellini declined to answer questions as to whether Ingrid was going to have a baby. He objected to the 'Morbid curiosity of the press' and questioned why he should have to answer such an intrusive question.

On 30 January a journalist phoned into their apartment, and Ingrid laughed off reports that she had been taken to hospital to have a baby. 'That's crazy', she said. A few days later the contractions started. Rossellini was in the mountains outside of Rome filming *Flowers of St Francis*, and rushed to the hospital in his Ferrari as Ingrid was taken to hospital. Their son, Roberto, known as Robin, was born on the evening of 2 February 1949.

The premiere of Anna Magnani's *Volcano* was being held at the Fiamma Cinema that evening, and Magnani was in attendance with a packed audience, including many journalists. The film had been delayed when a bulb in the projector had burst, and a bicycle courier had been sent to find a new one. When the film started up again, Magnani was surprised to see journalists leaving the audience, until the murmurs reached her – that Ingrid had given birth to a son. She was asked her thoughts and replied with the usual dignity that 'This is Miss Bergman's private affair.' But she couldn't help feeling sabotaged, and the film turned out to be a flop.

The baby weighed almost 8lb, was described as beautiful and definitely Rossellini's with its dark hair and blue eyes. While it was a calm scene inside the clinic, with Ingrid surrounded by flowers and breakfasting on orange juice and toast and marmalade, reporters soon descended on the hospital, all hungry for information and for a photo of Bergman with her baby. The gates were secured and iron shutters on her windows closed down. Such was the desperation for news, one journalist had his wife check in as a patient so he could get closer to Ingrid's room and there were attempts to bribe the nuns at the clinic. Reporters persuaded her doctor to answer questions on the birth, and he revealed she would breast feed for a month, and that 'she is one of the happiest mothers I ever known.' Newspapers ran up special editions to recount the 'torrid' story and 'The Bergman Affair', detailing every moment since she had arrived in Rome a year earlier.

When Hollywood woke up to the announcement, there was complete shock among the film community. As the *Los Angeles Times* reported on 3 February 1950, the news 'jolted Hollywood yesterday with the figurative effects of an atomic bomb explosion.' Lindstrom could not be reached for comment and the secretary at his Beverly Hills office told reporters he 'is not available to anyone'. Under Italian law, Lindstrom, as Ingrid's husband, had the right to take possession of the baby, and on the birth certificate, Ingrid could not be listed as mother. It said 'mother temporarily unknown.'

Hedda Hopper was enraged that Ingrid had denied her pregnancy when they met in Rome in August. Hedda wrote to her friend Helen Tubbs on 3 February:

> Well, you certainly had a red letter in Rome when Ingrid's son was born. That sure was a shocker, and I believe will kill *Stromboli* and her career deader than a smelt. In this situation I doubt very much if she will have much loving attention from Roberto. He doesn't seem the kind of person who can assume responsibility personally.

The new parents left the hospital in the dead of night, without even telling the nuns their plans, and bundled themselves and the baby into Rossellini's sports car. A friend of theirs blocked the road with his car to prevent them from being followed. Back at their apartment, Ingrid received hate mail, with comments that she would burn in hell, and that her baby would be cursed. Ingrid was denounced in the US Senate and her Hollywood career was all but over. Saint Ingrid, who had been considered such a role model as a wholesome mother and wife, was now tarnished. 'I didn't know they thought of me after they left the cinema, except as the character I played,' she said. 'I seemed to represent some kind of evil corrupting force and the absolute symbol of feminine shame. Ilsa could be forgiven in *Casablanca*, Alicia could be forgiven in *Notorious*, but Ingrid in Rome could not.' 1950 was Holy Year in Rome, and as millions of tourists and pilgrims descended on the city, Ingrid felt like the 'Scarlet woman … it became a matter of sheer physical and mental survival.'

The final version of *Stromboli* didn't turn out as those who had been involved in making it had hoped – Howard Hughes cut it extensively for its American release, taking away Rossellini's original intent. He also cashed in on the romantic controversy with sensationalist posters of a damsel in distress against an erupting volcano, with the tagline 'Raging Island…Raging Passions!' It was disappointing for all those who had worked under hardship on the volcanic island.

After the birth, Ingrid and Rossellini were hardly seen in public. At the end of April 1950, when two Italian news photographers took a picture of him and Ingrid as they left a restaurant in Rome, their first public appearance, Rossellini called for the police. The photographers were forced to hand over the negatives and Ingrid, who had been left standing outside the restaurant when Rossellini gave chase, was surrounded by a curious crowd, until she could escape in Rossellini's red car. Ingrid was supported by Roberto's sister Marcella and her daughter Fiorella, who threw stones at the photographers whenever they were followed. Ingrid scolded her, 'you know they are really only doing their jobs.'

On 24 May 1950, with their Mexican divorces secured, Roberto Rossellini and Ingrid Bergman were married by proxy in Juarez, Mexico. On the same day, they held a small ceremony at a little church near the Via Appia with a few guests including Federico Fellini.

As well as a new apartment in Rome on Viale Bruno Buozzi, the Rossellinis bought a beachside villa at Santa Marinella which became their main residence during the summer months. The white-washed home, on a rocky inlet, had long verandahs and was surrounded by a lush, fragrant garden of small pines, oleander and pineapple palms. It came with garages for Rossellini's cars, a boccia court, where Rossellini taught her to play boules, and tennis courts, a sport which she enjoyed when living in Beverly Hills. There were chickens and dogs roaming the grounds, and guests always arriving.

In October 1950 Ingrid was photographed looking fit and tanned in shorts and a shirt tied at the waist, playing boules with Rossellini, and in sunglasses enjoying the views over the sea. Protective of her child, she insisted that no photos were taken of her baby. The article in the *Los Angeles Times* noted:

You walk through the front door and into a small living room with a huge fireplace. On one wall there is a large pastel drawing of Ingrid and her baby, sketched from a photograph by an artist in Milan. Leaning against the back of an upright chair is an old-fashioned wind-up telephone. You step from this room onto a wide seaside porch where Miss Bergman spends hours playing in the sun with her baby.

Rossellini had grown up in a large house off the Via Veneto, where his parents would hold an 'open table', inviting anyone to come in and enjoy their breakfast, lunch or dinner. Roberto introduced the same open table to Santa Marinella, and often Ingrid would find their home filled with guests, without really knowing who they were.

Both their Santa Marinella villa and their large ten room apartment on the Viale Bruno Buozzi were fully serviced, with cooks and maids, leaving Ingrid with little to take care of. Though she never liked to cook, Ingrid enjoyed housework – throwing her energy and vigor behind the work of getting a home clean. While they could have some peace in Santa Marinella, their life in Rome was of constant scrutiny, with the blinds of their home often closed to prevent photographers taking pictures through the windows.

Ingrid, who never enjoyed seeing herself in evening gowns or cocktail dresses, strode through Rome in print dresses or trousers and shorts, which were quite controversial for conservative Italy around 1950. She enjoyed a wholesome diet of a big plate of pasta, meats and fish, plenty of fruit, and, like the Europeans, she avoided eating between meals. For Ingrid, the gelato must also have been tempting as she had loved ice cream in America, especially with hot fudge sauce.

However friends who saw her at this point commented on how thin she looked. When Italian actress Alida Valli visited Ingrid in Rome at the end of January 1951 she said 'she never saw her look so thin, beautiful or happy.' Helen Tubbs also reported to Hedda Hopper that 'she is thinner than ever before in her life and looks beautiful!'

This period for Ingrid wasn't all happiness and relaxation. While she was worried that she may never be able to act again, the most painful aspect of the situation for Ingrid was being cut off from her 12-year-old daughter Pia, who would read of the scandal in magazines and through classmates but wouldn't see her mother for the next ten years. Because Petter wouldn't allow Pia to be taken out of America, and Roberto wouldn't allow for Ingrid to return to America, hostile court battles for custody ensued over the next few years, playing out in the world's newspapers.

Hers and Rossellini's life continued to hold fascination, and in October 1951, they fought off rumours that they were separating. Newspaper *Paris Presse* reported that Bergman had moved from their villa into a two-room apartment in Rome following an argument. Upset at the reports, Ingrid invited a journalist to the beautifully furnished apartment on Via Bruno Buozzi, decorated with religious paintings, to prove they still lived together. Ingrid 'corrected her husband's English, adjusted his tie and kissed him tenderly while lunching with this reporter today'.

In February 1951 it was known that Ingrid was expecting another child, and that she wished for a girl. It was only when she received an X-ray at the hospital that she found out she was going to have twins. Ingrid's bump became enormous, and with no signs of labour by the tenth month, she was hospitalised with the possibility of inducing. While she waited for the birth, a court battle was taking place in Los Angeles, with Lindstrom opposing Pia from going to Italy to visit her mother. Eventually, Pia, admitted in court that she didn't want to go to Italy and that she would rather stay with her father. Out of this stress was the joyous eventual birth of her twins, born on 18 June 1952, first Isabella, and then a second girl, Isotta, each weighing seven pounds.

Despite worrying about never being able to act again, Ingrid would star in four more films directed by Rossellini. However, he possessively refused her 'permission' to work with other directors. Graham Greene had hoped for Ingrid Bergman to co-star with Gregory Peck for the film version of his novel *The End of the Affair*, and Fellini would have loved to have made a film with Ingrid. But the director admitted 'it was hopeless because Roberto was very possessive of his prize, his great jewel, and he wasn't going to let anyone have Ingrid for a film, and especially not an Italian film, and especially me. Our great friendship had turned into a certain rivalry.'

5

SOPHIA

The little blue tram, or 'transvetto', rattled into Cinecittà every morning from Stazione Termini, loaded not just with the film crew travelling to work, but with the hopefuls vying to be cast as an extra in whatever production was being filmed. On the journey through the countryside to the film studio, past hills and sheep, the tram conductor would lighten the journey with discussions and thoughts on the current films being made.

Passengers were dropped outside the studio gates, and while the labourers were allowed in to begin their day on one of the large soundstages, those without a pass crowded around outside hoping to be chosen as an extra. Cinecittà became known as the 'dream city', where anything was possible. These scenes were captured in Luchino Visconti's *Bellissima*, starring Anna Magnani as a pushy, ambitious mother who takes her daughter to the film studio in the hope she will be selected during a talent search.

In May 1950 Sofia and her mother Romilda took the tram to Cinecittà to find work as an extra on *Quo Vadis*, dressed in elegant black in the hopes of making an impression. Hundreds of people also had the same idea and they joined the crowds gathered around the gates.

They had only managed to come to Rome after Romilda persuaded her 15-year-old daughter to take part in a Naples beauty pageant in autumn 1949 to find the Queen of the Sea and her twelve princesses. Out of the 200 contestants taking part, Sofia, in her dress made from pink curtains, was selected as one of the princesses, winning 25,000 lire, a new dress, several rolls of wallpaper, which the family could use to cover the cracks in the plaster from wartime bombing, and a train ticket to Rome. The ticket and the prize money would take Romilda and her daughter closer to their dreams at Cinecittà – particularly when Romilda heard of the huge MGM production of *Quo Vadis*. Romilda had hopes that by going to Rome she could also reunite with Riccardo. But he had already married, so Sofia and Romilda were relegated to staying with relatives.

Louis B. Mayer had been planning *Quo Vadis* for many years, but it had been put on hold because of the war. When MGM executives arrived in Rome after the city had opened up again to film-makers, they surveyed the facilities and booked up Cinecittà, with the producers, art directors and costume designers arriving in the city two years before filming, in order to begin preparations. One of the largest sound stages was used as a warehouse for costumes, another acted as laundry and shoe-repair shop and on one sound stage sculptors created over 500 statues for the film.

One of the huge outdoor sets included a reproduction of the Circus of Nero, the exterior of Nero's palace, and ancient Rome with its houses and shops, was extensively researched in collections of museums and by studying famous Renaissance paintings. The film was truly of epic proportions, with 32,000 costumes, 15,000 hand-sewn sandals, 4,000 helmets and breastplates, 2,000 shields and 21,700 water bottles.

As *Quo Vadis* was the first Technicolor feature picture ever made in Italy, and the supply of power in Rome was inadequate, five large generators for hundreds of arc lights were sent from MGM studios to Rome along with more than 250 tons of electrical equipment. This was one of the first opportunities for Cinecittà to be given a boost with its furnishings from American studios.

Elizabeth Taylor had originally been announced to star as Lygia in the sword and sandal epic, with Gregory Peck as Marcus Vinicius, for filming in summer 1949. But with filming delays, and original director

John Huston dropping out, Robert Taylor was cast as Vinicius, Peter Ustinov as Nero, and the role of Lygia went to Deborah Kerr. Said Mervyn Le Roy, 'of all the tests I made in Hollywood, she stood out as Lygia. She has the fire, and that certain quality of beauty.'

Louis B. Mayer insisted the film be shot in summer, as his Ben-Hur in 1924 had been plagued by icy rain while filming in winter in Rome. Despite efforts, it proved impossible to install air-conditioning at Cinecittà, and with temperatures reaching forty degrees, actors had to be doused in cold water between takes.

Deborah Kerr arrived in Rome at the end of April 1950 with daughter Melanie. Her husband Tony Bartley later flew out to join her at her villa on the outskirts of Rome, which featured a shady garden, a terrace with flowers and a cook. 'I haven't seen all of the famous places in Rome,' she said, although she and the other leading cast and crew were given an audience with Pope Pius XII. 'I've been waiting for Tony so we can share the discovery of this beautiful Rome together. And Melanie, my daughter, two and a half, is the fatal attraction to keep me home when I'm not here in the studio.'

Deborah was up at 5 a.m. and in bed by 10 p.m. She said: 'The movie was made under terribly difficult conditions, enormous heat and many irritations … it was almost like making three movies, it went on so long.' On her days off, Deborah escaped the heat at a mountain resort in order to keep cool.

Quo Vadis went into production at the Cinecittà Studios on 22 May 1950. Mervyn Le Roy felt tense throughout as he knew how much was riding on the project – that if it went wrong, it could cause MGM to collapse. It was the most expensive film produced at that time and was ultimately a huge box-office hit around the world. With 235 speaking parts in the picture, and thousands more extras roles, more than 40,000 persons applied to the casting department.

Her mother told her just to say 'yes' to every question asked.

Standing outside those gates of the film studio, Sofia and Romilda managed to attract the casting scouts who selected the most promising from the crowds. They made it through the first round and were allowed through the gates. They were then placed in a line-up and director Mervyn LeRoy and his assistants reviewed them. He wanted faces with stand-out features, and who could deliver a line in English. Her mother told her just to say 'yes' to every question asked. So she parroted out 'yes' as an answer, until the director worked out that was all she could say, and burst out laughing at the charm of it. She won a non-speaking extra part in a crowd scene, where she enthusiastically threw flowers at Robert Taylor. Her mother was also given a bit part, where she held a bronze basket on her head all day.

The studio was noisy and hot from the lack of air-conditioning, as hundreds of extras were crowded onto the soundstage where they had to stand for hours. But the discomfort was beside the point, because it was the magic of the movies that was the attraction, in which a girl from a small town could be standing so close to the Hollywood royalty she read about in the magazines.

Sophia remembered in her autobiography that she:

> loved the hustle and bustle of the scenes, the noisy crowd of extras, the papier-mâché backdrops that each time would open up to a whole new world ... Cinecittà was a wonderland, a landscape of dreams in the making, all shuffled up like a house of cards. Ancient Romans sipped coffee with young soubrettes, great condottieri chatted with chorus girls, working-class women had a sandwich with men in tails.

Nineteen-year-old Elizabeth Taylor was in Rome on Honeymoon with hotel heir Nicky Hilton when the cinema quarter was in full swing for *Quo Vadis*. As a wedding gift, the Hiltons had paid for a three-month European honeymoon and Elizabeth and Nicky's tour of Italy also took in Florence, Verona and Venice, dodging the press and photographers. She travelled with a dozen suitcases and a poodle. They were young, rich and spoiled.

It had been a whirlwind romance and Elizabeth told reporters she knew the marriage would work 'because we both adore oversize sweaters, hamburgers with onions and Ezio Pinza'. But instead of the romance she was expecting, Nicky, a heavy drinker and gambler, dragged her to the casinos where he stayed all night, leaving her to go back to the hotel room alone. In Rome, after another violent fight, she needed to escape for a short time and contacted *Quo Vadis'* director Mervyn LeRoy, who had directed her in *Little Women*. As she told *Screenland* in December 1950:

> I just love Rome. The Colloseum is just like I read about in history. Isn't it wonderful seeing all of these famous places? For our first night in Rome, what do you think we did? We went out to Cinecittà to watch the night filming of Quo Vadis. It was so exciting seeing a movie being made again.

In the sanctuary of the studio set, she put on a tunic and joined the mob of extras to play a Christian slave girl for one day's filming. The *Los Angeles Times* reported that she 'found hundreds of Christian captives being herded towards the arena to be "fed to lions" or "burned to death". "Best fun I ever had," she said.' By the time she and Nicky arrived back in Los Angeles, their marriage had turned to dust. They divorced in February 1951. It was a bite of reality for someone who had always wanted to live their life in the movies. Her mother, Sara, once said: 'When other teenage girls were reading romantic stories and imagining themselves as the heroine, Elizabeth was living her dream world, by acting the role of the heroine – that is, at the studio.'

Similarly, the experience on *Quo Vadis* gave Sofia a taste of what could be possible, that she yearned to find fame in the movies. And the money Sofia and Romilda earned from being extras paid for two weeks' worth of their food. She and her mother tirelessly waited outside Cinecittà and visited production offices in the hope of being given small roles. She played a chorus girl in *Variety Lights* and briefly appeared as an abducted bride in *Bluebeard's Seven Wives*.

Sofia was left alone in Rome when Romilda had to rush back to care for an ill Maria. Without luck in being cast in other roles in films, she found work as a model. She appeared in *fotoromanzi* magazines, which were hugely popular magazines with photo comic strips that told a romantic story. They were given the nickname *fumetti*, as the photos of the models were captioned with their dialogue in puffs of smoke from their mouths.

Fotoromanzi reflected the new desires and experiences of Italian women and offered an escape from the post-war recovery and struggles, with their themes of betrayal and unrequited love. These magazines, such as *Grand Hotel* and *Sogno*, were constantly looked for new talent and new stories, and it could offer a gateway to the movies as it taught the models how to pose for a camera and to act out different expressions.

She was launched as the new cover star of *Sogno* on 2 December 1950 with an intense, passionate expression on her face to suit the character of a girl who wants to avenge the murder of her father. It was *Sogno* that came up with the idea of changing her name to Sofia Lazzaro – as it sounded much more exotic than Scicolone, and would suit the characters that she played, such as Persian princesses or gypsy girls. She was listed in a profile as having green eyes and chestnut hair, being a fan of Gregory Peck and a supporter of Lazio football club. She began to earn fan mail and requests for autographs, and *Cine Illustrato*'s serial 'Prisoner of a Dream', with Sofia as a singer in a Marseilles tavern, boosted their circulation to over half a million.

She continued looking for movie work, and entered a number of beauty contests where the judges were often powerful people in the movie business. These contests could be a gateway to fame, particularly as one of the finalists of Miss Italia 1947, Lucia Bosè, had a real fairy story. She had worked on the till in a Milan patisserie before winning Miss Italy and becoming a movie star. That same contest, Gina Lollobrigida had been discovered by influential producer Carlo Ponti.

Sofia came second in Miss Lazio, and took part in Miss Italy in Salsomaggiore in 1950. It was the first year Miss Italy winners were announced over the radio, and Sofia's photo, with her Lucia Bosè hairstyle, was placed in the newspapers as she had been given her own title, Miss Elegance, after coming second in the competition.

On a warm September night in 1951 she attended the Miss Italia contest at a terraced nightclub at the foot of the Colle Oppio, the smell of flowers being carried on the light breeze. While she was just with friends, and not planning to take part, Carlo Ponti, who was one of the judges on the night, had noticed her and sent her a message advising that she should enter. Sofia was excited to meet the powerful producer with twenty films under his belt, who had discovered Alida Valli and Gina Lollobrigida and was always on the lookout for the next big thing.

After dinner Ponti invited Sofia for a walk under the moonlight, and he suggested she do a screen test the next day. It turned out to be a disaster – she was too nervous and the cameraman complained her nose was too long. She was advised to 'soften' her features with a nose job, but she was secure enough to know that would completely change her face, whereas her unique beauty was the way these irregular features all came together. Yet Ponti could see something special in the 17-year-old, and not just in a professional capacity. 'I don't like actors, I like women,' he famously once said.

Carlo Ponti, born on 11 December 1912, in Milan, had at first wanted to be an architect and only got into the film industry by accident. After studying law, he was invited by a friend to join a film company, where he became an executive vice president and producer. After the war, he helped to kick start post-war Italy's movie industry with his partner Dino De Laurentiis.

Sofia began spending time with Carlo even though he was married and more than double her age. He helped to soften her Neapolitan accent by coaching her to read out loud, he advised her on how to dress, and one evening at dinner, when she began tucking into an omelette with a knife and fork, he subtly taught her the proper way – without the knife.

After a number of small roles, including with her first screen kiss with actor Walter Chiari in *Zorro's Dreams*, Ponti cast Sofia in her first leading role in *La Favorita* (1952). Her *fotoromanzi* fans were excited to see her come to life on screen. Sofia was offered the leading role in *Africa under the Sea*, winning the part after lying that she could swim. 'I almost drowned. I wanted to do that picture – it was very important to me,' she said. 'When they asked me if I could swim, I said 'of course, I'm Neapolitan. In Naples everybody's a champion.

When I made a big fuss about not wanting to get in the water the first day, they threw me in.'

It was with this role that her name was changed once more – with the spelling altered to Sophia, and with a new surname, Loren, after beautiful Swedish actress Märta Torén.

Sogno paid tribute to their star in her final photostrip and front cover, that the 'unforgettable interpreter of so many of our photo-romances, has been whisked away to the movies: but Sofia hasn't forgotten the readers of *Sogno*, and to them she fondly bids farewell and promises to remember them forever'.

Sophia, with her earnings kept under the mattress, was able to pay for a small room on Via Cosenza, to move in with her mother and sister, and where Romilda broke the rules of the patrona by cooking with a hot plate in the bathroom. As Sophia earned more with her work, she was able to upgrade to a small apartment on Via Severano.

Sophia was given another big break when Gina Lollobrigida dropped out of the operatic movie *Aida* after being told her voice would be dubbed. For Sophia, the success of *Aida* allowed her to pay her father a million lire to allow her illegitimate sister to take his surname. Riccardo was unwilling to be the father they needed, and Sophia continued to be the breadwinner. The money she earned from this film allowed her family to move to a larger apartment on Via Balzani. 'I was the head of the family, the husband, going out to work every day, my mother was the wife, and my sister ... was the child.'

During the making of *Quo Vadis*, director Vittorio De Sica had noticed 15-year-old Sophia on set, and saw something promising within her. When they met again, and he recognised her, he knew she would be perfect as the pizzaiola, or pizza girl, in *The Gold of Naples*, an affectionate tale of Naples in six episodes. Even though Dino De Laurentiis had wanted Lollobrigida for the part, De Sica insisted on Sophia. He taught her how to hide her shyness by expressing herself through her laugh, her walk and her body movements. Playing the pizza girl from Naples, only a short distance from her home town, would be a reminder of surviving the hunger of the war, without a father to guide her.

6

AUDREY

By 1952 film-makers from across Europe and the States were coming to Rome to film at Cinecittà and to absorb the excitement of the city. French auteur Jean Renoir directed Anna Magnani in *The Golden Coach* in 1952, while producer David O. Selznick hired Vittorio De Sica to direct his wife Jennifer Jones and Montgomery Clift in *Stazione Termini*. After *Quo Vadis*, sword and sandal epics were also becoming a mainstay for films being made at Cinecittà, including *Helen of Troy* with Brigitte Bardot. Rome was buzzing with stars on the Via Veneto, Fiat motorcars and scooters zoomed around the city, and the city had an excitement for film-makers with the echoes of ancient Rome in the walls of its palazzos, or its cobbled, narrow streets clad in ivy offering the perfect romantic moment.

'All over Rome today, almost everyone seems to be talking movies, making them, or helping in the process. The creative spirit flourishes, and discussions are not limited to the city's eight major studios or to the fashionable Via Veneto, that vital showcase for has-beens and want-to-be's,' said the *New York Times* in 1952. Movie stars were checking into the top-tier hotels across Rome, which were significantly cheaper than they would be in the States, soaking up the relaxed Italian lifestyle, and drinking in the best bars on Via Veneto.

In June 1952 a young actress and dancer named Audrey Hepburn checked into the Hotel Hassler to begin work on *Roman Holiday*, her first lead role in a major film. The sought-after hotel, situated at the top of the Spanish Steps, was a favourite for the film crowd, and for 22-year-old Audrey it was 'way over my head – I could never afford them before'. The luxury she was now surrounded by didn't go unnoticed, particularly because she had been close to starvation during a childhood spent in Nazi-occupied Holland. 'When you have had the strength to survive starvation,' she later reflected, 'you never again send back a steak simply because it's under-done.'

Screenwriter Dalton Trumbo first penned his story of a runaway princess in Rome in the mid 1940s, but after being blacklisted by the House of Un-American Activities for alleged communist leanings, he was shunned by Hollywood and his name would be left off the credits. Trumbo's story was adapted into a script by Ian McLellan Hunter and the rights were bought by director Frank Capra who envisioned Elizabeth Taylor and Cary Grant as a perfect pairing of princess and reporter. Capra ultimately passed on it and William Wyler was offered the script in 1951. Ben Hecht, known as 'the Shakespeare of Hollywood', worked his magic on the screenplay in 1951, John Dighton added additional dialogue, and Italian writers Ennio Flaiano and Suso Cecchi d'Amico contributed to the script once production was under way.

The script for *Roman Holiday* had resonance with Princess Elizabeth, whose fate was aligned to duty when she became queen after the death of King George VI in February 1952. Spirited, mischievous Princess Margaret, whose love affair with a divorcee, Captain Peter Townsend, caused upset in the monarchy in 1953, also had to sacrifice love for duty and the film, on its release, drew a parallel with her life. Hecht and Wyler researched articles on Princess Margaret in order to gain an understanding of life for a young royal. The British Censors were very nervous about any connection to Margaret and Elizabeth, insisting that it be made clear that the fictional princess was from a small European country. Of particular concern was an article by Helen Tubbs that appeared in *Hollywood Variety* in June 1952, and which insinuated their film was about Princess Margaret, despite producers' efforts to play down the connection.

In fact *Roman Holiday*, while it shared similarities to the two real-life princesses, could be considered a portrait of Audrey herself – a daughter of a baroness with an innocent *joie de vivre*, who suffered hardships during the war and found success through her talent and beauty. It was a fairytale that matched the type of film Audrey would make a career out of – the Cinderella stories of *Sabrina*, *Funny Face* and *My Fair Lady*.

When McLellan Hunter originally worked on the script in 1949, he included the hot spots in Rome where American visitors gathered. Café Doney, the favourite spot for the Hollywood crowd immediately after the war, was to feature with an establishing shot, Café Vento was to make an appearance, and newspaperman Joe was to take the Princess to Raphael's, the ivy-covered hotel at the back of Piazza Navona with its majestic terrace with views across the terracotta tiles to the city's towers and ripened domes.

By the time the film was being made in 1952, the shape of Rome was changing as tourists became more prevalent in the city. As Art Cohn, the screenwriter who worked on the script for *Stromboli*, conveyed to Hedda Hopper in August 1953: 'Rome has changed since you and I saw it in 1949. The chairs lining the sidewalk of Doney's, like the daily promenades on the Via Veneto, are the same, but the people in them are different. Four years ago they were wealthy Americans; today they are wealthy Italians.'

'Americans have changed too,' Mario, the bartender at the Excelsior, recounted to Cohn. 'Four years ago they kept the bar open until five or six every morning and almost everyone got drunk. Now the place is dead before midnight and we don't even get one drunk a month. Americans now drink like anyone else. Maybe it's because they don't have any war money left.'

Inspired by the success of films produced on location in Italy, such as *September Affair*, Wyler was convinced he could make a high-quality, cost-effective film in Rome. It would be completely filmed, edited, scored and dubbed in Rome, and many of the admired and trusted Italian crew who had worked on *Quo Vadis* were hired again for

Roman Holiday. To further save money, Wyler chose to film *Roman Holiday* in black and white, despite the vibrancy of Rome lending itself perfectly to Technicolor, and, as he recalled, 'by the time I'd realized my error it was too late to get enough color stock over to Italy.'

While the script was being developed, Wyler searched for an actress to play the princess – someone who had the poise and aristocratic air, while also revealing a playful and vulnerable side. 'I don't need a stellar leading lady,' he said. 'I want a girl without an American accent to play the princess, someone you can believe has been brought up as a princess. That's the main requirement – besides acting, looks, and personality.'

In July 1951, 22-year-old virtual unknown Audrey Hepburn, the same age as Princess Margaret, was brought to Wyler's attention and was described as 'a little on the thin side … but very appealing'. Audrey's mother Ella was raised in Doorn Castle, near Utrecht in Holland, and as a baroness, was a descendent of Dutch royalty. 'She is one of us,' Queen Elizabeth, the Queen Mother, was said to have told her daughters on meeting Hepburn. After marrying and divorcing a nobleman, Jonkheer Hendrik Gustaaf Adolf Quarles van Ufford, with whom she had two sons, Ella married an English–Irish businessman called Joseph Hepburn-Ruston, and they married in 1926. Audrey Kathleen Van Heemstra Ruston was born in Brussels on 4 May 1929, certified as a British citizen and travelling between Belgium, England and Arnhem.

Audrey's first visits to Rome actually took place in the 1930s, when her mother and father visited the city in support of Mussolini, a fact that would be painful to Audrey later in life. Sean Ferrer, her son, says that their support for Mussolini, as well as for the British Union of Fascists, stemmed from their noble background, when it had been fashionable to flirt with fascist politics in the 1930s:

> They came from a background of nobility, they liked the fact that things seemed to be running well under these particular political regimes and so they would spend holidays near Rome. Obviously being in England, lots of people liked to go south, and they could have picked Spain, but they spent time by the seaside in Rome. She didn't talk much about that,

but in retrospect as she grew up when she realised what it meant, she wasn't very proud of it. But she had been a little girl.

Audrey was photographed in 1937 at Ostia, the popular beach near Rome, in a large sun hat, shorts and a top – standing beside the wooden beach huts that once lined the beach. A photo from July 1938 showed a family picnic in the pine woods around Fregene with her mother and brothers, but absent from these photos was her father. Ruston walked out on his wife and daughter in 1935, when Audrey was 6 years old. She went to boarding school in England, seeing him in the holidays in Rome, but his departure was a tragic life event of which she said: 'I don't think I've ever recovered.'

At the start of the Second World War, Ella returned to Arnhem with Audrey as it seemed a safer place to remain than London which was facing the Blitz. But its safety was short-lived as the Nazis invaded Holland and what followed was five years living in fear under fascist control. By the end of the war, 16-year-old Audrey weighed 90lb and suffered asthma, jaundice, anaemia – all caused by malnutrition. She and her mother moved to London, setting up home on South Audley Street, Mayfair, while Audrey continued to study ballet. However her dreams of being a prima-ballerina were set back by the loss of training and strength during the war, and while she continued to practise, she also auditioned for stage roles. She was cast in the chorus line of musicals *High Button Shoes* and *Sauce Tartare*, showcasing her vivacious personality, and small roles in British films followed, before she was personally chosen by elderly French writer Colette, who observed that she would be the perfect *Gigi* for the Broadway stage adaptation of her novel.

Audrey came close to being chosen for a film production in Rome a couple of years earlier. While doing a small part in *Lavender Hill Mob*, British actor Alec Guinness was struck by Audrey's star quality and 'her faunlike beauty and presence'. He introduced her to director Mervyn LeRoy, who was in London casting for his epic *Quo Vadis*. Audrey was tested in Roman costume, but ultimately, she was too inexperienced to be considered for the main role of Lygia, which went to Deborah Kerr. But Rome would be on the horizon once more when she met

Wyler and his wife in a hotel in London to discuss the role. Audrey's *Roman Holiday* screen test was carried out at Pinewood Studios on 18 September 1951. Unaware that the film was kept running while she was interviewed, she recounted her childhood experience of delivering notes for the Dutch resistance. The test revealed how natural she was, yet also reflecting an air of regality, and William Wyler was won over by what he had seen. 'Everyone at the studio was very enthused about the girl and I am delighted we have signed her,' he said. With *Roman Holiday* Audrey found herself in the unique situation of going from being a chorus girl, to starring in smash-hit Broadway show *Gigi*, to winning the lead role in a major film.

On top of her *Gigi* and *Roman Holiday* commitments, Audrey also had a fiancé to spend time with, and who would visit her in New York for weekends while she performed on stage. James Hanson, whose millionaire father owned a Huddersfield transport company, had a reputation as a playboy who liked expensive motorcars and mixed in celebrity circles. Having previously dated Jean Simmons, an elfin beauty initially considered by Wyler for *Roman Holiday*, Audrey may well have been James' type, and his charming, confident traits measured up to the type of men she would fall for. Audrey and Hanson hoped to arrange a wedding in his home town of Huddersfield, but it became increasingly difficult as Audrey's schedule filled up.

The last performance of *Gigi* was on 31 May, and as soon as she finished, she left for Paris with James for a much-needed holiday, en route to Rome. After Hanson headed back to London, Audrey arrived in Rome on 12 June on a Pan Am flight from Paris, carrying her Edith-Head designed movie wardrobe with her to save Paramount import duty.

Gregory Peck also arrived from Paris with wife Greta and three sons, Jonathan, 8, Steven, 6, and 3-year-old Carey Paul, staying with him for his extended visit to Rome. Peck drove a hard bargain for his expenses, accommodation and transport when in Rome. Not only did he make three times the salary of Audrey, but he was offered a villa 15 miles from Rome, overlooking the vineyards of Albano, and featuring a marble swimming pool and exotic gardens.

The production officially opened on 23 June. It was a record-breaking heat in Rome over the summer of 1952, and while Audrey would wear one outfit for most of her scenes in the city, it was doubled up to take into account the wear and tear from the sunshine and sweat. Because Audrey's hair was cut into a fashionable crop, she required hairpieces and falls to be shipped in for the longer hair style of Princess Ann. With concern about the size of her chest, Edith Head also airmailed to the Grand Hotel several pairs of falsies to build her up.

Audrey was forever grateful for the opportunity so early in her career. She said she learnt 'almost everything' from William Wyler. 'I was a dancer and all of a sudden now I had to act, which I had never really done before. I'd done a play but I had never been in front of a camera. But then I was also joyfully innocent … somehow Greg and Willy made me feel good and were so helpful and so kind, but he was a very exacting director, although I never realized it.'

Filming in Rome over the summer of 1952 was not without issues – it was noisy, hot and crowded, and tourists and local people were all eager to catch a glimpse of filming. There were also political protests happening throughout the summer and fights in the streets as fascists, communists and Christian democrats all clashed.

The first day of filming took place in the late nineteenth-century baroque Palazzo Brancaccio, representing the embassy of Ann's country. Its gilt-edged frescoed walls and mirrored halls were filled with Italian nobility who had answered a casting call for the film, bringing along their jewels and gowns for the reception scene, as they rested on velvet chairs or carpeted floors while waiting for their turn. The heat was even more stifling indoors, particularly under hot lights, and Audrey, dressed in a flannel nightgown, had to run into another room and fling open a window to let the breeze inside.

Ben Hecht had detailed in his script a scooter chase through the streets of Rome, and Wyler was enthusiastic about this set-piece to take the audience on a fast-paced, mad cap journey through the city's main sites. Vespa offered Wyler two scooters to use in the film and for publicity purposes. They began filming the scooter scene on 30 July 1952, and it took five days.

In the original script, Princess Ann was to have made her escape from the embassy in the back of a milk truck, however deemed inaccurate to the story, it was changed to one loaded with crates of Cinzano and San Pellegrino, the bottles clinking as the cart rattles through the street. It suited perfectly the bustling Rome of young people on Vespas and in street cafés.

Some of the other sites included the Roman Forum, where Joe Bradley and Ann first meet at the Arco di Settimio Severo. He takes her back to his apartment at 61 Via Margutta, with its rambling terrace overlooking the courtyard. The ivy-covered courtyard leads out onto the bustling cobbled street, which in the early 1950s was a tin pan alley with cars, trucks and artist's studios. She had her haircut at a barbers' on the Via della Stamperia, directly opposite the Trevi Fountain, and enjoyed a gelati from Giolitti's while admiring the view from the Spanish Steps. At night they take the steps down to the Tiber, to a river nightclub covered in lights and in front of Castel Sant Angelo, which were popular meeting places for young people after the war.

For the scenes at Piazza di Spagna an estimated 10,000 people gathered at the foot of the Spanish Steps, which Peck described as being similar to acting in a 'huge amphitheater before a packed house of rowdies'. But Audrey found she could settle into it and enjoy it. She played around on set doing cartwheels or sharing jokes with cast and crew, and her youthful energy charmed those who met her. 'Those gams, that face' said John Huston, when he met her in Rome that summer while attending the Venice Film Festival to promote *Moulin Rouge*.

She told Modern Screen in 1953: 'The American method of picture-making was slightly diluted by the Roman and Italian atmosphere. I don't think I'll get the real American method until I work in Hollywood. I thought it was a great combination – good Hollywood organization with a bit of Roman sunshine thrown in.'

'It was a happy time, probably her happier times in Rome,' says her son Sean. She and Ella enjoyed the cafés and trattorias of old Rome, a chilled latte macchiato in the sunshine, or visiting Babington's, an English tea room by the Spanish Steps and only a few steps from the Keats–Shelley house. Often she enjoyed a glass of whisky or a cold beer around 5 p.m., and plates of pasta swimming in tomato sauce for dinner. But doing the rounds of nightclubs was not her style. She was far too conscientious. She would be in bed early to ensure she had seven and a half hours sleep before the early morning starts. 'My mother was very serious and she felt maybe she wasn't as good as other actresses and so she always wanted to make up for it by being professional, and being on time,' said Sean. 'So I would have thought, six day week in Rome, have a rest, go for a walk, eat some pizza, but she wasn't one who liked to go for hours sitting in a nightclub.'

'Even today, tourists don't really want to put their hands in there ...'

Production broke up for the Ferragosto weekend, an Italian celebration mid August to mark the Assumption of Mary. Wyler spent his weekend in the beach resort of Fregene staying on the Via Levanto and where he would have to make arrangements to pick up any telephone messages at the nearby bar.

Peck looked back on his 'wonderful summer in Rome', with great fondness, and he called it 'probably the happiest experience I ever had making movies'. One of the most treasured scenes between the two was the Mouth of Truth scene, capturing a moment of uncensored joy between the two. Audrey Hepburn told Terry Wogan in 1988:

> Even today, tourists don't really want to put their hands in there. It's a tourist site where everybody goes to, but when we rehearsed it I didn't know what he was going to do, and he didn't do it in the rehearsal, but he did it in the shot, this terrible thing with his sleeve. It was one of those tricks that was played on me.

The two co-stars' easy rapport and natural affinity was evident, and it led to a constant stream of rumours about a supposed affair, not helped that during filming Greta left to return to Finland, as cracks in their marriage began to show. Instead of a romance with Audrey, he had fallen for a French journalist, Veronique Passani, who interviewed him in Paris and they were soon married. Peck called Audrey 'wacky and funny, a very lovable girl who was always making faces and doing back flips and clowning around'.

Audrey's fiancé James Hanson arrived almost every weekend to see her, visiting her air-conditioned suite at the Hotel Hassler and then staying at an apartment on the Via Boncompagni that she moved into with her mother. While Ella was considered to be a woman of Victorian temperament, she was relaxed enough to allow James and Audrey to share a room together in Rome. He recalled, 'it was the first time in my life I had ever slept in the same bed as my fiancée – with her mother bringing the breakfast in. That was something I had never experienced. There was always a rather furtive dashing back to your room. But Ella was completely different. I remember her bringing the breakfast into that room.'

James Hanson spent time with cast and crew while filming throughout the city, relaxing in Audrey's trailer and watching her perform to the cameras, or playing gin rummy on marble-topped tables for hours with Gregory Peck at the Caffé Greco on the Via Condotti. Hanson was enthusiastic and encouraging of her career, but he also wanted to tie down Paramount to confirming a date for when she could be finished in Rome and they could be married in Huddersfield. Audrey's wedding dress was hanging in her wardrobe in Rome ready in wait for final confirmation of the wedding day, but with production behind schedule, there were worries she wouldn't have enough time between returning to New York on 1 October to report back for *Gigi*.

Securing a reservation on a steamship from Europe to America was proving particularly difficult over summer 1952, with places having to be booked up far in advance. Hanson wrote of his concerns to Paramount, asking that she be released in sufficient time. But despite Hanson's intervention, the production ran over and Audrey wasn't released until 25 September, only giving her a week before she had to get back to New York. Hanson's family expected a Yorkshire wedding and so they had to put their wedding plans on hold once more as she toured across American with *Gigi*. Paramount, had even been kind enough to give as a wedding gift the $3,000 worth of costumes from production, after she had asked Edith Head if she could keep them. The studio knew that they had a star on their hands, and they hoped that Gregory Peck would agree to sharing top-billing with her, despite his contract originally specifying only he receive billing over the film title. 'Audrey was the spirit of youth,' said Wyler. 'And I knew that very soon the entire world would fall in love with her, as all of us on the picture did.'

To capture this youthful spirit in the advertising and posters, the publicity people knew that the Vespa scene would help to make the film a hit, particularly with images of Peck and Hepburn riding the scooter in front of the Colloseum, while expressing 'happiness and abandon on the part of both the stars'. It was these photos that became one of the symbols of Americans in Rome in the 1950s.

Rome may have been the city of enchantment and romances for others, but for Audrey it marked the end of her engagement to Hanson. On 15 December 1952, it was announced that their engagement had been broken.

The ending was amicable – she told him she didn't think she could be married at this time. While James Hanson would have supported her career and encouraged her, she knew at this point that her life was destined for something else. 'I suddenly knew I'd make a pretty bad wife,' she told writer Anita Loos. 'I would forever have to be studying parts, fitting costumes and giving interviews. And what a humiliating spot to put a husband in … making him stand by, holding my coat, while I signed autographs for the bobby soxers!' *Roman Holiday* opened in New York in August 1953, and in the midst of a heatwave, it seemed to lift the spirits of all those who watched it. 'This is the most delectable romantic comedy I have seen in years. What makes it so outstanding?' wrote Lionel Collier in *Picturegoer*. 'There's the graciousness and range of expression of Audrey Hepburn, who plays the heroine's part with a sweep that sends her soaring.'

The final film was a love letter to the city; ice cream on the Spanish Steps, window shopping on the Via Condotti, dancing on a barge on the Tiber, champagne at G Rocca café by the Pantheon, a ride around the Colloseum on a Vespa and placing her hand in the Bocca della Verita, at the Basilica di Santa Maria in Cosmedin, lying in the shadow of the Forum. It was this scene of the Mouth of Truth that helped to make it one of the most-visited in Rome, with images of Brigitte Bardot and Alfred Hitchcock testing their hand in the grotesque sculpture.

On the back of *Roman Holiday*, Audrey Hepburn became a huge star and won the Oscar for Best Actress in 1954. Descriptions of her flew around: 'coltish', 'gazelle-like, 'elfin', 'enchanting'. She was described as 'Half nymph, half Wunderkind, wholly herself', and offering 'a curious combination of adolescent bounce and complete self-possession, whether she is whamming a cop, nibbling an ice cream cone or relinquishing a lover, she is completely believable'.

It was a favourite film in Japan, earning back a third of production costs there as the dreamy plotline allowed for a fantasy for Japanese teenagers also suffering from horrific defeat and occupation by the Americans. In fifties Japan, Audrey's look became a fashion trend, with Tokyo girls sporting cropped hair, and little Audrey Hepburn neckties. Audrey in her latte-coloured skirt, the white cotton blouse with its sleeves rolled up, and the necktie around her neck, was the inspirational style for holidaying in Rome. It was a film that showed the promise of rebirth, recovery and optimism and represented a new beginning for Rome in the 1950s. 'I remember the fifties as a time of renewal and of regained security,' Audrey said. 'There was a rebirth of opportunity, vitality and enthusiasm … a return to laughter and gaiety – the world was functioning again. Above all there was a wonderful quality of hope, born from relief and gratitude for those greatest of all luxuries – freedom and peace.'

As a follow up to its success, Cinemascope was utilised by 20th Century Fox that year for *Three Coins in the Fountain* – a tale of three perky American girls working in Rome while searching for love. It was a fantasy romance of sun-drenched piazzas and handsome Italians, the promise of marriage waiting round the corner, and fiestas and feasts set amongst the cypress trees and olive groves. It also brought further to prominence the seventeenth-century baroque Trevi Fountain, showcasing the custom of throwing a coin into its luminous blue waters, to be sure they would return to Rome.

7

AVA

Ava Gardner much preferred the night-time, when the sun had set, the drinks were flowing and the jazz was playing, and where magic happened under the stars and moonlight. 'It takes talent to live at night. Not many people have it,' she once said. From a childhood in the tobacco fields of North Carolina to being a major star in Hollywood, Ava left the United States in favour of Rome, Madrid and London where she mixed with the European jet-set and was constantly on the run from the photographers. As a nocturnal creature it suited her living in cities with a Latin beat to its heart, where dinner was served late and nightclubs opened until sunrise. 'When the sun sets, honey, I feel more, oh, alert,' she said in her autobiography. 'More alive. By midnight I feel fantastic. Even when I was a little girl, my father would shake his head and say, "let's just hope you get a job where you work nights."'

She may have been a party girl in the 1940s, drinking rum cocktails in pineapples at the tropical-themed bars near Hollywood boulevard – the Luau, Don the Beachcombers, the Mocambo – but Ava had never warmed to Los Angeles. It was a city she felt no connection with despite her years working there as an MGM starlet. To Ava, it was where marriages seemed to unravel under the spotlight, and ever since returning with husband Frank Sinatra, after their wedding in

Philadelphia on 7 November 1951, she had the feeling that the gossip columnists were in anticipation of her third marriage blowing up.

Ava and Frank had first met when she was a young bride married to Mickey Rooney. Frank, with his god-like charisma, particularly to the young studio starlets, made some comment that if he had seen Ava first he would have married her. They met again a few years later in Palm Springs at a party. After an evening of downing liquor they went for a drunken late night car ride, shooting off a gun in the desert town of Indio, hitting street lights and windows before being pulled over by the cops and let off with a warning and a $50,000 payment.

The first sparks of serious romance at the end of 1949 gained press attention and Ava was quickly billed as a marriage wrecker. Sinatra always maintained he was separated from his wife Nancy by this time, although she had only had their third child, Tina, the year before. Such was the scandal that Ava received poison letters calling her a tramp and a marriage wrecker. 'The year 1950 will go down in the records as the year of the open season on Ava Gardner and Frank Sinatra,' said *Modern Screen*. They were two young people in love, but 'the whole fucking world's press was on our necks', as Ava recounted. 'Reporters loved making a scandal out of our lives, and Frank's behaviour never helped. He hated the press. He loathed reporters with a passion. They were all sons of bitches. I don't know how they did it but those creeps always knew where to find us, and how to get a rise out of Frank.'

Ava and Frank had taken over from Ingrid Bergman and Roberto Rossellini as the most famous couple in the world, and were infamous for their blazing rows. The battling Sinatras drank too much (maybe four martinis to warm up, followed by wine with dinner and bourbon in a nightclub), they fought violently and then made up passionately. But 'he was good in the feathers. You don't pay too much attention to what other people tell you when a guy's good in the feathers.'

As well as the pressures of the media, Sinatra was flat broke from his divorce. After years as a singing sensation and top movie star, his MGM movie contract had been cancelled, and the young, teenage bobby soxers had stopped buying his records and moved onto another style of music. While Frank's career was fading, Ava's was thriving.

As part of her MGM contract she had signed a morality clause, facing instant dismissal for any scandalous behaviour. She was lucky to escape with her career intact, but she had proved she could ride the storm of a scandal and still be loved by the audience. The good money she earned from movies like *Show Boat* and *The Snows of Mount Kilimanjaro* paid for the Sinatras' rent and enabled them to travel. By 1952 Ava Gardner, according to Hedda Hopper, was 'hot as a heatwave in Texas'.

Frank, without any job offers, followed his sought-after wife to Kenya for her filming commitments for *Mogambo*. As a man prone to deep depression and self-doubt, Frank felt like the washed-up star he was being billed as, particularly when journalists referred to him as 'Mr Gardner' and 'Frankie' and asked his wife what she saw in a 120lb has-been. Ava continued to support and reassure her husband, appealing directly to Columbia Pictures boss Harry Cohn for Frank to audition for the part of Maggio in *From Here to Eternity*, a role he felt he was born to do. He won the role, and his career in 1953 was rejuvenated.

Ava was hugely jealous over his reputation as a lady's man, and whenever they were apart she imaged that he was with other women. 'I was so jealous every minute he was away from me,' she said. 'When I couldn't get him on the telephone right away at Las Vegas or wherever he was I wanted to kill myself.' They had another blazing row over the phone, she accused him of cheating, and that was it – an announcement in the press to confirm their official separation in October 1953 and she headed for Rome a month later.

After completing *Mogambo*, she had been scheduled to take on the role of a Parisian nightclub singer who falls for a young American about to go into priesthood in Rome, scheduled for Rome and Paris in spring 1953, although this part never materialised. When she heard that Joseph L. Mankiewicz's *The Barefoot Contessa* was being prepared for filming in Rome, a stay in the Eternal City was very appealing. She loved the Italian temperament, the anything-goes nightlife and the beauty of the Mediterranean countryside and coastline.

In early 1953, on a stopover after filming *Mogambo* in Kenya, Ava, with her co-star Grace Kelly and cameraman Robert Surtrees, spent a wild evening in Rome. Surtees acted as tour guide as he had spent a year in Rome for the filming of *Quo Vadis*, and Ava insisted they do a brothel-hop around the dens of Via Margutta, chatting to the prostitutes about their lives and buying them drinks. She got a kick out of touring the decadent, illicit parts of cities – Paris's demimonde, the gay bars of San Francisco, the rum bars and hot, sweaty clubs of Havana.

Pennsylvania-born writer and director Mankiewicz was considered one of the top directors and writers for women. His multi-award-winning *All about Eve*, released in 1951, nominated for fourteen Oscars and winning six, was a biting critique of the New York theatre world, and his line for Bette Davis, 'Fasten your seatbelt – it's going to be a bumpy night,' instantly became a classic.

His new script, *The Barefoot Contessa*, was to be an *All about Eve* for the movies, a commentary on café society and the jet set with thinly disguised versions of the Duke of Windsor, King Farouk, Howard Hughes and his right-hand man Johnny Meyer. But with its long monologues and indulgent prose, it was not that well received by critics or the public until it got a later lease of life in art cinema and an appreciation for its beauty and depth of Technicolor.

The story is of a poor Spanish dancer, Maria Vargas, who is discovered by a movie director and rises up the ranks of society, first as an actress and then by marrying into Italian aristocracy. The common assumption was Maria was based on Rita Hayworth, the movie star who began as a dancer in Tijuana nightclubs, before marrying Prince Aly Khan. But Mankiewicz visualised Ava Gardner in the role and he was desperate to cast her, despite strong interest from other actresses including Jennifer Jones. Ava could undoubtedly see the similarities with her own life and was certain that Mankiewicz based Maria on her, 'right down to the soles of my feet. Later he said she was based on Rita. That was crap.' Ava's was a Cinderella story, of a girl from the dust of the North Carolina countryside who was coached to be a Hollywood starlet at the age of eighteen.

Born on Christmas Eve 1922 to a poor farming family in Grabtown, North Carolina, her tomboy childhood was spent climbing trees and running barefoot through the tobacco fields of her family's farm in Grabtown, near Smithfield, as she loved the feel of the dirt and the grass between her toes. MGM coached out her accent, she was given lessons in singing and dancing, and taught how to pose playfully for the camera in a swimsuit or short skirt. After years of small roles, she got her break as a femme fatale in film noir, first in *Whistle Stop* (1945) and then as Kitty Collins in *The Killers* (1946), slinking on screen like a panther in black satin.

Her authenticity, along with her feline beauty, was what made her so appealing. Ava was 'a hot number', according to Miles Davis, 'the world's most beautiful animal', according to film posters, and had a wild reputation for being the last up at the party. She was the country girl who preferred going barefoot and flinging off her shoes to dance, and despite the after effects of too much booze, she would still look luminous on set the next day.

Journalist Stephen Birmingham said 'she would do her hair with toothpicks from the olives in martinis and it would look great. She could walk out of a hotel without makeup wearing flats, one of those kilt-type skirts with a big safety pin in it and a simple peasant blouse and she looked gorgeous. She had an ability to find the key light, the one that made her look the best.'

She wanted the role of Maria so much – it fitted her like a glove, and she 'knew that lady inside and out, in bed and out of bed. Especially in bed.' But MGM was refusing to loan her out, and when Mankiewicz arrived in Rome to prepare for the film, he thought he should consider another actress. He kept Linda Darnell in mind, having written part of the script while in bed with her. And when Elizabeth Taylor flew into Rome for a stay at the Grand Hotel, she was shown a script for consideration.

Finally, Ava sent a telegram to MGM's head, Nicholas Schenck, that she was 'desperately anxious to do this picture. I think the least that the company can do is to give me some measure of happiness in doing this kind of part. I want to do it at this time because I could leave for Europe immediately.' She had done every film that they had thrown at her, and she was insistent on this in return. MGM finally agreed, and an article in the *LA Daily News* on 23 November 1953 announced her imminent departure to Europe: 'Smokey-eyed actress Ava Gardner was packing for Rome and one of the things she did not slip into her suitcase was down to 118lb Frank Sinatra.'

News of her expected arrival in Rome dominated headlines with gossip and speculation around whether they would get back together again. As a tempestuous celebrity, and one of the most exciting, glamorous women in the world, she was considered fair game for the photographers of Italy, particularly as she had been married and separated three times, and she was still only 30 years old.

Press agent for *The Barefoot Contessa* was David Hanna, who considered the film a publicist's dream. He wrote in his memoirs: 'From Rome, where normally sensible journalists seize on anything to do with the movies like children reaching out for candy, there would be no trouble in doing a good job … publicity clichés wrote themselves – the closed set, the provocative title, the secrecy of the script and the casting of the caricatures.'

On the date of her arrival, photographers and reporters all jostled for a good spot on the tarmac at Ciampino airport. The plane touched down, all the other passengers disembarked, and then Gardner appeared at the top of the ramp. She was dressed in a light grey suit jacket, pleated skirt, a polka-dot scarf around her neck and with a coat draped over her arm. Having fixed herself up on the plane to be camera-ready before disembarking, she appeared serene and self-possessed. With a warm smile held in place, her eyes kept straight ahead, she walked briskly through the crowd.

'I just put the slightest scent on my fingers when I mix martinis,' she told him.

'No comment,' she replied firmly to those reporters who asked her about Frank. She was whisked to the Grand Hotel in a Cadillac, poised with the engine running, and her dozen or so pieces of luggage following on after her. Mankiewicz was waiting for her in her suite, which had been filled with flowers, and relieved to have arrived after a long journey, she cracked open the champagne, kicked off her shoes and launched into discussion with Mankiewicz on their film. 'You know, I've got pretty feet,' she said, wiggling her toes in the air. 'Hell Joe, I'm not an actress, but I think I understand this girl. She's a lot like me.' She hadn't read the entire script, she confessed, but she adored the synopsis.

A few nights later, Arthur Krim, United Artist's president, invited Ava to join and him and David Hanna for dinner, and arranged to meet in Ava's Grand Hotel suite at 8 p.m. Hanna arrived to find the door to her room slightly ajar, and after entering, he found Ava alone, shimmering in a beautiful gown and jewellery. She offered to make him a martini, and used her fingers to drop some ice from the bucket to the cocktail shaker and gently stirring the cocktail with her hand, so as not to bruise the gin with metal. 'I just put the slightest scent on my fingers when I mix martinis,' she told him. Arthur arrived and after drinks they headed to Alfredo's on Piazza Augusto Imperatore, the restaurant where celebrities went on their first days in Rome.

While the house band played music especially for Ava, the famous Alfredo di Lelio personally delivered to her a plate of his legendary fettuccine, with plenty of butter and parmesan cheese. He ceremoniously mixed it at the table with the golden fork and spoon given to him by Mary Pickford and Douglas Fairbanks when they paid a visit to the original branch on Via della Scrofa in 1927. David said, 'although she had dominated the evening, she was charming and vivacious, and unlike most celebrities, a delight to be with.'

Embracing a new start in a new city, this was a chance for Ava to make a new home in Europe, and rather than continue to live out of a hotel room she demanded she be given an apartment. In fact she had phoned David Hanna in the middle of the night, as she was prone to do when she was restless and couldn't sleep, and made sure finding a place was a top priority. After a few days of searching, she settled on a luxurious but musty and dark first floor apartment on the Corso D'Italia, a fashionable and busy street that runs along part of the Aurelian Walls and the outskirts of the Borghese gardens. It had rococo furniture, statues and muraled walls and a huge, untuned piano took up one section of the room. The bedroom looked out onto Corso D'Italia, which was noisy with car engines, scooters and night-time conversations from passersby, but Ava, an insomniac who would often stay awake until 4 a.m., she found these street noises comforting.

Her maid Reenie, her chef and driver were all tasked with tidying up the apartment, and as they opened up the shutters to let the light in, Ava wrapped a scarf around her head and helped to sweep up the dust and shift furniture around. In order to hang up and display her expensive gowns, she placed the glass-doored cupboards next to each other in her dressing room, creating the effect of a salon display.

A press conference for *The Barefoot Contessa* was held at the Grand Hotel ballroom to welcome Ava to Rome for the pre-production, although filming was not due to start until after the New Year, when Humphrey Bogart was scheduled to arrive. Before the press arrived, Ava asked for the lights to be dimmed and bulbs to be removed to ensure the most flattering illumination, for there to be no personal questions aimed at her and for there to be an orchestra to create a mood. Ava charmed Rome's media, and her photo at the event filled the papers and weeklies, as most celebrated star in town.

Over the next few weeks of pre-production Ava worked to develop her skills for the film by learning Spanish, rehearsing her flamenco dancing with instructor Giza Geert, and going for fittings with the costume designers for the film, the Fontana sisters, whose salon was based on Via Veneto. The three sisters Zoe, Micol and Jeanne Fontana were the leading designers in Rome, having gained a following after Linda Christian chose them to design her wedding dress. Ava went to the Fontana salon several times a week for the extravagant wardrobe of over twenty expensive, luxurious gowns.

As well as costume fittings, Ava was also required to model for a statue which was to depict Maria Vargas in the film. In sculptor Assen Peikov's cold, damp studio she posed in nothing but a slip for days on end as he studied her likeness and chiseled it into marble. Once production had come to an end, Frank bought the Barefoot Contessa statue to adorn his garden, a shrine to the one woman he couldn't forget.

While Ava was settling into Rome, Frank was left grief stricken in New York as he struggled to understand why she left the country. He was drinking heavily to escape his despair at losing Ava, and after making a feeble, attention-grabbing attempt to cut his wrists he was admitted to Mount Sinai for a 'check up and a rest'.

Ava took advantage of the break before filming to fly out to Madrid before Christmas and to celebrate her 31st birthday on 24 November, she also hoped to become reacquainted with Luis Miguel Dominguin, Spain's most celebrated bullfighter. Ava had been thinking about the handsome, lithe Dominguin since meeting him at a party in Seville after finishing *Mogambo*. He was tall, with melting brown eyes, and he was strong and poised and relaxed, and as soon as she met him Ava ensured that she had his full attention.

But she received a call from Sinatra that he would also be flying to Madrid, and planned to come to Rome too. 'It'll be a mess. Why the hell does he do it?' she told David Hanna. She had to say goodbye to Dominguin when Sinatra arrive by private plane on Christmas Eve, her birthday. They spent Christmas Day together acting like a united front as they opened presents and sang Christmas carols, and when a reporter from United Press managed to connect to Sinatra and ask him his plans for Christmas and for Ava, Sinatra replied 'I hope to spend Christmas with my wife the same way millions of people do all over the world.' They both came down with colds, and after a few miserable days spent bed-ridden, Ava and Frank arrived back in Rome on 29 December.

They were greeted by photographers, but this time there were no smiles from the couple still struggling with illness. Ava's glum face was disguised by sunglasses and she pulled a fur wrap tightly around her, while Frank, with misery etched on his face, held onto her arm tightly. He lashed out at a photographer as flashes popped in their face. They made it to the car with its engine running and were taken back to her Rome apartment.

By New Years' Eve they had recovered, and were photographed out for the first time at Hostaria del Orso, one of Rome's most fashionable restaurants, warming up for the new year with rounds of martinis. They continued on to Chez Bricktop on the Via Veneto with a handful of socialites and ex-pats, but it was a dull party and they escaped back home as soon as they could. They spent the first three days of the New

Year hidden away in the Corso D'Italia apartment, lamenting and arguing, discussing their past and what would happen in the future. A couple of photographers were camped outside trying to keep warm while waiting for any sign of movement. A journalist managed to make contact on the phone with Sinatra, and the wire service reported: 'Sinatra gave no hint of love or romance. Asked about reconciliation, he snapped "This doesn't concern anyone but us."'

Once Ava and Frank had talked and battled and said all that could be said, Frank slipped out the back door and fled back to America in time to begin production on *The Girl in Pink Tights*. However, his co-star Marilyn Monroe refused to do the role at the last minute and was put on suspension by 20th Century Fox, and the film was eventually cancelled. Frank felt he may as well have stayed in Rome.

Ava acted vague but cheerful, telling Hedda Hopper that she and Frank had a wonderful holiday but nothing was decided on reconciliation. Despite her love of Europe she was homesick for the United States, and after complaining of loneliness she asked her older sister Beatrice to come to Europe, and to make sure she was armed with a supply of American foods. Ava was still awake when Beatrice arrived one January morning, and she prepared breakfast and coffee while they caught up with gossip and Beatrice unpacked the Hershey's chocolate bars, Jack Daniels, popcorn, chewing gum, American cosmetics – all the things that weren't so easily available at Rome.

Beatrice, or Bappie as Ava called her, was invaluable in helping to organise Ava's life, having accompanied her when she first moved to Hollywood as a fresh-faced 19-year-old starlet, and looked after her through the early days of her career. While Ava had been lonely, she had also invited Luis Miguel Dominguin to her apartment in Rome and their relationship became more serious.

Some evenings she and Bappie cooked her mother's recipe for southern fried chicken, as a taste of her North Carolina childhood, and she drank grapefruit juice as a health kick before filming. In the lead up to the beginning of production, Ava was also occupied with practising her gypsy dance in the large mirror in her home, and took part in further wardrobe fittings and a final modelling of the sculpture.

Humphrey Bogart had signed up to star alongside Ava as director Harry Dawes, who discovers and mentors Maria Vargas. He flew to Rome on 4 January 1954 to begin the three months filming, which would start on 11 January and finish with location shooting in San Remo and Portofino. As a creature of habit, Bogart checked into the Hotel Excelsior, where he stayed every time he was in Rome. The bartender at the hotel bar knew how to make his martinis just so, he enjoyed watching those he called the 'Roman phonies' on Via Veneto, and he could order ham and eggs at George's across the street, rather than face the local cuisine served up in other restaurants. He considered spaghetti or any other Italian dish foreign and unappetising.

As with every Hollywood movie that came to Rome, extras crowded around the gates of Cinecittà vying for a role in *The Barefoot Contessa*, but casting director Mike Washinsky told the press he was really looking for those who could represent 'society figures, photographers, American movie fans, Spanish crowds, mannequins, obvious Hollywood types, facsimiles of the Monte Carlo international set, and of course, beautiful girls'. Real Italian nobility were brought in to appear at the wedding scene, while a gypsy troupe were discovered in the olive groves of Tivoli, where the location shooting would take place. Musicians from the Hungarian restaurant Piccolo Budapest, one of Ava's favourite hangouts in Rome, were also drafted to appear in a scene, bringing the actress's flavour of Rome to the film.

Ava was nervous on the first day of shooting, but when it came time for filming her first scene, she emerged from her changing room onto the Cinecittà sound stage, fitted out like a Madrid flamenco dive bar, and dressed in her gypsy costume, she confidently flicked a black shawl over her shoulders, turning on the smoldering hostility of Maria.

Ava maintained professionalism on set, always arriving on time and in between takes she retired to her dressing room or slept. Her entourage were on hand to entertain her – Miguel, Bappie, her good friend Mrs Doreen Grant, her driver Mario, and in the evenings they visited Roman bistros while trying to dodge the swarms of photographers.

It became obvious from the first day of filming that Ava wouldn't get along with Humphrey Bogart, a sardonic, at times curmudgeonly, actor who was not always the most communicative. Bogart, who had just won an Academy Award for *The African Queen*, resented that she had been paid more than him as she was considered the star. He complained about the circus of people who were always around her and he didn't think much of her talents. 'She gives me nothing. I have to lift her every time,' he grumbled.

When he first arrived in Rome, without anything like the fanfare and press attention Ava had received, Bogart wasn't too worried. Instead he questioned David Hanna about Frank Sinatra and Ava Gardner, and whether he thought they would get back together. 'I like gossip, I'm a busy body. I want to know about everything,' said Bogart. As one of the original Rat Packs, Bogart was very close with Frank Sinatra, a man's man, and when he discovered she was dating Dominguin, he couldn't understand why she chose a bullfighter over Frank. He told Ava: 'I'll never figure you broads out. Half the world's female population would throw themselves at Frank's feet and here you are flouncing around with guys who wear capes and little ballerina slippers.'

Bogart nicknamed her the Boon Hill Gypsy – 'do your bullfighter boyfriends know you're just a little hillbilly girl?' he teased one day. 'That's what attracts them, honey chile', she replied quick fire. Bogart was a natural stirrer who enjoyed 'a little agitation now and again'. But she did not appreciate these digs at her expense, or his 'casual' mention of any press articles about her love life. She was also annoyed at how his coughing fits would ruin take after take – the early sign of the lung cancer that would kill him. 'His dressing room was like a foggy day in London town every fucking day,' she complained, and this from an actress who enjoyed cigarettes herself.

'It wasn't the happiest movie I ever worked on,' Ava reflected years later. She called Mankiewicz a 'son of a bitch', and admitted their failure in chemistry. Knowing that he could write great roles for women – up there with Tennessee Williams or Ernest Hemmingway in her opinion ('I always felt close to Papa's women') – she wanted him to coax a great performance from her as he had done with Anne Baxter or Bette Davis. But she found there was little guidance. One day, when she was waiting for a set-up from camerman Jack Cardiff, Mankiewicz made a comment that she was the 'sitting-est' actress, and this comment made her feel even more resentful of him.

Bogart's wife, Lauren Bacall, known to her family and friends as Betty, arrived in Rome a few weeks after her husband, as she was reluctant to leave their children in America for too long. Bogart said he requested a double bed at the Excelsior for her imminent arrival. 'This is one marriage that isn't going to be ruined by separate sleeping,' he said. Although there was a rumour he had checked his mistress, wigmaker Verita Thompson, into the Excelsior in his wife's absence.

The Bogarts had been spending more time with Frank over the past year, particularly as he had been going through bouts of loneliness and depression on the back of the disintegrating of his relationship with Ava. Frank asked Lauren if she would do him a favour and deliver a present to Ava on her flight from New York to Rome. 'Frankie called me several times,' Lauren told a reporter in 1954. 'He kept asking me anxiously if I would take a present over to Ava. I kept saying "of course, why not, darling," wondering whether he expected me to fly a piano across ...'

Lauren agreed to do this and on the morning of her flight a large wrapped box was delivered to her. The gift wasn't a piano, but it turned out to be a large white coconut cake – a particular favourite of Ava's as it was a special reminder of childhood birthdays in North Carolina. As a Christmas Eve baby her parents were too poor to give her both birthday and Christmas presents, but from her first year of birth, her mother always baked two cakes – a chocolate cake and a white coconut cake.

Lauren kept the cake permanently in her hands and on her lap to stop it from getting crushed all the way from New York to Rome, via London. She was greeted at a rainy Ciampino airport by her husband, and was photographed in a warm wool coat and hat, with a fur coat draped over her arms and still clutching the patisserie box wrapped in striped paper.

Bogart whisked her back to their room at the Excelsior Hotel where the cake lay in wait for Ava to come and collect it. According to news articles at the time, Ava wept when she received 'that precious piece of pastry'. But Lauren, in her autobiography, recalled quite differently – that Ava appeared to show absolutely no interest in it and refused to turn up to the hotel to collect it. Worried that it would start to go stale after a couple of days, Lauren delivered the cake directly to Ava's dressing room at the studio but she was dismissive, angering Lauren by not even saying thank you. 'I stood there very much out of place and finally managed to get away. I was furious with her and never did get to know her on that film.'

Despite the coconut cake debacle, and without seeing much of Ava in Rome, except for a later visit to Portofino, Lauren had a wonderful time in the city. She explored the majestic piazzas and cobbled alleyways during the day while Bogart was filming, enjoyed meals in the evenings and on his days off they would go for trips to Florence or Venice. They frequently met with a group of friends who were also filming in Rome, including Howard Hawks, Harry Kurnitz and Edmond O'Brien, co-starring in *The Barefoot Contessa*, and they would enjoy dinner at Harry's Bar, originally on Via de Parione. Sometimes they would encounter writer William Faulkner at the bar at George's, and Lauren or Bogart would ask him if he would like to join them.

Location shooting took place in the olive groves of Tivoli, San Remo and Portofino. Because Bogie was not needed for the scenes filmed in San Remo, he and Lauren headed straight to Portofino for a week's holiday. Despite the chilly weather they enjoyed the pavement cafés and were photographed taking a boat ride in the harbour, Lauren in a duffel coat and Bogart in his customary trenchcoat and with a camera around his neck.

Photographers from across Italy arrived in Portofino, hoping to catch a photo of Ava with Luis Miguel Dominguin. One enterprising photo-journalist even hid in a tree waiting to capture that golden shot. She hated being captured unawares, and would do what she could to avoid it – so she arrived in the town at midnight, and without

Dominguin, who went ahead to Florence with the entourage. She may have been without a man, but Ava was pursued by photographers throughout her stay in Portofino, racing across the square to go in and out of her hotel, but she managed to keep her cool. Photographers captured her walking with David Hanna and in the company of Bacall and Bogart as they strolled through town. 'I've certainly been in enough pictures to last a lifetime, though most of them were posed and cheesecake,' she later recollected. 'I hate it when they snap me from a distance, when they hang in trees or hide behind cars. Who the fuck wants to have to go through life being made up?'

The gossip magazines in both Italy and the States portrayed Ava as a playgirl who was desperately disappointed in love. Her marriages to Mickey Rooney and Artie Shaw lasted a year, to Frank Sinatra only a couple of intense years, from 1951 to 1953, although they didn't divorce until 1957. Even though the movie magazines insinuated she was desperate for love and marriage, Ava had no plans to marry Luis Dominguin. She liked that he was fun and had many wild nights drinking and watching flamenco, that he was famous in his own right and was not using her for publicity.

As one of the most hyped women in the world, there was no end of speculation as to the men she was with in Rome, particularly when Dominguin returned to Madrid. Ava was spotted dining in Rome with Chilean actor Octavio Senoret one night, and with Vittorio Gassman another. There were reports of a romance with co-star Rossano Brazzi, rumours she was spending time at bullfights with handsome toreadors, and was doing the rounds of Rome's nightclubs with millionaire playboys and aristocrats. She was also said to be hosting wild parties in her home in Rome.

Ava was also reported to have taken three marine sergeants on a date to the wrap party for *The Barefoot Contessa* after being informed that they were on three days leave from Naples and were looking for something to do. Ava, dressed in a red and white cocktail dress, danced with the three marines and they continued onto a nightclub with Ava and her sister Beatrice.

Despite distractions like this, she was getting bored with Rome by the time filming wound up at the end of April. One of her final tasks for the film was to have publicity shots taken for the film. As a night-owl she much preferred to work when the sun was down, and so in a studio at Cinecittà, with liquor on hand and jazz being played on the gramophone, she posed for photos in one of Luis's bullfighter capes.

United Artists heavily promoting the film with a tagline of 'The World's Most Beautiful Animal'. If Audrey Hepburn was fawn-like with her doe features lauded in magazines, then Ava was feline, predatory, draped on a backdrop of leopard print. They were both up for the Academy Award for Best Actress at the ceremony in 1954 – Ava for *Mogambo*, and Audrey for *Roman Holiday*. Both were roles that reflected their true personalities with Ava's character of Eloise Kelly, a tough playgirl who can drink and has a fiery nature, and Audrey as a fun-loving but sweet princess.

8

AUDREY

It was September 1954 when Audrey Hepburn arrived back in Rome, this time to scenes of great chaos, of flashing bulbs and jostling reporters, having just been married a few days before to actor Mel Ferrer in a small, private ceremony on the shores of Lake Lucerne, Switzerland. The bride wore a Pierre Balmain gown and a crown of white roses, and they tried to maintain complete privacy by avoiding the photographers who had gathered in the area. At the wedding reception at the Bürgenstock golf club, when a photographer tried to take pictures, a guest grabbed the camera and smashed it.

Mel had taken four days' leave from filming *Proibito* in Rome to return to Switzerland, and so after a night staying at a chalet belonging to Mel's best man, millionaire Fritz Frey, the elusive Ferrers boarded the St Gotthard train to Rome as secretive and undercover as they could, to continue on with their honeymoon in a villa outside Rome. With their fifteen pieces of luggage loaded up, they locked the door of their sleeping car and drew the blinds. A porter revealed they avoided the 'diner last night, pulled down the shades and sent out at intervals for hot consommé, mineral water and coffee.'

The train pulled in to Terminal Station in Rome, and their blissful solitude was broken by the mob of photographers gathered on the platform. They had been angered that Mel's press agent, Hank

Kaufman, had denied Mel was going to Switzerland for anything but a holiday. 'We want to be alone,' Mel told them as they scrambled for photos and interviews. Audrey, noted by the *New York Herald Tribune* to be 'a bit pale', said her Roman Holiday 'isn't make believe now – it's real and I'm happy to be here. I know Italians love lovers and I love Italy.'

The Ferrers were driven in a Mercedes Benz to Cinecittà Studios, followed by five carloads of photographers. In the pursuit, one reporter complained, 'that crazy chauffeur of theirs drove so fast we were almost killed following them.' Another pleaded that all they wanted was to ask some questions.

The Ferrers waited in an office to shake off the photographers, and were then taken to their secluded villa in the Alban Hills, near Anzio Beach. Villa Rolli was the same one that Paramount had hired for Gregory Peck and his family during the making of *Roman Holiday* and which he may have recommended to his friends Audrey and Mel for its relaxing, luscious gardens and quaint farmhouse feel. They bolted themselves into the stone villa, but the photographers soon found out where they were staying and arrived en masse, knocking on the doors and windows of the 20 room villa. With her meteoric rise to fame as one of the most popular movie stars, it was expected there would be press interest in her marriage. But the Roman photographers had geared up in fervency since Audrey's days with *Roman Holiday*, more than they would have imagined. Mel recalled: 'We had to establish a cordon of security around the farm, so that she could continue to rest while I went off each day to the studio. It was a beautiful and peaceful spot.' To satisfy the needs of the media, Audrey and Mel held two press gatherings at the Grand Hotel. They were asked when they fell in love and she said it was in New York that she realised she would like to marry him, but there was no particular moment, it just happened. She revealed her plans for returning to work but her future hope was 'based on my great faith that marriage and a career will work out, and one day, yes, I hope we will have children'.

Gregory Peck was the matchmaker in Audrey and Mel's relationship, having introduced them at a cocktail party in London in summer

1953, in anticipation for the release of *Roman Holiday*. Sean Ferrer says: 'I believe that Gregory Peck came back from *Roman Holiday* and he and my father and Deborah Kerr were putting together La Jolla Playhouse. He came home and said, I just made this film with this lovely girl, you should meet her, she's just your type.'

Audrey was similarly bowled over when she met him. 'The way he looked me in the eyes – the way he just penetrated me with his eyes,' is what Audrey first remembered about their encounter. She added: 'It was quite simple. I saw him, liked him, loved him …'

Ferrer was still married to his third wife Francis and so for some time they kept the pretense that they were just good friends, even as they lived together in an apartment in Greenwich Village, New York at the start of 1954 for the stage production of *Ondine*, of which he was directing and she was starring. The hectic schedule for *Ondine*, with eight performances a week, press interviews, speculation of her love life, all became overwhelming. She smoked a pack of cigarettes each day, chewed her fingernails and later admitted to a journalist she had 'suffered a complete breakdown in New York'.

After 157 performances, *Ondine* closed on 3 July 1954, and she and Mel retreated to Switzerland for complete rest and to relax her nerves, and where the clear air would help her asthma. At fashionable, exclusive alpine village Gstaad there were too many photographers, so they went to Bürgenstock – a quieter retreat on Lake Lucerne where she found a villa that looked out onto the Alps. 'I love to wake up in the early morning, throw open the shutters and drink in the sight of the tall mountain peaks and the lake down below,' she said.

While she stayed in Switzerland, Mel went to Rome to film at Cinecittà. For his 37th birthday in August 1954, she sent to him a platinum watch inscribed 'Mad about that Man'. The gesture spurred him to fly back to Lake Lucerne and propose to her.

She loved the travelling that her career allowed her, and said in 1954: 'If I had my choice, and if I had the money, I'd have an apartment in London, an apartment in New York, and someplace in the country— providing, of course, I could travel a lot and go to Paris and Rome a great deal! But of course, the day I marry a man I'm very much in love with, and he lives in Timbuktu, that's where I'll live.' She was willing to push back on her career and fit around her husband's work commitments rather than be apart.

While they were technically on honeymoon, Mel was given another week off work before reporting back to Cinecittà to continue filming. They spent time in the exotic garden of fruit trees and grapevines, and enjoyed cocktails by the pool. Once he returned to the studio, Audrey was content staying at the villa to play housewife. 'When I get married I want to be very married,' said Audrey. She was kept company by two watchdogs and three cats, a donkey and countless chickens pecking for grain on the courtyard. She read scripts in the garden, learned to cook Italian food, and when alone, she ate her lunch on the floor to stretch out her spine and keep her chin up. She still showed the discipline of the years of ballet training, and with her sudden and huge fame, movie magazines wished to inform their readers how she maintained such a slim figure. 'I don't say I eat a lot,' she told *Modern Screen* in 1953. 'I eat small meals, but I love to eat quantities of the things I like. I love meat. I love a steak. And I adore sweets and chocolates and things like that.' She was loyal after discovering new fashion designers who could create sleek, practical, beautiful clothes for her. She first met shoe designer Salvatore Ferragamo in Florence in 1954, and would favour his shoes from then on.

Audrey was hoping to keep out of public life while trying for a baby, but the main work project occupying the Ferrers was an idea for making a screen version of *Ondine*, and in November 1954 the British film-making partners Michael Powell and Emeric Pressburger were guests at Audrey and Mel's villa to discuss their interest in the film.

Michael Powell had first met Audrey and Mel backstage of the 46th Street Theatre after a matinee performance of *Ondine*, where he observed Mel's lean height and self-confidence, and Audrey's charm. 'They were madly in love. That is to say that she was whole-hearted in her love for him. She is the kind of woman who gives all or nothing. I don't know how he lit this torch, but by heaven it flamed.' He noted that at this point they were planning an escape to Europe. 'Mel had been offered a part in a picture to be made in Rome and they planned to escape there, look for work without appearing to do so, and live on his salary.'

For their meeting in Rome, Mel had met Powell and Pressburger at Terminal Station and after a private screening of *On the Waterfront*, they went for dinner at a Roman nightclub. They drove back to the Ferrers' home in the vine-clad, olive grove hills, following a private road that led to the villa, with the sound of barking dogs to greet them and the night sky lit up with stars. Powell recalled being woken in the morning by numerous cats who jumped on him and padded his stomach with their paws.

After breakfast, they spent a cold, misty morning discussing and working on their ideas for *Ondine*, despite the interruptions of 'telephone calls and hysterical servants. Audrey and Mel were, amiably, the worst listeners in the world. They were always wandering off in the middle of a sentence, and none of us allowed any of the others to finish one.' Mel was insistent in staying true to their Broadway production depicting a heroic knight and a water-nymph, despite Powell and Pressburger's modern vision, perhaps along the lines of their critically acclaimed *The Red Shoes* and which went back to the original La Motte Fouqué fairytale. 'Audrey looked at him adoringly. There had obviously been extended pillow talk throughout the night,' remembered Powell, as Audrey backed up her husband in his vision.

The following evening Mel and Audrey held a dinner party for Powell and Pressburger with cinematographer Jack Cardiff and the two top movie producers in Italy – Dino De Laurentiis, with his wife Silvana Mangano, and Carlo Ponti with his fiancée Sophia Loren. Powell recalled that Mangano 'sat smoldering in a heap of black and silver tissue all evening', while the statuesque Loren, in a striking red dress, 'a very large girl with gaps between her teeth,' loomed over slight Audrey. The fire had gone out by the time the guests had arrived, and so the women sat in their furs until the servants could rekindle the flames. A dinner of roast venison was served, as the guests tried to communicate in mixed Italian, English and French.

Despite these discussions over dinner, Mel was unwilling to experiment with alternate visions and ideas, and the film of *Ondine* never came to fruition. But Mel and Audrey were in discussion with Ponti and De Laurentiis for a big budget adaptation of *War and Peace* to be directed by King Vidor.

With Mel cast as Prince Andrei, Audrey agreed to play Natasha for a salary of $350,000 and expenses – the highest fee for any actress in the world at this time. It was only her third Hollywood movie, but she had experienced a monumental rise in fame since her first time filming in Rome in 1952, earning just $12,500 for *Roman Holiday*. She couldn't help but feel that the huge salary was undeserved. 'I'm not worth it!' she said to her agent when he showed her the contract.

The Hepburn and Ferrer marriage inspired headlines around the supposed controlling nature of Ferrer, despite Audrey earning three times his salary. It had been reported that he refused to let Hepburn have a solo curtain call in *Ondine*, and that he was riding on his famous wife's coat tails for his role in *War and Peace*. Audrey was defensive and rushed to take her husband's side. 'He was asked to play Prince Andrei long before I was even approached – as a matter of fact, before we were even married … After it was decided, Mel and I were thrilled at the thought of being in the same picture together. But from that moment on, we were put on the defensive. Imagine!'

Her marriage to Mel was a continuation of her relationship with her father's, where she looked for a figure who was a little older, more experienced and who she could rely on to protect her. If she chose him because he was older and experienced, he responded to her vibrancy and youth, and unquestionably, with professional respect. Audrey was very traditional and 1950s in her view of marriage as she heldher husband as the one in charge of any decisions. 'It's so nice being a wife and having your husband take over your worries for you,' she said. 'American women have a tendency to take over too much, and in that way they miss out on a lot of fun that their European sisters have.' He was also protective because she had suffered a miscarriage in March 1955, a traumatic event 'that was the closest I came to feeling I was going to lose my mind,' she recalled.

They arrived back in Rome at the end of June 1955 to work on *War and Peace* for the next four months, ending her romantic year away from the spotlight. Publicist David Hanna, who had looked after Ava Gardner during *The Barefoot Contessa*, greeted Audrey when she stepped off the plane with Mel. Many of the newspapermen had appeared with her in *Roman Holiday*, and she smiled at them in recognition. Audrey was serious and ambitious about her career – 'This, I believed, would be a welcome change from Ava and her supreme indifference', said Hanna. He added that 'Audrey and Mel were fair bait for the Rome press corps when they arrived, but by choosing to face the problem directly they succeeded in throwing off some of the snide insinuations then circulating.' These insinuations included the continued rumours of his controlling nature, which she began to find very annoying.

They held a press conference at the Grand Hotel, with Hanna using his expertise on lighting, which he had learnt from Ava, to ensure Audrey was as comfortable as she could be sitting in front of a roomful of reporters. The pressures from the media at times could be overwhelming, particularly that there were 'so many people pointing cameras, especially in Europe'. Sometimes she felt bombarded with the personal questions, about her views on love, about how it feels to be a star. Audrey preferred to remain neutral. 'Here I am, an innocent little actress trying to do a job, and it seems that my opinion on policy in the Middle East is worth something. I don't say I don't have an opinion, but I doubt its worth.'

They rented the same pink villa near Albano, with its garden bursting with flowers and grapevines, with views to the hills dotted with monasteries and the ruins of castles. It was reported she was 'radiant from being married,' and 'visitors to the villa come away impressed by Audrey, the wife. She searches the countryside for just the right bread, the perfect cheese, the correct wine. She supervises the servants. She tiptoes around Ferrer when he is one of his moods.' Halsman, who photographed her at the villa said, 'There are so many girls with absolutely perfect features and that's all you get. But with her, the entire girl is as if she were illuminated from the inside.' Looking over the brilliance of Rome, and the future, Audrey told him, 'I've never been so happy.'

Norman Parkinson also visited during the summer to take pictures of the couple in their blissful surroundings, with Audrey in a pale pink dress and white gloves against a backdrop of bursting bougainvillea, or posing with a baby donkey in Capri pants and ballet slippers beside one of the old farmhouse doors.

Audrey and Mel were private people, preferring a life of domesticity and early nights rather than cutting loose with the Rome nightlife. An Italian family held a party for Audrey during *War and Peace*, but the Ferrers left early. 'I have a difficult day tomorrow,' Audrey explained, to the disappointment of her hosts. Unlike some of her colleagues, who had to be dragged out of bed after being out all night and then revived with strong coffee and good make-up, Audrey preferred to be up early. 'I would have never dared to do what they did.' She would wake around 5 a.m. if filming, so she could go over her lines while eating breakfast – boiled eggs with toast fingers, coffee and milk.

Producers Carlo Ponti and Dino De Laurentiis spared no expense for their four-hour epic, with cinematographer Jack Cardiff operating in VistaVision Eastman colour. It had a budget of around $5 million, with all 48 acres and nine soundstages of Rome's Cinecittà Studios being used to recreate early nineteenth-century Moscow and Siberia with artificial snow shipped in from England by the ton. The production involved 15,000 extras, 7,000 costumes, 8,000 horses, 5,000 guns and sixty-four doctors dressed as soldiers in case of any accidents. Fifty tailors in Rome closed up their shops after being drafted in to keep up with the demand of making uniforms. There was a call for additional tailors across Europe, and an entire button factory was taken over by a huge order of 100,000 rare buttons for the Cossacks, hussars and French army. The Rome summer heat and lack of air-con in the studio was stifling for those wearing period costumes for ten hours a day. Audrey at least was dressed in cooler empire-line dresses with plunging necklines, as always, inspiring Rome fashion designers, this time to introduce a Napoleonic style to their collections.

The quiet countryside and fields around Cinecittà were also utilised as outdoor locations. As the *New York Times* reported from a visit to the set:

A lazy timelessness is perhaps the first impression one got on approaching the scene, sprinkled as it was with grazing horses, ambling extras in period costumes, open carriages moving through the woods and out into the open under a sunlit sky. Then under a giant tree, the discordant note: machinery, trucks, technicians, the camera.

Mel and Audrey involved themselves in all aspects of production including the script and the costumes – and their influence extended to the miscasting of Henry Fonda as Pierre, who at 50 was almost double Audrey's age. Mel, Audrey and Henry Fonda occupied their time on set by playing card games, by joining the crew for three hour lunches as they consumed wine and pasta and relaxing with King Vidor in the Cinecittà bar, its counter filled with bowls of lemons and coffee cups.

Audrey helped match-make Henry Fonda with a friend of hers, the Contessa Afdera Franchetti, a social butterfly of Rome's nightlife. He had been lonely in Rome while filming *War and Peace*, as he was separated from wife Susan Blanchard. He wrote in his autobiography, *Fonda: My Life*, 'Week in and week out, I had nothing to do. So I'd call her or she'd call me and we'd go out.' They married in 1957, shortly after his divorce to Susan came through, but she was so busy as a socialite, and he was absorbed in acting, they divorced six years later. 'She wasn't any more a contessa than my flannel shirt,' he said. Afdera retaliated: 'I wasn't a good wife because being married to him was so dreary, I could weep. I left him because he was the biggest crashing bore I've ever met. One should never marry crashing bores – just see them on stage.' Being with him, she said, was like 'permanently taking a sleeping pill'.

'*War and Peace* was a very happy time and I think they were very happy on this film. But she lost a couple of pregnancies,' says her son Sean Ferrer. 'She was a young girl, 24 or 25, and (Mel) was a film producer. If Ella carried the baton up until the very beginning of her career, once they were together he always made sure she was surrounded by the best cameraman, the best crew, and screenwriters.'

It was reported that Ingrid Bergman received one of the highest payments – $50,000 for doing one day's work, playing a woman whose small child is saved by Henry Fonda's Pierre from a burning house. She was said to have done it as a favour to her friends Silvana Mangano and her husband De Laurentiis.

If Audrey preferred quiet nights in her villa with Mel, far away from the antics of the Via Veneto, there was one actress on the set of *War and Peace* who would have a penchant for placing herself in the heart of Rome's nightlife all the while staying on the second floor of the Grand Hotel.

Brilliantly blonde, statuesque and with awe-inspiring measurements, Anita Ekberg was born in Malmö, Sweden in 1931. After being crowned Miss Sweden, she caused a sensation as a guest at the Miss America pageant in Atlantic City and was then signed up by Universal in 1951. Playing Princess Helene in *War and Peace* was to be her big break, as over the four years in Hollywood she had only been given bit parts in three films. But plenty of gossip had been generated around her love life and 'continental' attitude to men – that Gary Cooper had taken her to dinner after meeting at a party for Marilyn Monroe at Romanoff's, that she was in Palm Springs with Frank Sinatra and that she was set to marry Tyrone Power after his divorce from Linda Christian.

> '... Her limbs are beautifully shaped, her lips are provocatively kissable.'

'What is there about this blue-eyed, honey-haired Scandinavian beauty that makes her such a temptress?' asked *Modern Screen*. 'The obvious answer lies in Anita's obvious charms. She has more of everything than practically any other actress in Hollywood. She stands five feet ten in high heels. She boasts a forty-inch bust. Her limbs are beautifully shaped, her lips are provocatively kissable.'

As soon as Anita arrived in Rome for three months of work on *War and Peace*, she set alight the gossip magazines and caused a sensation in a city that was used to beautiful starlets. It was said that around thirty-five reporters interviewed her during her first week in Rome, and that there were always 'a dozen or so wealthy stagedoor Giovanni's waiting at the studio entrance, hoping to take her home after a day's work'. Hedda Hopper wrote of her in September 1955: 'Since Anita Ekberg landed in Rome they've got the old tape measure working overtime again since she's giving Lollobrigida and Sophia Loren competition. I like Anita. She's co-operative too, but if she worked harder learning to act she'd have a longer career.'

Staying just a few doors down from Anita, in room 227 at the Grand Hotel, was love rival Linda Christian, and one of the big stories was that there would be sparks if the two ran into each other, with reporters and photographers tipping hotel staff to keep their eyes open. Ekberg said: 'I am too busy to deny all those stupid stories that are being circulated about me.' When they ran into each other in the lobby, Anita swished past Linda, on the arm of Mario Bandini, an Italian actor and good friend of Audrey and Mel's. Audrey was photographed on the set of *War and Peace* with Ekberg, who was dressed in tight white dress and sunglasses with her little dog, and who Audrey fussed over. During filming of *War and Peace*, the two couples were said to have gone to Capri together.

Despite her sultry image, Anita was keen to assert that she had the brains as well as the looks. 'As a matter of fact I have just finished *War and Peace*, the book. How many girls do you know have read *War and Peace*? No matter what they write about me, I am not a femme fatale and I am not all body. I have a brain and I use it.'

After an intensive four-month, six-days-a-week shoot, Audrey left Rome on 13 November to rejoin Mel in Paris. They then went on to their newly purchased chalet in Bürgenstock, which looked onto the Alps and the clear waters of Lake Lucerne. With permanent residency in Switzerland, it also saved them on the huge taxes imposed in America and the UK. Ferrer gave her a Yorkshire terrier puppy, the fashionable dog for women in the mid 1950s, whom she appropriately named Mr Famous. He would be her companion wherever she travelled, and she was often snapped taking the little terrier for walks around Rome when staying at the Hassler Hotel, her first choice of hotel ever since her arrival in the city for *Roman Holiday*. She regularly walked passed Trinità dei Monti with Mr Famous on her way to and from the Hassler Hotel, where she would be greeted by photographers or young fans who she would sign autographs for. She was often spotted in a heavy herringbone tweed coat, her hair pulled up in a chignon or with a silk scarf wrapped around her head. In February 1960 she was snapped coming out of the Hassler with Mr Famous, dressed in a black frock coat and low heels, with the passenger in a car grinning in amazement at seeing her.

Seven years after first staying at the hotel during the filming of *Roman Holiday*, she was photographed on the terrace of the Hassler opening the telegram that announced her as Best Actress of 1959 by the New York Film Critics for her role in *The Nun's Story*. Filmed at Cinecittà and on location in Belgium and the Congo, it had been the surprise hit of the year for Warner Brothers and the role of Sister Luke, with her strong convictions, was one she felt was deeply suited to her nature. On the Hassler balcony, surrounded by views of the auburn Rome cityscape, Mel, holding Mr Famous, kissed her on the forehead and pulled her close as he congratulated her. They had more reason to celebrate when she found out in autumn 1959, after several miscarriages, that she was pregnant once more.

9

SOPHIA

Naples was buzzing with the news of *The Gold of Naples*, an adaptation by well-loved Neapolitan author Giuseppe Marotta, being made in town in spring 1954. Sophia, dressed in a blouse designed by Pia Marchesi, was to perform her lively scenes in an especially-built pizzeria in a Naples alleyway which attracted crowds of spectators. Vittorio De Sica admired her impulsiveness, a Neapolitan spontaneity, which he believed was perfect for the role, despite De Laurentiis wanting a bigger name. De Sica advised her not to take acting lessons, but to teach herself and to use instinct. 'He helped me create an explosive, sexy, blowsy Neapolitan pizza girl who sprang from a part of me I didn't know existed,' Sophia said.

As publicity for the film, Sophia was photographed in pizzerias around the country, dressed up as the pizzaiola, or pizza girl, in her peasant blouse falling off her shoulders as she prepared the pizza herself. In Milan she handed out hundreds of pizzas to fans in Piazza San Babila against a backdrop of Christmas illuminations.

The Gold of Naples was a hit when released in December 1954, and her character became an icon for a new Italy. She was used in advertising, such as for a lighter mozzarella that promised to help women achieve a figure like Sophia's. But it wasn't just in Italy that she was noticed. The *New York Times* in April 1954 reported on 'a buxom newcomer named

Sofia Loren' playing the Pizzaiola, and she was described in the *Daily Mirror* as 'as delectable as the pizza she sells!'

Her relationship with Carlo Ponti was also strengthening, but she still felt like the girl from Pozzuoli, with strict morals around having a relationship with a married man. His wife was aware of his affairs, and tolerated them as long as they didn't become too serious. She was very attracted to him, 'his open smile, the quality of his eyes, his diffident but forceful manner'. But, as she recounted, 'at eighteen I still had the mentality of a Pozzuoli girl, an affair with a married man was unthinkable ... this did not mean that I did not "pet" with Carlo, but there is a vast difference between petting and real sex involvement.'

She also dated a young Italian singer Achille Togliani, having met on one of the fotoromanzos, and would come to support him when he performed at festivals. But she was looking for a father figure, and one who could guide her through her career at every step.

By 1954, Sophia Loren was ranked third most popular Italian actress, behind Gina Lollobrigida and Silvana Mangano, and after several more leading roles only she and Lollobrigida were the stars in Italy who could carry a picture. Another sign that she was making it was a supposed feud with Lollobrigida. It began when *The Gold of Naples* rivaled with Vittorio De Sica's *Bread, Love and Fantasy* on release at the end of 1954. It was a sequel to the hit film *Bread, Love and Dreams*, where Gina Lollobrigida famously played the sparky village girl who rode a donkey, transforming its setting, the hilltop hamlet Castel San Pietro Romano, 40km outside of Rome, into a tourist attraction, with drink bottles now served on ice and the barmaid dressed in local costume.

In the third installment, *Scandal in Sorrento*, released in 1955, Sophia Loren stepped into Gina's role as she danced the mambo and captured men's hearts. It was considered a declaration of intent in overstepping Gina's career. Loren and Lollobrigida were both invited to London for a Week of Italian Cinema in 1954. Speaking only a little English, when Sophia was asked about her supposed rival she generated headlines such as 'Why La Lollo Hates Me'. Their rivalry was a way of demonstrating that diva behaviour at Cinecittà could rival that of Hollywood, fulfilling the statement in the *Los Angeles Times* that 'Life on the Tiber is more gossip-ridden than at Hollywood and Vine.' Similarly, during the filming of *The Barefoot Contessa*, a story went around that Ava Gardner had refused to meet Lollobrigida when she paid a visit to the set – the Hollywood diva versus Italy's biggest star.

'There was no rivalry between us,' said Lollobrigida dismissively, 'because at the time I was already a star and Sophia Loren was still a beginner. Italian journalists lack imagination. If someone succeeds it's not because someone else fails.' In interviews, Sophia also rejected any idea of antagonism. 'I do not even know her. I met her only once for five minutes,' she said of Lollobrigida. 'They wrote about which one would come to the States first. There is a place not only for the two of us but for many others.'

... by 9 a.m. several hundred girls had gathered outside Titanus Studios.

As the 1950s progressed, Italian cinema was becoming less political, moving away from neorealism towards comedy. In *Too Bad she's Bad*, Sophia's first teaming with Marcello Mastroianni, she played a bad girl thief, and in autumn 1955 they teamed up again in *Lucky to Be a Woman* depicting Rome and its starlets, photographers, and gossip.

Following Sophia's monumental success, stardom seemed only a jump away for many young Italian hopefuls. When Vittorio De Sica announced that he was looking to cast an unknown for the role of Luisa in his new film *Il Tetto*, he put out a casting call, and by 9 a.m. several hundred girls had gathered outside Titanus Studios. Said the *New York Times*: 'Many had turned up as Lollobrigida-type vamps, and over-ripe, over-age candidates. Seventeen-year-old Gabriella Pallotta, a tiny, plain girl with a nice smile and an inner depth and strength that she manages to project, was cast at Luisa.'

In August 1955 Sophia made her first appearance on the cover of *Life* magazine – her first American publication, and she won the biggest deal in Hollywood a foreign actor had ever received – a contract with Paramount Pictures for $200,000 per movie as well as percentages of the profit.

Stanley Kramer, the producer of *High Noon*, was in Spain to prepare for a Napoleonic War drama, *The Pride and the Passion*, originally to star Marlon Brando and Ava Gardner. Frank Sinatra replaced Brando, and when Ava dropped out, Carlo Ponti recommended Sophia to Kramer, who was being described in Italy as the new Ava Gardner.

Sophia arrived in Madrid in April 1956 to be greeted by fans shouting '*Guapa! Guapa!*' (Beautiful!) and met her idol Lucia Bosè, who was now married to Luis Miguel Dominguín, Ava's former lover. Sophia still at times struggled to understand English, particularly at the big Hollywood parties with producers, journalists, influencers, where she smiled and nodded and tried to converse. It was at one of these cocktail parties in Madrid, organised by Kramer to herald the start of the movie and to present his stars to the press, that Sophia and Grant were first introduced. Frank Sinatra and Cary Grant both arrived late, and Sophia had been so nervous that she changed her outfit a dozen times.

'Miss Lolloloren, I presume? Or is it Miss Lorenigida? You Italians have such strange last names I can't seem to get them straight.' She heard that recognisable Cary Grant voice, as he made his introduction in an irreverent way. But rather than finding him witty, Sophia was annoyed at all the talk of a rivalry.

Despite this, she and Cary saw each other every night, dining in little romantic restaurants on hilltops and moonlit terraces, and they soon fell in love. He called her 'dearface', gave her two little gold bracelets to wear and had begun to talk of marriage. 'Cary Grant – he has a wonderful relaxed look. He puts you at ease. You wanted to tell him your life story. You just want to tell him what happens to you,' she said.

They celebrated Christmas of 1956 in John Wayne's hotel suite in Rome, as Wayne was in the city to do screen tests for *Legend of the Lost*, her next American movie. The crew went to Piazza Navona to buy gifts of nougat and nativity figures from the Christmas market, with the sound of bagpipes and the smell of roasted chestnuts clinging to the night air, as the festive square filled with tourists and locals.

Despite the relationship with Cary, Sophia was still secretly engaged to Ponti, as she had been for the past three years. She had only been 19 when she met the 39-year-old Ponti, and she was well aware that he was a father figure in lieu of her absent one. That he could also be her companion, lover, manager and adviser of her career added to the attraction. Romilda disapproved of the age gap and that he was already married and living in a country where divorce was illegal.

After filming *Legends of the Lost* in Libya, Sophia and Carlo made their first trip together to Los Angeles. Greeting her at the airport in LA was a crowd of studio executives, agents and reporters who asked her whether it was true she owed her figure to spaghetti and which American men she found most attractive (she said William Holden).

One of her first appointments was a Paramount cocktail party at Romanoff's in Beverly Hills, held in her honour and which they had decorated in a Mediterranean style for the occasion. Guests included Gary Cooper, Barbara Stanwyck, Fred Astaire and Gene Kelly, and photographers buzzed around her. And then Jayne Mansfield arrived, spilling out of her low-cut dress. She made her way straight to Sophia's table, and as Jayne sat next to Sophia, she suffered an accidentally-on-purpose wardrobe malfunction. It was a publicity stunt for the latest blonde bombshell to upstage the new Italian sex symbol and the photo of Sophia, looking alarmed and disapproving of Mansfield, went around the world. Sophia would always refuse to autograph the photo whenever presented to her.

LA was full of Cadillacs, huge hacienda-style mansions with swimming pools, drive-in cinemas and ritzy steak restaurants. 'When you fly over Los Angeles and see all the cars – all the different colour cars and the swimming pools, it is amazing. We are not used to it – I am not used to it in Italy,' she said. But she missed her country and its humour and history, whereas in Hollywood the conversation seemed to just revolve around the movies. 'Ordinary people just didn't seem to exist in Hollywood.'

When she wasn't at parties, Sophia recovered in her Beverly Hills hotel suite surrounded by flowers and notes from well-wishers, but kept thinking back to the Pozzuoli of her childhood and how she fantasised about her favourite stars on screen. She told Hedda Hopper in 1961:

I have never been a child really. When I was a child, I never had the thoughts a child can have to go and play with other children. I stayed with my mother. She needed me. I never had a chance to be a child. My thoughts were what are we going to eat. I always wanted to become an actress, always. I never collected pictures of movie stars, never wrote for autographs.

In 1957, on that first arrival in Hollywood, Hedda interviewed Sophia in Audrey Hepburn's former dressing room on the Paramount lot. Sophia wore a linen dress the colour of a ripe watermelon and white stilettos, and hungry from not having had lunch, she nibbled on cheese and crackers. Hedda commented that she was looking thinner, maybe she wasn't eating enough and working too hard. She had observed that 'Sophia has trimmed her 38-24-38 body to a more svelte 37½, 22, 36½ because she knows Americans like their stars bosomy but not too fleshy.'

Sophia recounted she was up at 5.30 a.m. every morning after eight hours sleep, she ate cottage cheese and fruit for lunch, but started the day with a big breakfast of bacon and eggs. Sophia's appetite, and a supposed love of pasta, was a source of fascination in the press. Hedda recounted that 'spaghetti is what keeps her thin. Ingrid Bergman says the same thing. Must be true. Many Italians practically live on it, even children.'

The last scenes of *The Pride and the Passion* were finished in California, and once Carlo had left Los Angeles she began seeing Cary again, who was still pursuing Sophia and sent roses to her every day. From Los Angeles she took the Super Chief to Washington DC, where she would make *Houseboat*, to meet Cary. But Carlo realised he was in danger of losing Sophia, and so he had to take action by applying for a Mexican divorce and proxy Mexican marriage.

She would have married Cary Grant if Carlo had been unable or unwilling to get a divorce. But, she said, 'Carlo was Italian; he belonged to my world,' she said, and she knew she needed to keep her Italian links close to her. She also chose Carlo because: 'I wanted a husband who was not good-looking. I have a Neapolitan temperament. If I had

had a handsome husband, he would have attracted the attention of other women and I would have become jealous.'

Two days before the shooting of *Houseboat* ended, Carlo and Sophia were together in Washington DC, eating croissants for breakfast, when they read in the paper that their marriage by proxy had taken place in Mexico the day before. Ponti's lawyers had gone ahead with the Mexico marriage without letting them know. It wasn't exactly the white wedding, but it was all they had been able to manage. The day after the marriage was announced, Cary Grant, always the sport, congratulated Sophia and wished her well.

They were due to take a honeymoon cruise from California to Italy but they cancelled it after The Vatican's official newspaper, *L'Osservatore della Domenica*, stated that the marriage of a 'young, beautiful Italian film actress' was illegal, that her husband was a bigamist and living together would make her a concubine because a civil divorce and marriage were not recognised in the eyes of the church. With her own country condemning her as a 'public sinner' and facing excommunication, it was one of the saddest, and most shameful, days of her life. After all she had been through with her father, a legal, happy marriage proved the hardest to come by. 'What I wanted to have was a legitimate family,' she says, 'a legitimate husband, children, a family like anybody else. It was because of the experience I had with my father.'

The official publication of Italian Men's Catholic Action urged all Roman Catholics to shun her pictures. They said 'being loaded with money and desire to enjoy it every day does not place him and her beyond the moral law'. Sophia receiving angry letters, a call in *Oggi* for her to be burnt at the stake, and a Milanese housewife Luisa Brambilla, brought charges of bigamy against them. In Italy, members of the public could press the court to prosecute and so there was the real threat of being charged and convicted. The Christian Democratic Party, the political wing of the church, still held staunch influence over 1950s Italy.

To escape the pressure in Italy Sophia and Carlo moved to a home in Bürgenstock where their neighbours were Audrey Hepburn and Mel

Ferrer, who they would often meet on their walks and whose chalet was along a peaceful trail and on a hill, overlooking the lake. While Sophia and Carlo faced prosecution and were condemned by the Catholic Church, she watched the marriage of the Ferrers with fascination, as it 'seemed to me like a dream – far away and unreachable … In those days, she was so happy, she inspired my dream.'

One time when Mel was away, Audrey invited Carlo and Sophia for lunch. Audrey, dressed in white to match the table setting, served them raspberry compote and crispbread, while they held pleasant conversation about life in Switzerland. Sophia thought that the crispbread was an appetiser, but when the maid cleared their plates and Audrey announced she was full, Sophia realised that was the extent of the lunch. 'I was dying of hunger, and as soon as we got home I made myself a sandwich,' she said.

The Pride and the Passion was released in 1957 to acclaim, but for some in Italy Sophia was betraying her Pizza Girl roots as an icon of Naples by being too Americanised. At the same time she was facing huge criticism, and felt relieved that she could be protected by her Paramount contract. She didn't want to go back to Italy because of the hostility and accepted a role in *Black Orchid* with Anthony Quinn.

The last film to be made as part of the Paramount deal was *It Started in Naples*, with Clark Gable, and filmed on the Island of Capri in 1959, the playground for the glitterati who were entranced by its limestone cliffs, glowing blue waters and the quaint, colourful houses of its fishing villages. The word Capri came to represent a certain carefree lifestyle, of casual pants, bikinis and dripping wealth. On the set Sophia was reunited Vittorio De Sica, who had a part in the film. He hadn't approved of her Americanisation and wanted to bring her back to her Italian roots. However in her role in *It Started in Naples*, *Il Giornale D'Italia* wrote that she 'recaptures the free and easy, tongue-in-cheek, sizzling tones of the pizzaiola'. She performed a song in the film *You Want to Be Americano*, which would become a huge hit – a song which satirises the American influence of Italy following the war, and represents the carefree, beatnik Italian freedom of the time.

10

ANNA

During Rome's long, hot summers, it was as if, according to Tennessee Williams, 'a paralyzing heat' descended, where 'you can hardly creep through it, and nothing gets done. I don't think I will be able to stick it out for long, for one thing it makes work all but impossible.' But he found during his long friendship with Anna Magnani that she provided the inspiration for a number of his strong characters, including in *Orpheus Descending* and *Sweet Bird of Youth*.

His play *The Rose Tattoo*, portraying a Sicilian woman's devotion to her husband and daughter, was written just for her, capturing that southern Italian personality he adored. Magnani similarly felt affection for the American playwright, and while she loved the character of Serafina, she had been too scared to act on stage in the States and to leave her son behind – a move which bitterly disappointed Williams as the replacement, Maureen Stapleton, was 'too young and too American'.

Anna's son was the most important person in her life, and to do theatre was too much of a commitment. 'If I don't do theatre, it's because theatre takes up your entire life, and life for me is my son and my son matters to me more than theatre,' she said in 1963. 'I've spent too much time away from him for me to go off again. Don't forget that for eighteen years I have been the man of the family, so if I go off, who will take care of this family?'

Producer Hal Wallis saw Williams' *The Rose Tattoo* on its opening night in Chicago and 'knew at once that I had to buy it. It was sure to be a great success. Audiences would identify with its earthiness, its sexuality, its deeply felt emotions and naturalistic dialogue.' Wallis met Tennessee Williams backstage, and the writer was not as flamboyant as he had thought – 'quiet, sober, professional and very personable', and who always seemed to be with a raincoat draped over his arm, to hide his flask of whisky. They quickly signed the deal for a film version to be directed by Daniel Mann.

Anna Magnani was seriously interested and free during the summer of 1954, and Tennessee and Hal Wallis only wanted to do the film with her. 'As far as I was concerned, there was only one actress on earth who could play his tempestuous Italian heroine, the warm passionate, angry and exciting, utterly feminine Serafina,' said Wallis.

Magnani was not as well-known in America as she was in Italy, and the terms that she presented to accept the role were considered exorbitant, leading Audrey Wood, Tennessee's agent, to push Hal Wallis into accepting, or risk losing the film rights. 'I am sure you are not going to get Magnani at a cheap figure,' she warned him. 'Magnani has been good enough to say she will wait for a certain period (but I will have to) push towards other producing bodies unless you have arrived at a concrete approach to a deal with Magnani.'

Hal Wallis flew to Rome to meet Magnani, and with Pilade Levi, head of Paramount's Italian office, they were invited for drinks at her apartment at the top of the pale-pink, baroque Palazzo Altieri. Because there was no air conditioning, she kept her windows wide-open, letting in all the noise from the street – the whistles, the horns, the shouting drivers. After the nervous-looking maid showed them into the apartment, they waited and waited for Magnani to make herself known. A handsome young man, one of her lovers, wandered in and out of the room, and they helped themselves to the Johnny Walker Red Label and bucket of ice that had been left out for them. 'We waited for her for a very long time. Tennessee told me that in

Italy the longer a star keeps someone waiting, the bigger they are. We realised how important she was as each hour went by,' recalled Wallis.

Eventually Anna made her entrance, striding in wearing a tight, low cut black satin dress that clung to her curves. She surveyed her guests with her feet wide and her hands on her hips and looked directly into Wallis's eyes. She smiled, then frowned and burst into laughter. She had a 'lusty, bawdy attraction', but her English was limited and Pilade tried to keep up with her fast flow of words as he acted as translator. She poured herself a glass of wine and topped up their drinks with whisky, and they went out onto her terrace as she told them *The Rose Tattoo* was so beautiful and wonderful that she would die to play Serafina.

Magnani insisted she drive them back to their hotel, and they took the private elevator from her apartment down to the courtyard before stepping into one of her cars. Tipsy from the glasses of wine, she weaved through cars and traffic lights as she talked breathlessly.

Anna owned a beach house south of Rome, in San Felice Circeo, and she invited Wallis down one afternoon. The rambling beach house was on a rocky promontory overlooking a sandy bay. Her house was filled with people, and a maid showed Wallis down a pathway to her private beach. Bursting from the sea, like a bawdy Venus with wet black hair, was Magnani, dressed in a tiny bikini that flaunted her 'Rubens-like glory'. She tossed her damp hair from her face as she embraced him, soaking his shirt with salt-water. She put her arm around his waist and they walked up the steep steps to the beach house. Magnani supervised a large Italian lunch of pasta, veal, tomato sauces and flowing vintage wines. After eating to bursting point, the other guests fell asleep on the beach or in their bedroom while Magnani, her agent, Pilade and Wallis launched into negotiations over her contract.

Wallis met Williams back in New York to discuss the adaptation of the script to the screen. The play was considered shocking with its depiction of 'lust and sex', while the American Production Code, which acted as a moral censor for films, felt that 'Serafina's primitive confusion between religion and superstition seems calculated to put religion in a rather ridiculous light.' Magnani's lack of English was a concern, particularly as the script had long monologues that would require for her to learn them in English.

Daniel Mann wrote to Tennessee Williams in July 1954:

> The whole Wallis organisation and everyone I have met and talked to in Hollywood so far, are tremendously excited about the idea of Rose tattoo with Magnani. I also had a talk and spent the better part of a day with Burt Lancaster, discussing characterisation, make-up and problems in general. I am happy to tell you he is most enthusiastic and quite eager to get to work. ... I can only tell you that I share with you, from what my responsibility will be, a full desire to fulfill the beauties of *The Rose Tattoo* the way they were received and dreamed by you.

Location shooting was carried out in Key West, with interiors in Los Angeles. Going to Hollywood and leaving her son behind was a big deal and before sailing to New York, she felt under great stress to close up her apartment, and find care for her son.

She travelled with Williams from New York to Los Angeles on the Super Chief to Los Angeles and they spent the journey working on the script together; she went over her lines again and again. In her first readings, Magnani was struggling with English and the anxieties around her performance. She worried that if she faltered over a word she would be made to do the line again which would hurt her dramatic flow.

> She did, however, fall for Burt Lancaster and his broad-shouldered ruggedness.

Ahead of her arrival in Los Angeles, Anna Magnani was dramatically described by Paramount as a dark Garbo: 'born in direst poverty, brought up on the streets of Rome, Magnani found acting an avenue of escape from her slum beginnings.' They added that 'she began as a nightclub singer specialising in rowdy street songs or "*stornelli*" ... then, as today, she did not care how she looked. She wore no makeup, combed her hair with a rake and flung herself into her parts with wild abandon.'

Just as when Sophia Loren arrived in America, Anna was said by the gossip columnists to have dieted to fit 'American standards', while still remaining voluptuous. They advised that:

> she likes slacks and sweaters, buys them by the dozen. Her windblown, earthy looks are her trademark, she feels, anything else false ... she brushes her teeth with soap, any soap, follows this with toothpaste. She washes her hair in the shower, dries it in the sun. She scrubs her face with soap, hot water and brush, rinsing in ice water, using no creams.

Once in Hollywood, Anna worked quietly in the sanctity of the set, avoiding parties and studio gatherings until she got back to Rome. She did, however, fall for Burt Lancaster and his broad-shouldered ruggedness. Despite his reluctance for any romance, they became good friends.

On completion of the film, before she sailed back to Rome from New York in February 1955, Anna wrote to Wallis that she hoped to see him in Rome and promised to find him a beautiful dog to add to his pack. She told him her Hollywood experience 'is like a big emotion because I found so much comprehension and so much friendship'. In return, Hal promised to send her a jeep from America, to help navigate the rough, unpaved roads around her beach house. She promised to paint a rose on its hood and told him 'my son and I are looking forward to receiving the nicest of all toys!'

Hal Wallis advised Magnani that Hedda Hopper would be in Rome in mid June 1955, staying at the Excelsior as usual and that she should take the time to meet with her. 'Miss Hopper as you know is very important here – both locally and through her column,' he told Magnani. 'She is particularly anxious to see you and I think it is advisable that you arrange to have lunch or cocktails or dinner with her. You will find that she is very easy to be with, and she can be most valuable to you.'

The Rose Tattoo's premiere in New York, designed as a benefit for the Actor's Studio, was completely sold out and throughout the screening the audience applauded her performance. The film, and Anna, was the talk of the town.

Anna was invited to the States for the premiere but she turned it down as she wanted to spend Christmas with her son. Thirteen-year-old Luca was at boarding school in Lausanne and was about to undergo an operation to straighten his feet. He was unable to walk after contracting childhood Polio. 'There is nothing in the world that would take me away from my son on Christmas,' she said, and she liked nothing more than spending time with her son, making him 'a cup of goats' milk cocoa'. 'Love for one's children lasts forever, love for the men that take us to bed comes to an end. And when it ends, you cry a bit, but then it passes,' she said. She had no desire to remarry as she would rather have had her freedom without being tied down.

Playing Serafina had been incredibly hard for her as she struggled with English, but she felt that despite her fears, some sort of miracle must have happened that allowed her to bring out the performance. Tennessee would tell her that she shouldn't have any fear as she was always able to do miracles. After taking home the New York critics award and the Golden Globe, at the 1956 Academy Awards Anna Magnani was named best actress for her performance as Serafina. She was the first foreign actress to win the award, such was the impression that she had made on Hollywood.

She had been told of her Oscar win by a reporter who had called her up at 4 a.m., and thinking it was a joke, she hung up on him. When he called her back and the news sunk in, she spent the next four days and nights without sleep and in a state of high-emotions. Her home was invaded by reporters from around the world, and she received hundreds of telegrams. 'Rome was completely drunk with victory', she said:

> The common man, as well as the important people, the man in the street, the policeman directing traffic, all of them sent their congratulations because they felt that my victory was a national affair … my Oscar inebriated Italy entirely. It was a deluge of love that dropped over me from the public.

She posed for a photo on her balcony in Rome holding her Oscar up over her head, dressed in a black shirt, long skirt and leopard trim shoes, with the tiled roofs and domes of Rome in the background. She sent the image to Hal Wallis, and he replied to her that the photo brought back memories from when they first stood on her terrace discussing the project. 'Little did we dream at that time the events that were to take place – and the final triumph for you. It has all been most wonderful, and I look forward to our continued friendship and association.'

Finding a follow up project to suit the volcanic talents of Magnani proved to be difficult. She had hoped to star opposite James Dean in *Cherie*, but was shocked and 'flabbergasted' by his sudden death in a car crash in September 1955, as the young actor had 'conquered all of Rome' with his singular role in *East of Eden*. As well as *Cherie*, Hal Wallis thought she might do a film called *Lioness*, but she felt it was too similar to *The Rose Tattoo*. 'I immediately do or do not feel the part,' she said. 'This is my thermometer … it never misses.' Anna always gave her opinions and thoughts, and she was respected and deferred to, with the rights to approve her co-stars. Another actor she was excited to work with was Paul Newman, a name she had heard on the grapevine. Anna wanted Hal to consider *La Lupa*, about a mature woman who loses her head over a younger man, and she told him 'the ending will bring goose-pimples to your skin!' Ponti and De Laurentiis had made an earlier version which she had refused to be in because it had owed nothing to the original novel, which she begged Wallis to read.

Tennessee wrote *Orpheus Descending* for Anna and Marlon Brando and, finding it to be one of his most interesting comedies, she was desperately trying to bring this film to the screen. But getting the film made proved almost impossible, with Marlon Brando playing a tiring game of 'yes' and 'no' as he kept Tennessee hanging in suspense as to whether he was going to do both the play and the film. Anna told Daniel Mann:

> Marlon still doesn't know what he wants, what he wants to be, or what he wants to look in respect to others! Marlon will destroy himself. I saw *Guys and Dolls*. Well it was not a step forward for him. Not even his presence was able to save the picture.

The project wouldn't get off the ground until 1959, when it was released as *The Fugitive Kind* in 1960.

Anna was an animal lover, and locals such as Federico Fellini would regularly see her around the Pantheon with a large bag, giving out food to the stray cats and dogs. She was an animal lover who was particularly devastated when her big black wolf of a dog, Micia, 'one of the seven wonders' and her best friend, was diagnosed with throat cancer. Micia was treated in a veterinary clinic in Pisa, with Anna phoning up to six times a day to check on her. However there was no cure, and Micia had to be put down. She told Daniel Mann in a letter that the loss of her beloved dog 'was a shock that left me lifeless for 20 days at least. I cried, I cried so much. I wonder if I should feel ashamed of this, but truly I don't. Anyway, even today when I think of her I feel like crying.'

She had been looking forward to working with Danny on an adaptation of the novel *Furia* but her emotions took a hit Hal Wallis failed to find a screenwriter to adapt it in a way that would suit her talents after her spectacular Oscar win. Eventually it was renamed *Wild is the Wind*, a western love triangle directed by George Cukor, filmed over summer 1956 in America's South West. It was not the happy experience that making *The Rose Tattoo* had been. Magnani found fault with the script, and on one occasion was spotted driving on the freeway, the script propped up against the windshield, shouting and gesticulating.

She was grudging and ill-tempered, and hated the location shooting in snowy rugged Nevada, where they trekked to the locations, waiting for the roads to be cleared. She had Italian food ordered in from her favorite restaurant in Los Angeles, but, as Hal Wallis recounted, her motel room was a mess as she threw the food around in a fit of rage, with spaghetti sauce and pasta on the walls. There was no telephone which further angered her, and the room had to be completely repainted after she checked out.

Co-star Tony Franciosa and Magnani were mutually attracted to one another and they began an explosive affair, their quarrels and make-ups filling the night air. Franciosa had been dating actress

Shelley Winters, whom he had promised to marry. When she heard the rumours of a romance she called the motel each night for reassurance, and when that wasn't enough she travelled to the location to claim him from Magnani. They held a quickie wedding in Carson City but when she returned to Hollywood, his affair with Magnani continued.

Working with the explosive Magnani had been an experience for Hal Wallis that he would always remember. 'I never worked with Magnani again, though not from choice. It was just I was unable to find a vehicle suitable for her unique talents. But she forgave me and I forgave her and I shall never forget her.'

11

AVA

By the mid 1950s tourism was thriving in Rome, with a gleaming new thirty-two-passenger bus whisking visitors from the airport into the city, along the crumbling Appian Way, dotted with the ancient, vine-clad villas that housed those famous movie faces.

Fast, noisy cars and scooters, blasting their horns, boiled around the Colloseum. The *Los Angeles Times* described the city in spring 1955: 'Ponderous buses, tiny trolleys, automobiles, erratic drivers, hundreds of darting, weaving motorbikes, bicycles and motor scooters, chattering, roaring, tooting, shouting – no system, no direction, no right of way, no boulevard stops.'

The Via Veneto was one of the major attractions for visitors, and the street now heaved with traffic – a stream of Topolinos or brand new Cadillacs. In its sidewalk cafés there were the obvious attention-seekers and wannabe movie stars, where the glamour girls could be seen at Doney and Strega. On the opposite side of the Via Veneto, considered the 'left bank', was where the intelligentsia could be found, along with the journalists, artists and tourists looking for a more relaxed scene at places like Rosati and Carpani. 'It's hard to say which side has the most fun,' noted the *Los Angeles Times* in 1954. 'But there's no intermission along Via Veneto. Its small span comes to life early to serve continental breakfast, steps up its tempo for the noontime rush and stays in high gear long after midnight.'

The women of the Via Veneto seemed as smart and well coiffured as anywhere in the world, accompanied by poodles and little Yorkshire terriers, seated with immaculately-turned out gentlemen with their Homburgs and Italian suits, or with canes for the Englishmen. They enjoyed the pleasure of veal scallops, spaghetti, and fettuccine. For luxury, private dining they went to Hostaria Dell'orso, a fourteenth-century hostel said to have been frequented by Dante Alighieri.

Nights on the Via Veneto would often finish at Bricktop's, or Brick Toppo, which Virginia-born Ada Bricktop had opened in 1952, after being integral to the Lost Generation in Paris with her Bricktop's nightclub in Montmartre. She mused that it was the sons of her clients from Paris in the 1920s and 1930s who now arrived in Rome to visit her club, after hearing wild stories from their fathers. She was said to send money from her takings every morning to the orphanages around Rome, persuading her wealthy clients to help her out with donations or with used clothes.

Rome's nightlife by 1955 was back to its 1920s bohemian peak; cabaret clubs had sprung up in the city's cellars and vaults, futurist artists displayed their young art, there were improvised poetry sessions and the streets pulsed to the rhythm of jazz. At The Grotto of the Augusteum, young people drank wine, listened to poets and danced the foxtrot as the sun dropped behind the Seven Hills.

In 1923 there was a bohemian bar called The Devil's Cabaret which was divided into three rooms – Paradise, Purgatory and Hell – and which had gimmicky cocktails such as Liquid Fire and Beelzebub's Blood. Pina was a modest trattoria visited by foreign journalists and the Anapadrama in Via Margutta was another popular spot. But in the 1930s the fascist head of police had began a purity campaign, raiding bookshops for pornography, and shutting down bars that were considered too deviant.

Via Margutta was a rambling enclave for bohemians and artists who set up studios in the former stables, now covered in ivy, and by 1954 it was becoming a popular party place for beatniks, celebrities and society people. Painter, existentialist and society girl Novella Parigini's open studio attracted the café society set. It was also the street that Federico Fellini would live for most of his career, watching and observing all of Rome's life to use in his films, including the antics of Parigini. One of the people who frequented the street was a teenage Ursula Andress who shared an apartment with Brigitte Bardot, while filming *Helen of Troy*. You could find the bohemians and existentialists at the bars of Margutta, dressed in black and with their long hair hanging around their shoulders.

By the beginning of 1957 there were said to be around 3,500 permanent American residents in Rome, and they were served with an daily newspaper in English, the *Daily American*, and American bars in every hotel where the bartender had been taught how to make a proper dry martini. To make them feel at home, there were counter-style greasy spoon diners serving real American hamburgers, hot dogs, ham and eggs, Silex coffee. Jerry's was a small downstairs bistro on Via Veneto, just a block and a half from the Excelsior. It was owned by Jerry Chierchio, a New Jersey cook, who after working for King Saud, opened up his bistro serving a side-order of recommendations to help Americans find apartments and jobs.

The *New York Times* noted in 1956 that it was American women who were the predominant groups of tourists – travelling in groups, in pairs or on their own. 'You can see them sitting at the sidewalk cafés in Sorrento and on Rome's Via Vittorio Veneto,' drawn to Rome rather than France because 'Italy is less expensive, they like the genuinely warm welcome they get from their Italian hosts and the people they meet on their travels.'

As Hollywood made films about Rome in Rome, the romantic factor of the city had been geared up a notch. Seeing Audrey rollicking on a scooter, or getting soaked in the Tiber with Gregory Peck, or the American girls of *Three Coins in the Fountain* finding love, must have made an impact on young college-age American women who now found that they had new opportunities and new freedoms to travel. They may also have been inspired by the photos of their favourite film stars living the glamorous life in Rome.

Life photographer Slim Aarons and actress Joan Fontaine spent time together in Rome in 1949, and he captured her during a visit to the Colosseum. (Slim Aarons/Hulton Archive/ Getty Images)

Ingrid Bergman at a press conference at the Hotel Excelsior with Roberto Rossellini, *left*, following her hyped arrival in Rome in March 1949. (INTERFOTO/Alamy Stock Photo)

Anna Magnani, an animal lover, pets a dog while enjoying drinks at the Doney on the Via Veneto. (Keystone Pictures USA/Alamy Stock Photo)

Elizabeth Taylor and new husband Nicky Hilton touring Rome's ancient sites during their erratic honeymoon in 1950. (AF archive/Alamy Stock Photo)

The Italian poster for *Roman Holiday*, or *Vacanze Romane*, released in 1953. (Author's collection)

Audrey Hepburn and Gregory Peck play cards during a break from the filming of *Roman Holiday*. (Author's collection)

The former terrace restaurant at the Hassler Hotel in the 1950s, with stunning panoramic views of Rome. (The Hassler Hotel)

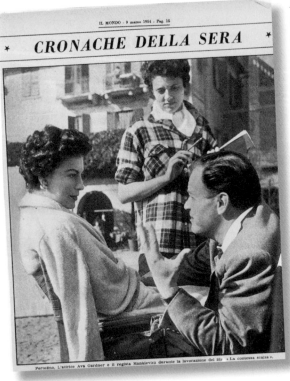

Left and opposite: Countless newspaper articles celebrated Ava Gardner's arrival in Rome for the filming of *The Barefoot Contessa* in 1954. (The Ava Gardner Museum)

barefoot girl with cheek

While making UA's exciting film, The Barefoot Contessa in Italy, with Humphrey Bogart, Rossano Brazzi and Valentina Cortesa, Ava impressed one reporter as being a refugee from a psychoanalyst's couch.

abroad with Ava

In spite of the title, Ava wears 26 pairs of shoes in the film. Also, she speaks Spanish for a scene in the drama.

Italian actresses may be all the rage . . . but they still can't hold a candle to the fabulous charms of that American charmer, Ava Gardner . . .

In Italy, where she's playing the title role in UA's "The Barefoot Contessa," Ava cools her tired tootsies.

20

Ava Gardner poses for publicity shots on board a yacht during filming of *The Barefoot Contessa* in San Remo, 1954. (The Ava Gardner Museum)

A publicity shot of Ava Gardner taken one night at Cinecittà in 1954 for *The Barefoot Contessa*. (Author's collection)

Audrey Hepburn playing table tennis with Mel Ferrer in the grounds of their villa near Rome during the filming of *War and Peace*, May 1955. (Willy Rizzo/Paris Match via Getty Images)

Ingrid Bergman and Roberto Rossellini on the terrace of their home in San Marinella. (New York Times Co./Getty Images)

Kim Novak meets Anna Magnani, who is filming *When Angels Don't Fly* at Cinecittà, in May 1956. (Bettmann/Getty Images)

Ava Gardner cuts the Thanksgiving turkey on the studio lot in November 1958 with Zoe Fontana, cameraman Giuseppe Rotunno and Giuseppe Bordogni, following completion of *The Naked Maja*. (The Ava Gardner Museum)

Anita Ekberg walking down the steps of Trinità dei Monti in Rome with photographer Pierluigi Praturlon, whom she formed a friendship with. (Pierluigi Praturlon/Getty Images)

Marcello Mastroianni and Anita Ekberg on the Via Veneto set at Cinecittà for *La Dolce Vita*. (Author's collection)

Anita Ekberg in *La Dolce Vita*, in a scene set in the nightclub Caracalla's. (Author's collection)

Anita Ekberg set a trend for jumping into the Trevi Fountain after the release of *La Dolce Vita*. (Author's collection)

Sophia Loren enjoying pizza with co-star Jean-Paul Belmondo during a break film from filming *Two Women* in 1960. (Pierluigi Praturlon/Getty Images)

Elizabeth Taylor and Richard Burton are served by the famous Alfredo at his restaurant in Rome in September 1961, during the filming of *Cleopatra*. (Keystone-France/Gamma-Keystone via Getty Images)

Richard Burton and Elizabeth Taylor chat off-camera during filming of *Cleopatra* at Cinecittà in January 1962. (Paul Schutzer/The LIFE Premium Collection/Getty Images)

Elizabeth Taylor and Richard Burton snapped by paparazzi as they leave Tre Scalini restaurant on Piazza Navona in July 1962. (Keystone Pictures USA/Alamy Stock Photo)

Sophia Loren photographed in Rome in December 1962, after visiting the clinic where her sister Maria had given birth. (Keystone-France/Gamma-Rapho via Getty Images)

Audrey Hepburn with Mel Ferrer and Mr Famous looking out over Rome from the Piazza della Trinità dei Monti in January, 1960. (Trinity Mirror/Mirrorpix/Alamy Stock Photo)

Sophia Loren in a scene from Vittorio de Sica's Academy award-winning
Yesterday, Today, Tomorrow (1963). (Author's collection)

Brigitte Bardot is captured by paparazzi walking through Rome's streets in April 1969.
(Keystone Pictures USA/Alamy Stock Photo)

Platinum blonde Kim Novak took a break from making movies to do a tour of Europe, from Cannes to Rome, where she checked into the Excelsior. She visited the city's top sites – the Colloseum, the Forum, the Trevi Fountain to throw a coin in – and was photographed at Doney's sidewalk café, until she had to leave as the crowds gathered around her.

Kim had travelled to Rome to meet with actor Mario Bandini, whom she was dating. Kim had read in her guidebook that travellers should not drink the tap water and should choose mineral water instead. Mario kept trying to tell her that some two million people in Rome were living on the tap water and none of them were getting sick. 'After all, you don't brush your teeth with Aqua Minerale, do you?'

'I do,' she replied.

Kim and Mario were photographed in Villa D'Este, holding hands; there were so many flashes from the cameras going off in their faces that they couldn't see the fountains. She learnt about Italian food from the head chef at the Grand Hotel. Bandini took her to the Catacombs, and to the Mouth of Truth, where she placed her hand in the sculpture, and then for dinner at Hostaria del Orso, with its different floors for cocktails, dancing and dining. Kim was also invited to a private showing at the Fontana salon, located discreetly by the Spanish Steps, where their latest autumn 1956 was collection was being displayed, and she watched the elegant models parade in front of her while sipping on Coca-Cola. Kim was desperate to meet Anna Magnani, and so introductions were arranged at the studio where the Italian actress was working.

Ava Gardner, despite her time spent in Rome previously, had never toured the city's attractions. So over the Easter Weekend in 1955, while staying at the Excelsior after having returned from filming *Bhowani Junction* in Pakistan, she and her press agent David Hanna decided to play tourists. She took a camera with her to record images of the Vatican city, and Sistine Chapel, the Piazza san Pietro and the Forum, and because she was recovering from a cold, she had a fairly subdued evening, only visiting a couple of nightclubs this time.

By the end of 1955, Ava had chosen to make Europe her permanent home. She bought a villa in La Moraleja, outside Madrid, as she had fallen in love with the culture and romance of flamenco and bullfights, the music, the men and the colours of the Mediterranean. Rome was a place she would still travel to frequently for filming at Cinecittà Studios, and where she enjoyed the shopping and the Via Veneto nightlife, despite the increasing irritation of the photographers. Like Kim Novak, she often visited the studio of the Fontana sisters, her favourite designers, to be fitted for that season's gowns.

Ava arrived in Rome again in July 1956 to commence filming on *The Little Hut*. She stepped off the plane in the company of her co-stars Stewart Granger, David Niven, and Italian comedic actor Walter Chiari. Ava, in sunglasses and her shoulder-length hair neatly waved, was presented with a huge bunch of flowers and she smiled and laughed with her co-stars as they posed for the photographers.

'he had been flirting with me almost from the first day we met, but you expect that from Italian males.'

The Little Hut was a silly sex comedy by French writer Andre Roussin which had been adapted into a West End play by Nancy Mitford. The cast of high-profile actors, Niven, Granger and Gardner, were not overly thrilled about the quality of the film, but it was a money-earner and so they thought they may as well get on with it. Ava said of *Little Hut*:

> I hate it, that's all. Every minute of it. It was a lousy story. I shouldn't have done it. The director was awful. It's not going to be much but what could I do? If I took another suspension they would keep me at Metro the rest of my life.

A press conference was held with the stars, but the media almost shoved Niven and Granger out the way to get to Walter Chiari, who was, unbeknown to Niven and Granger, a huge star in Italy. He could sing, dance, act and put on a comedy show, and rumours spread that he was in a relationship with Ava Gardner. Chiari described Ava as 'a good friend'. He had also been linked to Italian actress Elsa Martinelli, who he said is 'also a very good friend'. Asked who was the better friend, Chiari replied: 'You put me on the spot. That's like asking a little boy who he loves best, his papa or mama.' Ava also fought off rumours of romance with Porfirio Rubirosa, a Dominican playboy. 'He's not even worth talking about', she snapped when questioned at the airport. Ava took her favourite apartment on Corsa D'Italia where Chiari would also stay, confirming how their relationship stood.

Ava had been in the audience at one of Chiari's comedy vaudeville shows in Rome at the end of 1953 when he did an impression of Frank Sinatra, who she had only recently split with, and it caused her to crack up with laughter. She said, 'he had been flirting with me almost from the first day we met, but you expect that from Italian males.'

Chiari visited Ava on the set of *The Barefoot Contessa* several times and fell head over heels for her. But she was with Domínguín, and Chiari was with his girlfriend of four years, Lucia Bosè. In a crossover of relationships, Lucia Bosè would marry Domínguín after Ava turned down his marriage proposal, and Ava and Chiari met up whenever she returned to Rome for her visits to the Fontana studios.

Walter was nice, she said – 'amusing, good-looking, even-tempered, highly intelligent, and a delightful companion. He followed me all over Europe, all over the world in fact.' They lived together at times, but 'the distance that separates liking from love is as wide as the Pacific as far as I'm concerned.'

During filming *The Little Hut*, Chiari and Ava disappeared at lunchtime together, not coming back for several hours and leaving the rest of production at a loose end. Chiari would make the most of the summer and autumn by taking her on trips around the countryside of Lazio and she followed him on his tours to Turin as a supportive face in the audience, as she had often done with Frank. And just as she fought with Frank, Chiari and Ava would have blazing rows, followed by passionate make-ups.

Photos of Ava having rows with Walter Chiari, or on set in her skimpy grass skirt or black lace underwear costumes, were highly prized by the photographers, who realised they could get a good price in the Italian and overseas productions.

It was a photographer named Tazio Secchiaroli who got himself a golden shot on the set of the film. He hid in a cardboard box at Cinecittà for hours before spotting Ava Gardner with wet hair and wearing nothing but a towel. The photos he captured were of the actress at her most relaxed, showing a double chin as she laughed with David Niven. They were syndicated worldwide for the novelty of seeing a beautiful star in such a candid, unpolished way.

Tazio knew the movie stars and their business well. In 1943 he had worked briefly as a gofer at Cinecittà Studios, 'the dream factory' that rivaled Hollywood for movie productions. He lost his job when the studio was forcibly closed because of the war, instead finding work as a scattino, or street photographer, charging American GIs and tourists for snaps and discovering a natural flair for photo-reportage.

Tazio had cut his teeth on one of the biggest scandals in Italy, where a major figure in the communist party, Giuseppe Sotgiu, went to watch his young wife, painter Liliana Grimaldi, sleep with an accountant, Sergio Rossi, and other men and women at a brothel at via Corridoni. Secchiaroli staked out the building, photographing Sotgiu entering the brothel, and leaving four hours later. The photos caused huge embarrassment when they appeared in *Momento Sera*, particularly as Giuseppe Sotgiu had criticised the bourgeois society linked to the death of Wilma Montesi.

Wilma Montesi had been found dead on the beach at Tor Vaianica on 11 April 1953, with the police initially stating she had accidentally drowned after washing her feet, despite drowning not being the cause of death. She had been seen in the car of a well-known political personality, but her parents, wanting to preserve her reputation, confirmed she had gone to Ostia to help a skin condition.

Anna Maria Moneta Caglio, intriguingly known as the Black Swan, was a society woman who claimed Wilma had died during a sex and drugs party held by Ugo Montagna, a friend of the Popes' physician, and Piero Piccioni, son of Christian Democrat minister Attilio Piccioni. Tazio was photographed dancing with Caglio, his camera bag still slung over his shoulder as he recorded the people involved in the case. It was Tazio who got the photo of the suspects, Montagna and Piccioni, together in a car, after waiting outside Piccioni's home for two days.

Over the next four years there were countless reports and details revealed, with seedy new characters coming to the forefront. The case would even involve Ingrid Bergman and Roberto Rossellini, who were asked to make statements in the defence of Piero Piccionni. It was reported that Ingrid and Rossellini saw Piccioni in a bar at Amalfi in April 1953, the day before Wilma is believed to have died. It backed up Piccioni's statement that he was in Amalfi with actress Alida Valli and had no involvement in Wilma's death.

In 1957 Montagna and Piccioni were acquitted of murder. The victim, Wilma, had all but been forgotten amongst the society names, but the Montesi and Sotgiu scandals revealed a corrupt and hypocritical Italy. Yet papers on both the left and the right of the political spectrum would rather lay the blame on the photographers for their salacious, 'gotcha' style of snatch photographs.

'I was obsessed with her. She was the most beautiful woman I had ever known.'

Tazio's previous life at Cinecittà stayed with him, and he would return to the studio fifteen years later, this time hunting the celebrities who had flocked there. The photographer was an instantly recognisable figure in his crumpled suit, a camera and battery pack slung over his shoulder and riding on a Lambretta. He was always scouting for faces, his keen eye watching people tumbling out of the pavement cafés and coming up with ingenious new ways to catch candid celebrity photos.

In 1955 Tazio opened the Roma Press Photo agency with Sergio Spinelli, who did the marketing and PR, phoning around news desks to sell Tazio's images. They worked from an apartment on via Nazionale with Tazio covering nights, and Spinelli working by day, with both clocking in twelve hours each. Their agency proved so popular that they moved to new offices and could afford to hire Velio Cioni and Giovanni Lentini, and by 1960 they had twelve employees working for them.

In 1957, Ava, who had put on a little weight, according to her publicist David Hanna, decided to cut and dye her hair into a platinum blonde crop, in the mode of Marilyn Monroe. 'I wanted to be fresh and wisecrack that she looked like a chubby albino but held my tongue,' he said. Ava went for dinner with Hanna at Hungarian restaurant Piccolo Budapest, one of her favourites in Rome. She was particularly paranoid about the paparazzi this time, as she knew they were desperate to catch a photo of her as a blonde. So she checked both ways down the street before jumping into her chauffeur-driven car to be taken to the restaurant. Walter joined them at Piccolo Budapest, but when he arrived Ava greeted him indifferently, and switched moods, becoming quieter in his presence. But despite her seeming cold to him, she continued onto a jazz bar with Walter for a night-cap and checked again that the coast was clear for photographers. She hadn't succeeded in avoiding the photographers completely, as images from the evening appeared in print a week later, with unflattering photos of Walter and Ava being caught in the flashlights.

Ava was beginning to be fearful of ageing, of seeing lines on her face, and not recovering so quickly from the night before. She felt afraid of photographers and the candid shots that would try to capture her at her worst, demanding they be barred from her set so they couldn't sell unapproved photos. She was only 34 but it felt like she was the oldest star at MGM.

Back in Rome in July 1957, Hedda Hopper reported that Ava won't marry Walter Chiari and that 'she treats him with silent contempt'. It wasn't far from the truth – she was losing interest in Chiari and didn't have the heart to tell him. Ava withdrew her affection and tried to sting him with tales of her infidelity, and even accused him of using her for his growing fame. But when she was lonely she would call him up and he would come running. 'I was obsessed with her. She was the most beautiful woman I had ever known,' he said in 1967.

Ava made headlines again in Rome in March 1957, but this time not for her love life. She caused a small scandal with the Catholic Church when she was pictured in a black hat and high-collared dress which resembled the cassock of the Catholic priest and was worn with a large crucifix. It was designed by the Fontana sisters, who had named it the Pretino dress, meaning 'little priest'. The controversy forced the

Fontana sisters to withdraw the outfit from their collection. It also demonstrated a clash between glamour and the movie industry and the Catholic Church, which sought to condemn some of the actions of the industry. Large posters of a scantily clad Brigitte Bardot, or of Anita Ekberg, pasted to the side of buildings were considered to be shocking enough to taint the morals of the public.

12

INGRID

In June 1955 Hedda Hopper visited Ingrid Bergman's home in Santa Marinella, '45 minutes' drive from Excelsior', which she described as 'modern and comfortable but that's about all'. She noted how Ingrid had changed into shorts and a blouse and 'I've never seen her looking better'. She noted the Rosselinis had four dogs, a lamb and two goats, and how little Isotta cuddled into her mother's lap. Asked if she would return to America, Ingrid said, 'I don't think so. I am European, you know, and love the life over here.' She said she had 'slimmed down on spaghetti. She lunched on fresh figs, lobster, squash, green peppers, cheese and eggs.'

During the interview at their beachside home, Rossellini was silent and refused to speak to the gossip columnist – he was suspicious since the hammering they had received in 1950 on the birth of their child, who was now 5 years old. Hedda in return sarcastically referred to him as 'Roberto the genius', and that he had ruined the career of Ingrid Bergman. 'She was treated as a goddess when she first arrived, the first great star to come to Rome and to give the film industry an impetus.'

Louella Parsons visited Ingrid Bergman in November 1956 and described how she was dressed in black slacks which highlighted her slim figure, that 'The round girlish face is gone but the schoolgirl complexion remains. Her cheeks are pink and she uses no rouge or makeup. She is still a very beautiful woman, so animated and so fresh looking. Neither has she lost that well-scrubbed appearance.'

Being directed by Roberto Rossellini had not been easy for Ingrid. His neorealist style was the opposite of working in Hollywood, where scripts and storyboards were prepared in advance. But Rossellini refused to plan out his movies or rehearse dialogue, and the films they made together only drew in niche audiences.

Producers began to lose faith in Rossellini that he would be able to complete the picture on time and that it would make a profit, and so the money for Rossellini's arthouse films was hard to come by. Offers to direct a film for 20th Century Fox, *Sea Wife*, with Richard Burton and Joan Collins, had not worked out for Rossellini, and he was becoming increasingly depressed that he could not reach the heights of the acclaim he had won for *Open City* and *Paisan*.

'Roberto did not think much about money unless it wasn't there, for a film or for pasta. Of course, we always had money for pasta,' said Ingrid. Rossellini preferred the finer things in life, often living outside of his budget. Ingrid could have commanded large salaries from the many important directors who wanted to work with her, but Rossellini refused to allow her to work for anyone else.

Sometimes the furniture in their home would be taken away to pay Rossellini's debts, leaving just mattresses when the beds and headboards were removed. However, Ingrid was devastated when a lampshade made from a black hat from playing St Joan was taken – it was a link to her past life as a Hollywood actress.

Concern about their lack of money made it impossible for Ingrid to be truly content, as she had worked hard and earned money since she was a teenager. Ingrid suggested that they could start living within their means, and try to clear their debts by moving into a small apartment without servants, where she would do the shopping and cooking. He shook his head solemnly. 'Life like that wouldn't be worth living.'

In 1954 George Sanders co-starred with Ingrid on *Voyage to Italy*. George struggled to adapt to this style of film-making and found it very stressful to have to improvise and invent his lines at the last minute. Ingrid's heart went out to him as he broke down in tears over the stress of the situation. However as they travelled to Naples and then Capri for location shooting, George and Roberto both realised a shared a passion for skin-diving. When the sun blazed in the sky and they needed a break from the long hours, or they were feeling hung-over, Roberto, George and the crew would change into mask and flippers and dive into the water to catch fish.

Another project worked out more successfully. The oratorio for *Joan of Arc at The Stake*, which Roberto hastily planned on the back of an envelope, was critically acclaimed and made a profit, but still Rossellini was not being inundated with offers. Rossellini, in an interview with the Roman weekly *Epoca*, in August 1955, insisted that over the six years she had been in Italy, Ingrid had only been offered a couple of interesting roles from Hollywood. He said she was 'a precious capital that should have been exploited. Instead nothing.' He said he understood why Hollywood had to 'dismantle the Bergman myth, but of what interest was it to us Italians to devalue a capital asset which came to us gratuitously?'

However, the truth was that it was Rossellini who had stopped her working with Italian directors like Franco Zefferelli, Federico Fellini, Vittorio De Sica, and she began to feel resentful. 'All wanted to work with me and I wanted to work with them; and they were furious with Roberto that he wouldn't let me work for them … but in Roberto's terms, I was his property …'

If she even suggested working with another director it would lead to a row, with him asking whether it was because she wanted to sleep with other directors. Eventually, she summoned the courage to stand up for herself, telling him that she wanted to make a successful film that people would want to see, and that she would like to be able to buy her children new shoes.

Their silences grew longer, and she was scared to broach subjects with him for fear that he would overreact. She began to realise that it was Anna Magnani who had been his ideal actress, the one who could work with him. Ingrid recounted that 'the world hated the Rossellini version of me, so nothing worked. And he was stuck with me … by this time we both knew it … the traumas of our artistic life, our increasing debts worried me enormously.'

She was asked by friends why she didn't just leave him if she was unhappy – but for Ingrid, it was impossible, not after all she had gone through over the last five years in Rome. 'There was no thought in my mind that I would ever divorce Roberto. I would have gone through hell and still stayed with him, having had such hell to marry him in the first place.'

Jean Renoir visited Santa Marinella during the summer of 1955 with a screenplay for a period comedy called *Elena et les Hommes*, which he wanted Ingrid to read. She loved it, particularly the idea of having a complete script, and decided that she would do it whatever Rossellini thought. To her surprise Rossellini agreed, and she felt Jean Renoir had saved her, just as he had promised at the height of her career: 'I shall wait until you are falling and then I shall be holding the net to catch you.'

Ingrid and her children moved to Paris to work on the film with Renoir, and where she would co-star opposite Mel Ferrer and beat icon Juliette Greco. She was then offered the role of *Anastasia* by friend Kay Brown, which would mark a triumphant return to Hollywood after her self-imposed exile. Roberto objected to the idea of his wife returning to Hollywood cinema and threatened to drive his Ferrari into a tree. She had heard all this before, from when they were in Sicily and he had threatened to kill himself if she went back to Petter. But this time she wanted to do *Anastasia* so much, and the excellent salary would also allow them to pay the bills. While Ingrid was in London filming *Anastasia* in 1956 the children stayed with Rossellini in Rome.

In mid 1956, Rossellini was asked to direct the French stage production of *Tea and Sympathy* at the Théâtre de Paris, and which Ingrid could star in. Rossellini was unimpressed with the play, thinking the theme of homosexuality was too distasteful, and turned it down, expecting Ingrid to do so too. She refused to give up the part, and stayed on in Paris for the play: 'I suppose that two or three years earlier I might have been a submissive little Italian wife, but I don't think so because I've never been submissive as far as my work is concerned.'

Rossellini had been certain it was destined for failure, and he was there on its opening night, watching Ingrid from the wings, ready to commiserate. Instead she received a standing ovation, and *Tea and Sympathy* was sold out over its nine month run. The next day Rossellini left for India, having decided to take up the opportunity to do the documentary he had been thinking of for a while. 'I remember his suitcases were full of spaghetti. As we stood there in the noise and the smoke amid all the people. I had this strange feeling that this was the end of an episode and that things would never be the same again.' It would be almost a year until she saw him again.

'He's so jealous of Ingrid Bergman's success, he couldn't stand it.'

The salary she received for *Tea and Sympathy* was the first she had earned without having to give to a husband since being a teenager in Stockholm. She had to learn for herself how to take care of taxes, whereas Roberto had managed to avoid paying tax as much as possible. 'I came from a time when women didn't think so much about careers, and expected to marry and have a man take care of them,' she said.

In spring 1957 news broke of an affair between Rossellini and a married Indian woman. Rossellini phoned Ingrid from India in the middle of the night: 'If any newspaper people call you regarding some romance of mine, you will deny it. Not a word of is it true!'

For him to phone her like that could only mean that it was true – that he had fallen in love again and now this new woman would take care of Rossellini. Ingrid sat on her bed and smiled, as all the problems with her marriage and the question of a separation had now been resolved.

Hedda Hopper, who had never forgiven Rossellini for his rude treatment when she had interviewed him with Ingrid, reported that 'people keep asking why Rossellini would make such an ass of himself in India. There's only one answer – jealousy. He's so jealous of Ingrid Bergman's success, he couldn't stand it. He's been a failure ever since they started Stromboli.'

Rossellini met Sonali Dasgupta at a cocktail party at the Taj Mahal Hotel in Bombay, as she had been hired to advise him on local customs. She was married with two young sons, but a couple of months later she had left her husband and moved next to Rossellini's Taj Mahal suite. Sonali was described as 'a tall, shapely Bengali' and 'a college graduate who speaks good English, has musical talent and is trying to write film scripts – with encouragement from Rossellini'. Rossellini told Sonali he was going back to Italy to tell Ingrid their marriage was over, and he wanted Sonali to come with him.

Sonali's husband, an Indian producer called Hari Dasgupta was in Calcutta with their 5-year-old son Raja when he was inundated with international journalists trying to get a quote from him. His family and Sonali's were all mobbed with requests until they had to hire security to protect them.

Ingrid, still starring in *Tea and Sympathy* in Paris, was forced to frequently deny that her husband was having an affair, and sounded tired when she suggested that 'it may be blackmail for all I know.' She was parroting what Rossellini had tried to convince her – that the romance was just rumours from people trying to make trouble for him. The play closed in July 1957 and Ingrid returned to Rome, thrilled that 18-year-old Pia, who was known as Jenny in the United States, was arriving in Italy to stay over the summer. It would be the first time they had properly seen each other since she left for Rome in 1949 and she had been nervous about their reunion.

A trip to New York to publicise *Anastasia* had ended in disaster for a planned meeting between mother and daughter as Ingrid had been too busy with interviews to arrange a time to meet with Pia. But over the summer Pia was finally able to stay in the room kept for her at Santa Marinella. Pia loved her summer in Italy, telling her mother, 'why in the world should I stay in America when it is so wonderful here?' Ingrid and Pia photographed travelling in an open-top car through Rome, with Pia smiling and turning to the camera. Ingrid took her on a tour of Rome's tourist sites, and they drew in a huge crowd when they stopped in front of St Peter's Basilica.

All the while Ingrid continued to deny the end of her relationship with Rossellini. 'There will be no divorce,' she smiled, when asked in July. 'They just made up those stories in America to hurt him. When he finishes his picture in India he will come home to us.'

The 27-year-old Sonali arrived in Paris on 6 October 1957, pregnant and with a baby in her arms and asked if she could meet Ingrid. Reporters found out from Air France that she had arrived in the country but were unable to confirm her whereabouts. Sonali had left her oldest child behind with her husband. The 1-year-old child was also her husband's, but Ingrid realised that it was Rossellini's child she was pregnant with. Sonali's situation was strangely similar to her own, all those years ago when she had left her husband and child and was pregnant out of wedlock in a new country. Sonali complained to Ingrid about how intrusive the press had been, how they had spread the scandals around, how she had been harassed by photographers, and Ingrid was empathetic as she had had this experience too. In an American interview in January 1957 Ingrid has stated that publicity about her private life has 'brought me unhappiness'. She said people don't 'have any right at all' to know all the details of a film star's personal life. 'Unfortunately I know what human beings are like; they like gossip and they like to hear what other people are doing, and the worse it is, the more they seem to enjoy it.' She had also been incensed that the media, on her first trip back to America since her scandal when publicising *Anastasia*, had the right to allow people to judge whether she had sufficiently redeemed herself. American talk show host Ed Sullivan asked his audience on air whether or not they wanted to see Ingrid on his show. He said that she had seven years of penance, and while his comments drew criticism for being overly judgmental, the letters he received suggested the American public were still not ready to forgive her.

Rossellini followed Sonali to Paris about two weeks later and Ingrid arrived to greet him at Orly airport. In full view of the photographers and reporters who had gathered they hugged and kissed, and Rossellini announced that the divorce rumours were nonsense. They drove off from the airport in a car with diplomatic plates, but once in the privacy of their hotel room they spoke quietly of a separation. Rossellini and Ingrid obtained a legal separation in Rome on 8 November 1957 after seven years of marriage, citing incompatibility.

For Christmas 1957 Ingrid flew from London to Rome so she could spend time with her children and help them decorate a 6ft Christmas tree. She was greeted at Ciampino airport by Rossellini's sister Marcella and Ingrid's three children, with the twin girls dressed in matching tartan bonnets. Marcella had been caring for the children while Ingrid was in Paris. Now that she was back in Rome Ingrid found the full weight of the press on her again as they recorded her arrival.

On Christmas Day Ingrid, Roberto and the children were holed up inside the Bruno Buozzi apartment as the press gathered outside in the cold winter air. They gathered around their tree and drank glögg, a Swedish mulled wine, while Roberto rested his head in her lap. Ingrid laughed at this domestic vision and their amicable relationship. 'My goodness, all those people down there in the street. They should see us now. It would be the picture of the week.' She sent a bottle of glögg to the press, who were freezing while waiting for something to happen.

After her separation, Ingrid had the freedom to choose her own career path. There had been rumours in July 1957 that she would be co-starring with Sophia Loren and Audrey Hepburn in a Carlo Ponti produced adaptation of Anton Chekhov's *Three Sisters*. This never came to fruition, but she was paired once again with Cary Grant in *Indiscreet*, eleven years after their huge success with Hitchcock's *Notorious*. Nonetheless she wondered if she could ever fully recover from her years away from Hollywood and the endless speculation around her life. Arriving in London for *Indiscreet*, the press at the airport asked her, 'you've ruined your career by marrying Rossellini, and now you are ruining it again by leaving him?'

She cried with happiness in her bathroom in Paris when she heard the news that she had won the 1958 Academy Award for *Anastasia*.

Hedda Hopper told her readers after speaking with her that she sounded just like the old Ingrid – 'vibrant, healthy and happy the way she used to be oh, so many years ago when she was a neighbor of mine in Beverly Hills.' Despite the sense of embrace from the Hollywood community after winning the Oscar, she had no intention of returning there. For one thing she liked that in Italy and France she could work with a wide range of people, including communists – the perceived enemy of 1950s America.

'Here in Europe, we don't have the problem of communists as you have it in America, because here it isn't a crime, and I worked long enough in Italy and France to know that half of the people I work with, if not more, are communists, and we think nothing of it,' she told CBS in an interview. She said that Hollywood lost some of their best talent because of their communist witch-hunts, and that they would surely regret it.

Ingrid met and fell in love with a Swedish film producer, Lars Schmidt, and after they married in London just before Christmas 1958, the real trouble with Rossellini began. Despite having left Ingrid for Sonali, Rossellini expected Ingrid to never marry again. Shouldn't being a mother be enough for her? When the news of her marriage broke he began a lawsuit for custody – that she was a Protestant, had no family, and her name wasn't even on the birth certificate.

A French court granted Ingrid custody, with Rossellini given weekend custody, but he appealed to Italian courts. After endless fights over the children, taking them out the country covertly, Roberto stealing their passports – eventually Ingrid gave in. 'I could never abandon my children, but between us we were tearing them to pieces.' She agreed Roberto would have custody, they would be raised in Rome by his sister and his mother when he was not around, and that she would move between London, Paris and Rome.

At the end of August 1959 Rossellini appeared in public with Sonali for the first time at the Venice Film Festival, while Bergman was in the French Riviera with Lars Schmidt. Rossellini vowed never to allow his children to be reared by a 'foreigner'.

Under Hindu law Sonali needed her husband's consent for divorce, and Hari das Gupta announced from Calcutta that he would not stand in her way. Rossellini was determined to settle the custody battle before remarrying. In 1959, at the Palace of Justice in Rome, Ingrid was granted a divorce from Rossellini, looking tanned, in a suit jacket and skirt, photographed with her lawyer.

Sonali settled into Rome, giving birth to her and Rossellini's daughter Raffaella in 1958. Sonali always wore saris, and at 5ft 8, she was a glamorous, exotic sight in Rome. Despite living in Rome until her death in 2004, Sonali never felt exiled, and would often return to India, visiting her parents in Lucknow with Raffaella.

She opened an Indian-inspired boutique, Varuna, on Via Borgognona – the first of its type in Rome in the 1960s and where she sold clothes, jewellery and Indian handicrafts which became very popular amongst fashionable Rome society. On her trips back to India she would take the opportunity to buy handicrafts, cottons and silks to create her designs. She also brought Margo soap, Neem toothpaste and panjika almanac from Calcutta – all the things that reminded her of her country of birth, ensuring she retained the Indian Bengali identity she was so proud of.

Speaking to *Times of India* in 2014, her brother said:

> She was close to all her siblings, one in Oxford and another in Kolkata. She travelled with her daughter, Raffaella, to India to visit our parents in Lucknow. She was not 'cut off' as it has been written about her. Her son, Gil, used to travel to India on a regular basis on business. He made it a point to visit his grandmother (my mother) in India ...
>
> Her clothes, jewellery, furnishings and handicrafts sold at Sonali, her store, were much sought after and her clientele included the film fraternity of Itlay and Hollywood. And she certainly remained in touch with her family back home.

Her son Raja, whom she had left in India when he was 5 years old, was given a ticket to Rome by his mother when he finished school.

For the seven weeks in Rome he was showered with attention, and was embraced by Rossellini as a son. 'We would spend hours together discussing so many things,' remembered Raja. 'He would take me to his shoots and take me on drives in his Ferrari. He even introduced me to Enzo Anselmo Ferrari, founder of the Scuderia Ferrari Grand Prix motor racing team.'

Ingrid remembered, 'I did have marvelous happiness with Roberto as well as deep troubles. But trouble is part of one's life ... if you have never cried, if you have never been really miserable and thought that you could not go on, what kind of understanding would you have for other people who are in trouble?'

13

AVA

'It's no secret that I've had some terrible experiences with the press. You can't understand what it's like living with it. People ask the most amazingly personal questions and get furious if you don't answer,' Ava Gardner lamented in her posthumous autobiography. She said that Howard Strickling, MGM's famed publicity chief, taught her never to sue, 'no matter what lies the scandal sheets wrote about me – and I never did. He said that magazines like *Confidential* wanted you to sue because the publicity would boost their sales, and they had no money to pay you damages anyway.'

The photo reporters restlessly and regularly prowled the Via Veneto for celebrity sightings and they were becoming even more fervent, riding up and down the curving street on their Vespas. Because Ava often tried to avoid the cameras, but still lived a glamorous whirlwind of a life in jazz bars and at bull-fights, her photos were often more valuable and she would be pursued by the photographers in reckless car chases. Any pose or expression was twisted to suggest something that was not necessarily the case. She would also be paranoid that friends were tipping them off, according to her one-time press agent David Hanna. He witnessed how quickly word spread that she was on the Via Veneto, and in no time there would be eight photographers lurking outside a club.

Ava arrived in Rome in January 1958 for her last film under MGM before she could be released from her contract. To avoid the packs of photographers stalking the airports of Rome, she flew to Nice from Madrid, where her driver Mario picked her up in the Cadillac and drove her across the border into Italy and down to Rome.

In *The Naked Maja*, she was signed up to play the beautiful Duchess of Alba, believed to be the mistress and model of Francesco Goya. Filming was originally to take place in Madrid, but the Spanish Government would not approve the controversial script on the subject of a member of the powerful Alba family, with the insinuation that the Duchess had posed nude for Goya, and so the production was forced to move filming to Rome. Ava would later dismiss *The Naked Maja* as 'not my most memorable effort' but praised the vivid colours of the cinematography, which reflected the artistry of Goya and the rich decadence of Spanish nobility.

She moved into the Grand Hotel while searching for a flat. Corso D'Italia, where she had stayed during the filming of *The Little Hut* was not available, but she didn't want to stay in one of the large, cold Via Appia villas that were so popular with movie people and which she regularly passed on her way from Ciampino airport into Rome city centre. Instead, she took her eighteen pieces of luggage to a beautiful penthouse apartment at 9 Piazza di Spagna, with a balcony looking out over the cobbled, palm tree lined square and onto the baroque Fontana della Barcaccia and the Spanish Steps. Sister Bappie moved in with her, as did Walter Chiari, although their relationship was a stormy battle of fighting and making up. Sometimes she felt paranoid that he was using her to further his career, or that he was working with the press as they relentlessly pursued her.

Ava and Walter had been together for three years but by 1958, Ava Gardner was reminiscing about her Frank Sinatra, who she had finally divorced in 1957, when in Mexico filming *The Sun Also Rises*, and Chiari was drifting further from her mind. Walter was devoted to her, following her to wherever her next assignment would be and he would have married her if she would accept his proposal.

For this visit to Rome, Ava was not in the best mindset. A few months before, in October 1957, the impulsive actress had been swept up in the excitement of a bullfight in Seville while visiting with Bappie and Chiari. Woozy on solysombras, a heady mix of absinthe and cognac, she was cheered on by the crowd to go into the bullring on horseback. This was a dangerous enough move when sober as she was ill-equipped to take part in a bullfight, and when the bull charged and the horse bolted she was thrown onto the ground. She was dragged to safety from the angered bull but the side of her face took the brunt of her fall, and she was left with a large solid hematoma on her cheekbone. For months she fretted over it, feeling the lump with her fingers and looking at her reflection in the mirror to see if the beautiful symmetry of her face really had been ruined. She was all too aware that her career depended on her carefully honed image as a great beauty, and she was devastated as she thought it was gone. She would feel the bump, looking obsessively in the mirror. 'I'm ruined, just ruined. And why did it have to be this side? Damn, what a fool I was.'

> She was all too aware that her career depended on her carefully honed image as a great beauty …

Ava travelled to Switzerland for special treatment and massages, and sent a telegram to David Hanna who was in Munich, asking for him to send her a Gesicht Sauna, a face bath which she thought could help ease the lump. Gradually the swelling came down, but she was still left with a hardened blood clot on her face which would serve as a reminder of the over-excited stupidity of one fleeting moment. She would have preferred to wait in her Madrid home, La Bruja, for her face to mend as news of her injury was in the papers, with plenty of speculation as to just how bad it was.

This time in Rome she shied away from the press, terrified that they would capture her face at a bad angle. Because Ava tried to avoid the cameras, her photos became more valuable and so the street photographers were even more desperate to get a shot. Any pose or expression was twisted to suggest she was distraught or depressed or angry. Whenever she paid a visit to a night spot on the Via Veneto, eight photographers lurked outside a club until she left. She would do interviews, and they would follow the same line – that she was lonely, frustrated, wishing for marriage and the simple days of North Carolina.

One evening during the hot summer filming *The Naked Maja*, Ava and Hanna went for a beer at a trattoria round the corner from her Piazza di Spagna apartment. Two photographers insisted on taking photos until she was back in her apartment. Later, when the photos appeared, they were captioned that he was her lover and that she looked depressed because she was not the beauty she once was. It was cruel, and played exactly on her fears over her looks.

When Titanus offered her the script of *The Naked Maja* for approval, she bluntly told them it was terrible, and the delays for months while they rewrote and amended gave her more time for her face to heal. To occupy some of her time, she and Walter Chiari travelled to San Remo where they spent evenings at the casino. Ava made an entrance in a Fontana gown, because she still had to put on the glamour when she was out, and she proceeded to lose a four figure sum on the roulette table.

Because of the production delay, instead of working in the spring, filming took place in the peak of Rome's summer, under hot studio lights and with limited air conditioning in Cinecittà. She was wearing heavy costumes and with corsetry pulling in on her body, the heat was making her stir-crazy. She wished she could act the film as the title might suggest – completely naked. She also wandered the set barefoot. 'Seventeen years in pictures and I've never picked up a nail or splinter yet,' she said.

Ava, feeling lonely, set her eyes on co-star Tony Franciosa. The American, who had had a tawdry affair with Anna Magnani two years before, was a method actor who would throw himself into the character of Goya before going on camera. He had studied the biographies of Goya intensely, as well as his works of art and favourite Madrid haunts, and contorted his face as if trying to absorb himself completely into the artist. 'A few moments of concentration offstage, then the intense vibrant projection into his part, his face changing contour, his mouth hardening, his eyes seeming to reach out to capture the image before them,' wrote the *New York Times* in July 1958 from behind the scenes of the production. They reported that an admiring Roman extra had declared, 'Even bedraggled, he looks handsome!' Yet he prepared himself as a drunken Goya by 'sticking his finger down his throat to make himself nearly sick and groaning and moaning to get his self in the right psychological mood,' according to Ava.

Franciosa had eagerly written to wife Shelley Winters in March 1958: 'I doubt if you'll notice me in the Goya film. The first four pages of the script have Ava Gardner in the nude. After visiting Italy I now know where I belong – Italy. After seeing the Colloseum and beauties of Rome, which have lasted so many centuries, I feel we've got a chance too.'

With his wife Shelley Winters in the United States, at first Tony made it clear he wasn't interested in any on-set liaisons with his beautiful co-star. In fact, many people on set got the impression the two actors couldn't stand each other. Instead, Ava developed a friendship with the other American actor on-set, Mickey Knox, and when Tony found about this, he suddenly asserted his rights over his leading lady and they began spending their evenings exploring the nightlife of Rome.

Mid afternoon the champagne was cracked open in one of their dressing rooms, and by nightfall they would giddily head out to the hotspots on Via Veneto. All Franciosa's hard work in researching and preparing for the part of Goya went out the window while he drank and cavorted with Ava, who was notorious for her ability to hold her drink. She would begin the film a picture of radiance, having given up alcohol and attended health spas in preparation, but during filming old habits would die hard, and she would fall back into her usual pattern of martinis and local spirits, staying up until dawn. Tony would later comment that it seemed as though she could go for days without sleeping, yet would still arrive on the set glowing and radiant. The photographers would chase Ava and Tony whenever they ventured out together – the two of them thrillingly speeding through the Roman boulevards or up into the ancient hills in a Thunderbird to escape the press pack.

This chaotic, heat-soaked lifestyle was the backdrop to the events of one Friday evening, 15 August 1958, the Feast of the Assumption, which would infamously become known as the night of *la dolce vita* and would inspire Federico Fellini to make his seminal film of the same name. That evening there was a sense of restless frustration in Rome's humid air. The lazy, paralysing heat during the height of summer had caused a Roman languor, a '*febbre tevere*', as Tennessee Williams called it, where productivity seemed impossible, and all one could do was drink.

That night, a number of photo-journalists, including Tazio Secchiaroli, had been prowling the strip, keeping an eye out for the two movie stars who everyone thought had been having an affair and which had been gossiped about in the scandal rags. The photo-reporters were desperate for that one golden shot that would confirm the relationship between Ava and Tony. As the press reported, Tony was 'the current leading man in Ava's fickle heart'.

> Ava's sleek chauffeur-driven car was chased at 4 a.m. through the quiet streets of Rome by two photographers in an open-top car, their cameras raised ...

The outdoor café shots became ten a penny, and the photographers had to move on to more exciting things if they were to make an impression. They would provoke the celebrities to do something, anything, which could make them a sale. In early summer 1958 a leading paparazzi, Elio Sorci, captured shots of Walter Chiari chasing and attacking photographer Tazio Secchiaroli after he had taken a photo of the couple in a blazing row. Secchiaroli, Sorci and two other photographers, had been following Ava and Chiari as they did the rounds of nightclubs, but these were too similar to the other photos they had. As the couple were coming out of the car and into the apartment building, Secchiaroli, warning Sorci to get ready, went up close to Ava and set off the flash in her face. She screamed out and Chiari rushed at the photographer. Sorci started shooting, capturing the moment as if Chiari and Secchiaroli were fighting. The photos were first published in magazine *Settimo Giorno*, and subsequently made it into several newspapers.

On another occasion during the summer of 1958, Ava's sleek chauffeur-driven car was chased at 4 a.m. through the quiet streets of Rome by two photographers in an open-top car, their cameras raised up to try to catch an image of her.

Unofficially, Secchiaroli was the leader of the photographers, perhaps because he was the boldest, and his manner was earning him the nickname '*volpe di* Via Veneto', or, 'the fox of Via Veneto'. He was the one who developed the reputation as an 'assault photographer' for the way he lunged at his targets as if he were a paratrooper and the Via Veneto was his theatre of war.

Ava had been involved in media scandals before, whether it was being falsely accused of drunkenly trashing a hotel room in Brazil when on the South American tour of *The Barefoot Contessa* or a false story in *Confidential* magazine over an affair with Sammy Davis Junior. But her press coverage would reach a crescendo on the Via Veneto in the summer of the 1958. As her publicist David Hanna wrote, 'during the shooting of the Naked Maja, Ava's private war with the Italian press was at its height.'

Tazio and his colleagues had spent the evening prowling the Via Veneto looking for suitable subjects for candid shots and by 2 a.m. they were restless. That's when they spotted the glutinous former King Farouk of Egypt sitting in the 'Left Bank' of the Via Veneto, at the Café de Paris, wearing a light summer suit and with his plump, raven-haired companion Irma Capece Minutolo, and another woman, reported as her sister, but believed to be a paramour. Farouk was living in exile in Italy after being forced to abdicate in 1952 and had been a common sight on the Via Veneto for many years. He was known for his excessive lifestyle, including the rumour that he consumed 600 oysters a week.

The five photo-reporters charged at the table to get close enough for a night shot with their flashguns. In the rush, Farouk's bodyguards mistook these photographers for assassins, as they later claimed, and immediately tackled them, sending chairs, tables and drink flying. Farouk joined in the attack, captured on camera mid motion as he fired down on the photographers with punches, trying to break their cameras. It was photographer Umberto Guidotti who captured the moment while the others were assaulted.

Before the police turned up, the photographers heard that Ava and Tony were arriving across the road at Bricktop, or the 'Right Bank', and shook themselves free of Farouk and his bodyguards to get close enough to capture the two movie stars embracing. As the photographers charged forward and stunned them with the bright flashlights, Ava cried out and Tony fought back, lunging at Secchiaroli as he came toward him. The other photographers stood by to capture that moment mid tussle and Tony and Ava sought refuge inside the club. The photographers, now in an enraged mood, waited for them to emerge at 4.30 a.m., and followed Ava all the way back to her apartment on Piazza di Spagna.

The next day these photos hit the news-stand, and Tazio Secchiaroli found his own fame as both the photographer and subject of these controversial images. *Il Giorno* blazed the headline: 'Photographer attacked by Farouk and Franciosa,' and the story was written up in *L'Espresso* with the headline 'that terrible night on Via Veneto'. Even though it was just an average night with the usual activity, the article caught the attention of director Federico Fellini. He had been planning a film based on the decadent café society of Rome, and this incident captured his imagination as an example of the many stories of celebrity clashes on the Via Veneto. 'Today,' Fellini said in 1958, rather than the bohemians and artists of only eight years before, 'there is journalism, photo-reporters, motorisation, the branch of café society.'

This iconic moment in Italian history would, of course, also impact on the lives of Ava and Tony. Now that the images had been widely circulated, Shelley Winters informed her husband she was coming to Rome herself to keep an eye on him. She was a formidable presence, Brooklyn born, street smart, and with a wry humour. Tony hadn't plucked up the courage to inform Ava his wife would be arriving, and so when Shelley turned up on set, Ava was taken by complete surprise.

Shelley recounted that she found her husband a wreck, having not slept or eaten properly for days, with Ava's bad influence in encouraging him to binge drink. She ordered Tony to go to Capri with her for a rest while they had some days off filming, and he in turn begged for forgiveness for his wrongdoing. Ava came to Naples and suggested she could also go to Capri with them, and Shelley laid down the law in clear terms – if Ava so much as stepped on that island, Shelley would put out a contract on her. Italian press reported on 25 August 1958 that a physical fight had broken out between Ava and Shelley over Tony at a Naples hotel, and they they had had to be separated by a waiter and an elevator boy.

Ava wasn't fazed by the press attention. For her, Tony had simply been a passionate distraction, a man to entertain her during the film production and to distract her from her recent divorce from Frank Sinatra. She often thought of Frank in a wave of regret and nostalgia and had been shocked when she saw the headline in the *Examiner* in March 1958 that Frank was set to marry Lauren Bacall.

Lauren had not wanted news out on their engagement so quickly, and neither had Frank. After having read the article, Ava confronted Sinatra on the phone and he denied his new engagement. 'I was never going to marry that pushy female,' Frank told Ava, and he quietly slipped out of contact with his supposed fiancée, never to speak to her again for twenty years. Lauren Bacall later recounted in her autobiography: 'he behaved like a complete shit.'

Later in April 1958 Frank contacted Ava asking if she would like to meet him in Rome as he was stopping over as part of his world tour. She agreed but had been further upset by articles on his relationship with a socialite, Lady Adele Beatty, who sounded like she should be English aristocracy, but was really from Oklahoma having risen through the ranks of polite society in America's south.

After finding this out, Ava refused to take Frank's calls and his messages to her apartment went unanswered. One morning as she took Rags, her corgi, for a walk, she got the urge to see Frank. After walking out of the heavy doors of her apartment building, she found herself making the short walk around the Piazza di Spagna and up the Spanish Steps to the Hassler Hotel, where Frank was staying. Rags had been a gift from Frank for Christmas 1953, and he jumped up on Frank in recognition, but Ava coolly handed back a ring he had given her, and told him he could give it to his English lady. She regretted this move as soon as she got back to her apartment, and Frank, upset at Ava's actions, called for a car to take him to the airport.

The wounds left by their split were still raw: Ava would sit on her balcony late at night, looking out over the palm trees of the Piazza di Spagna with a martini and cigarette while Frank Sinatra played on the gramophone, his crooning voice drifting out over the Roman night sky. Maybe on these melancholy nights she thought of her time in Rome four years previously, painful days spent together in the New Year, when they finally called it quits on their marriage.

14

ANITA

The photographers who prowled the Via Veneto and staked out Cinecittà were still not earning a lot despite the costs of their pictures and it had become a battle, a survival for money. 'We had nothing, and they, the rich men who were living *la dolce vita*, had everything: beautiful women cars, money,' said Tazio Secchiaroli. The photographers had discovered that if they could create a situation that provoked a narrative, they could make almost one hundred times more money than the meager 3,000 lire they would receive from the newspapers for a photograph.

As death and violence captured in photography are particularly appealing, so are images of the subject of a celebrity under the glare of the spotlight, or trying to escape the lens. It not only places the viewer in the heart of the action but also adds to the vulnerability and makes those famous faces seem more human.

Tazio Secchiaroli was interviewed in September 1958 in *Epoca* weekly magazine, describing his tactics as a photographer – to never let his subject get away from him:

On these occasions, nothing will stop us, even if it means overturning tables and waiters, or raising shrieks from an old lady who doesn't quite get what's happening … even if the police intervene or we chase the subject all night long, we won't let go, we'll fight with flashes, we'll help each other out … the increasingly ruthless competition means we can't afford to be delicate; our duties, our responsibilities as picture-hunters, always on the look-out.

He added, 'of course we, too, would like to stroll through an evening, have a cup of coffee in blissful peace, and see Via Veneto as a splendid international promenade, rather than one big workplace, or even a theatre of war.'

Anita Ekberg had become a regular, glamorous face on the social scene since arriving in the city to film *War and Peace*. The actress was usually dressed in black, or with a huge fur coat on, no matter what the temperature was. At the airport in Rome on one occasion, when a reporter asked if it was mink, she snapped, 'what do you think it is – rat?'

She married British actor Anthony Steel in May 1956, and during the ceremony 200 fans burst through police guards. They spent a few days of their honeymoon in Florence where the groom was presented with a 'colossal' bill of $1,360 after four days of living the high life, and which Anita, it was reported, bailed him out of. It was an indicator of the excessive, drunken lifestyles which made them so captivating as subjects in photographs.

As the newly-weds flew from Rome to London right after their wedding, on a roasting day in May, she waved goodbye from the top of the plane in her glamorous mink coat for the benefit of the photographers. She swept into her coat again when she disembarked in London after spending the flight brushing her famously blonde hair. People 'could hardly keep from hooting with laughter,' said Hedda Hopper in *Modern Screen*.

One evening in 1958 Tazio tried to ambush Anthony Steel and Anita Ekberg as they were leaving a nightclub at 3 a.m. on a deserted Via Veneto. As Tazio got close with his flash, drunken Steel rushed for the photographer, trying to grab the camera. 'There was no call at all for it, it was a peaceful situation,' said Tazio. 'The situation was almost comical because as I ran away, weaving between the tables, I would photograph him, throw a chair behind me and he would trip over it.'

Some stars who wished to get in the papers and to become part of the narrative of challenging the aggressive tactics of the photographers would phone ahead of time as to their whereabouts. Thus the surprise shots were sometimes set-ups by those looking for some extra fame. What differentiated this type of photographer in 1958 from the reportage that came before was that they created a new method of assault photography. These photographers now placed themselves within the story, becoming part of the narrative of the surprise photo, whether it was a genuine scenario or not.

Peter Howard Vanderbilt was the 26-year-old American playboy and son of the Howard family that owned the racing horse Seabiscuit. On a Wednesday night, 5 November 1958, he organised a small party in the Rigantino restaurant in the maze-like Trastavere area of the city, with the Contessa Olga di Robilant, a 25-year-old socialite from an old Venetian family, who was looking to become an actress. The party was a way of launching her name, while for Howard it was a goodbye party as he was returning to the United States. They split the costs of the restaurant, a small buffet and five policemen to keep out gatecrashers and invited 200 members of café society and Roman aristocracy including Novella Parigini, Anita Ekberg, Linda Christian, Elsa Martinelli, Prince Borghese and Prince Hercolani.

The party was at first sedate, and as the jazz band played Anita Ekberg, dressed in a black velvet dress, got up to dance. Just like Ava Gardner, Anita always flung off her shoes to dance – partly because she was so tall that it made it easier to move without them. She moved to the sounds of the jazz band, the cha-cha-cha, the rumba, trying to encourage the others to have a good time.

A dark-haired Turkish actress in a tight white dress, Aïché Nana, who no one had really noticed before, went up to the bandstand and asked for a drum roll to perform a belly dance, after being encouraged by Ekberg and Novella Parigini. Aïché unpeeled her white dress to reveal black lace underwear and as she stripped and danced, a crowd of guests gathered around and the gentlemen flung their coats down to give her a blanket. She slipped off her stockings and then her bra, and as she writhed on the coats, the female guests looked on with remote amusement and the men crouched down closer.

Tazio, seeing the situation unfold, stood up on a table with his camera to take in the full view of the dancer and the crowd, as he knew that these respectable society people were also part of the story. He took as many shots as he could before the battery of his flash died, while Ekberg looked on at him disapprovingly. The policemen broke up the dance, and the party, arresting the Turkish girl for indecent exposure as she tried to plead that someone had undone her zipper.

No one would have known about the event if the photographers hadn't captured the action and sold it to the papers as an orgy. An article in *L'Espresso* in November 1958, with the headline 'Striptease at Rugantino' and using the photos taken by Tazio, caused an outcry as the editorial asked whether these high society people had the right to decide on their own morals. The photos also ended up in *Life* magazine, creating this sense of hedonistic Rome overseas.

When the Vatican condemned the party in their paper *L'Osservatore Romano*, scandal erupted. Peter Howard was asked to leave the country, although he insisted he had been planning to leave anyway. 'She wasn't doing anything you couldn't have seen on New York's 52nd Street ten years ago,' Howard told American reporters.

Director Federico Fellini had been interested in the vibrancy on the Via Veneto, the street he used to gather on with his writer friends like Ennio Flaiano and had wryly observed the action as the movie people flocked there throughout the 1950s.

Fellini noted that he was always being asked by acquaintances visiting Rome to please bring them there to meet Anita Ekberg:

> When I reply that I can do nothing, that I don't know the password to the world of 'Roman Holidays', no one believes me. They would believe me even less if I told them the truth, which is that in my movie I invented a Via Veneto that doesn't exist, exaggerating and molding it with the freedom of fantasy to the dimensions of a large allegorical fresco.

The miracle scene in *La Dolce Vita* was inspired by the mocked up photos Tazio took, after he read a report of two children who had seen a vision of the Virgin Mary in a tree. On a particularly quiet news day he found the countryside village where the children lived and convinced the parents to have the children recreate the scene, while a small crowd gathered around them and acted for the camera.

Fellini's imagination and the idea of *La Dolce Vita* was sparked by the stories he read in *L'Espresso*, of Ava Gardner and King Farouk, of Anita Ekberg, the Turkish dancer and the striptease at a pizza restaurant in Trastevere. Fellini got in touch with Tazio Secchiaroli, and after buying him drinks and dinner, Tazio was only too keen to introduce him to his fellow photographers, who shared the stories of their exploits and their tips on getting the perfect snatch shot. There was plenty of material that Fellini could use in his work with stories around Ava and Anita. Later, Ava may well have recognised her life playing out on the screen in Fellini's film – the wild, heavy drinking, divorced actress who was always in close range of a camera flash. She had another memorable run in with photographers at the end of October 1959, when photographer Lino Nanni filed a complaint of battery against an unidentified escort of Ava's. Nanni said he was assaulted by a 'distinguished-looking' man at the top of the Piazza di Spagna. Nanni had followed their limousine from her hotel on a scooter, and when the limousine stopped, the man pushed Nanni off his scooter, took his camera, hit him on the head and kicked him.

Fellini spent evenings observing the photographers and chatting to them about how they created the narratives of their photos, who they chose to target and how they spotted them. He was interested to hear about how they marketed the photographs to the papers and laughed at their stories of their inventive methods.

The photographers got a kick out of sharing the stories of their exploits and all their inventive ways of finding a story and so when Fellini offered to buy them all dinner one evening in November 1958 they gathered at a restaurant, Da Gigetto er Pescatore, near the Milvian Bridge. Photographers including Tazio, Ezio Vitale and Pierluigi Praturlon talked to Fellini as the white wine flowed, sometimes over-embellishing or exaggerating their tales.

A couple of months earlier Pierluigi Praturlon had taken photos of Anita Ekberg bathing in the Trevi Fountain. He and Anita would often go out dancing together at a place near Casalpalocco, and she was always barefoot. One night in August 1958, when they were driving back from the nightclub, she asked to stop the car by the Trevi Fountain as she wished to cool her sore feet in its water. As she hiked up her skirt and waded in, Pierluigi took out his camera and began shooting, Anita lit up by the glow of the lights of the fountain as two policemen watched, entranced by the vision. It provoked one of the most famous scenes in the movie.

In 1958 Fellini, Ennio Flaiano and Tullio Pinelli worked on the screenplay, picking up on an old idea of Flaiano's of a man from the Italian countryside who arrives in Rome to be a journalist. Fellini wanted to, as Flaiano described in his diaries, 'depict this "café society" that flits between eroticism, alienation, boredom and our sudden prosperity.'

When choosing the name of their photographer Flaiano and Fellini found inspiration from George Gissing's *By the Ionian Sea*, with the character of a hotelier in Catanzaro called Paparazzo. The name also had a similarity to 'papataceo', a word for large mosquito, a pest that was always buzzing around, waiting to draw blood. It was a name that seemed appropriate to this new wave of journalism and their clicking cameras and indefatigable approach. Tazio, considered more intelligent and inventive than the other photographers, was the one who Fellini trusted and relied on the most. In fact Tazio was almost cast as Paparazzo, a character whom he had inspired, but Walter Santesso was ultimately chosen to play the part.

Fellini was concerned Marcello Mastroianni was too innocent and good-looking to play his sinister reporter Marcello Rubini, and so insisted he lose 10kg, added fake eyelashes and a yellow tint on his skin, 'and a black suit and tie that reeked of mourning'.

As a statement of the artificiality and 'subjective reality', rather than shooting on the actual Via Veneto, he ordered set designer Paolo

Gherardi to reconstruct the vibrant section of the street on Studio 5 at Cinecittà. It was built to almost exact measurements, except for flattening the street's natural gradient. *La Dolce Vita* was set over the course of seven days and nights, with eight segments asking questions on the sanctity of the Church, of fathers and sons, of the nature of celebrity. Scenes depicted real life events in Rome – Aiché Nana's drunken striptease became the basis for the striptease at a party in Fregene, while the Wilma Montesi case became the basis for the girl being humiliated at a party.

Filming began on 16 March 1959 in a recreation of the dome at Saint Peter's. Anita Ekberg was dressed in a black gown and priest's hat, much like the Fontana dress worn by Ava Gardner which caused such controversy the previous year. As the actress Sylvia, Ekberg's figure was a representation of Italy's economic boom. Sylvia's volatile relationship with Lex Barker's character was a reference to Anita and Anthony Steele, whose drunken excessiveness and arguments were often in the news.

The opening scene depicts the giant statue of Christ suspended over Rome as it is carried by helicopter, passing sunbathers by a terrace pool before being brought to Saint Peter's. This representation of the coming of Christ is a fakery, much like the artificiality and superficiality of culture and religious values.

When *La Dolce Vita* hit cinemas in 1960 it immediately caused scandal among conservative Catholics with accusations of blasphemy and pornography. *L'Osservatore Romano*, the Vatican's official paper, called for it to be censored. At the Milan premiere Fellini was assaulted, and there were even calls for his arrest. In spite of, or because of the controversy, the film surpassed box office expectations, became the hit of the year and drew acclaim from around the world. It won the Palme d'Or at Cannes, Fellini was nominated for the best director Academy Award, and Piero Gherardi won an Oscar for his set design and costumes. It would also have a huge cultural impact. The relentless photographers now had a collective name, 'the paparazzi', turtleneck sweaters became fashionable as '*la dolce vita*' sweaters, and jumping into the Trevi Fountain was a new sport for university students, uninhibited tourists and starlets looking for some extra publicity. When three British tourists were arrested and taken to court after being found in the fountain, Rome's *Il Messagero* wrote: 'Before you know it the dry land in front of the Trevi Fountain will soon be surrounded by striped beach umbrellas, brightly coloured cabanas and prancing bikini-clad females.'

Tazio was becoming as reported on as some of his subjects, with interviews and features, including in *Oggi*, in January 1960, where an article entitled 'I Had a Fistfight with Farouk in Via Veneto' featured the photos of Ava in a towel on *The Little Hut*, Farouk at the Café de Paris and the fight with Walter Chiari.

> Anita one night fired a bow and arrow at paparazzo Felice Quinto, who had been cast as an extra in the film.

After *La Dolce Vita* was released, and having gained experience as a set-photographer, Tazio was able to give up working nights as a photo-reporter, in order to take photos on sets and as a portrait artist on Fellini's films. He said that Fellini had opened the doors to Cinecittà for him, and teaching him how to capture the world in an amusing, disenchanted way. When he took photos of Fellini on set he wanted to capture the artist in action – as the ringleader at the circus, always impressing and drawing people to him. His photos of Fellini in *8½* capturing the director guiding his own autobiographic film, and later he was trusted as a photographer for Sophia Loren.

1960 was a year of change in Rome, and it marked fifteen years from when Rossellini's *Rome Open City* and neorealism had made such an impact. They marked two different cities – from the tragedy of squalor, deprivation and war, to a city of hedonism, luxury, and with a glittering surface over the flagstones of its piazzas. With Fellini's masterpiece, film became the artistic movement of Italy for the twentieth century.

Famously, at the same time as *La Dolce Vita*, Anita one night fired a bow and arrow at Quinto, who had been cast as an extra in the film. Pushed to annoyance after being tailed home from a nightclub in the company of Guido Giambartolomei, she ran into her villa and emerged with a bow and arrows, which she began firing off at the photographers. Quinto tried to disarm her and she began kicking at him, injuring his hand, while another photographer, Marcello Geppetti captured the images. There were threats from both sides that the police would be called, and Geppetti kept the peace by handing over a roll of film – however it was the wrong one. He kept the images and they were soon splashed in papers around the world.

'I was so mad that night,' Anita told Hedda Hopper. 'I'd been making a picture and was exhausted. My producer took me out for some spaghetti and the paparazzi followed us. We tried to lose them but they came right into my garden, I'd been practicing archery and my maid handed me the bow and arrow so I walked out and began shooting. I broke two flashbulbs and hit one man in the shoulder; they screamed for mercy and never tried breaking into my property again.'

By 1960 the war and memories of fascism had been forgotten and Rome was a pleasure capital to spend money, to show off, to be seen living the good life. That year the city hosted the Olympics to rapturous appreciation – Rome was the first of the Axis powers to hold the games since they were defeated in the war. It was also the first to be shown on television and was the chance for Italy to show a new modern country to the world. At the same time the Cold War was raging. Cuba had fallen into Soviet hands and a wall about to be built through Berlin, dividing Germany into two worlds. This made the competition between countries even more dramatic and the Olympics heightened the tension between the USSR and America. Bruised by Sputnik, the Americans worried the Russians would take more gold medals, which they did, particularly asserting themselves in gymnastics. 'One of the standout events was when Ethiopian barefoot runner Abebe Bikila won the torchlight marathon, taking victory at the Arch of Constantine twenty-five years after his country had been invaded by Italy.

The Olympic Stadium and area around it had actually been constructed by Mussolini in the 1930s as part of his Foro Italico complex, and some of the more obvious fascist symbols of the

Mussolini era were eradicated in advance of the games. The Olympics also led to the building of vast underpasses through the city, cutting through Corso D'Italia and opening the city up to even more traffic.

The Via Veneto was even more appealing to visitors to Rome, where it was referred to as 'the beach' because of the stretch of coloured parasols shading the pavement cafés. And where there was always the possibility of seeing drama and spectacle. Where else could you see a leopard or a lion cub being led down the street on a lead? French actress Irina Demick took a leopard to the Doney, causing some consternation to the uniformed staff who had to move chairs and tables out the way.

Another fixture was Jayne Mansfield. One moment she was divorcing Mickey Hargitay, the next she was playing a violin for him in a Rome restaurant. In October 1962, Marcello Geppetti captured Hargitay carrying a laughing Jayne Mansfield to the car, her blonde hair gleaming, her cleavage spilling out of her skintight dress, and clutching her shoes in her hands.

Marcello Geppetti, the man whom a barefoot Ekberg grabbed by the hair after firing arrows, took some of the classic photos of that era: Audrey Hepburn walking Mr Famous, dressed in an elegant belted shift dress as a group of sailors followed in the distance; Joan Collins, Jack Lemon and Robert Wanger at the counter of the Caffe dell' Epoca; and, in one of his most famous photos, the one that would change the way we consider the paparazzi snatch shot, Elizabeth Taylor and Richard Burton entwined on a sun-covered yacht deck during the making of *Cleopatra*.

15

ELIZABETH

Elizabeth Taylor knew how to make an entrance. She would say: 'Never look anyone in the eye, ever. You have to walk with your vision about two inches above the heads of everyone in the room, and with a smile that is as meaningless as it is broad.' Her arrival onto set on the first day of filming *Cleopatra* in Rome in September 1961, finally after a year of setbacks and millions of dollars wasted, was purposely dramatic. She glided onto the soundstage in a full-length black mink coat, followed by her entourage of hairdresser, costume designer, secretary, maid and assistant. She didn't much acknowledge her co-stars Rex Harrison and Richard Burton, instead going directly towards her director, Joseph L. Mankiewicz, bowing to him, offering up her hand, and letting the mink coat fall to the floor to reveal her Irene Sharaff-designed tunic.

Producer Walter Wanger had hoped to make *Cleopatra* for many years. He considered it 'the last word in opulence, beauty and art … the story of a woman who almost ruled the world but was destroyed by love'. In September 1958 Wanger met Spyros Skouras, president of 20th Century Fox, and they looked out the old Theda Bara *Cleopatra* script from the 1920s, which they thought could be rewritten and updated.

Little did they know that there would be more interest in *Cleopatra* in 1962 than any other world event. It was possibly the most written about movie in Hollywood history, and the production was almost beside the point. It was Elizabeth Taylor's affair with Richard Burton and the break-up of her marriage to Eddie Fisher, with the indulgent, paparazzi-ridden Rome backdrop, that led to what was dubbed '*Le Scandale*'. Headlines blasted out the latest on 'Liz and Dick'. The *Los Angeles Times* noted in April 1962 that: 'Probably no news event in modern times has affected so many people personally. Nuclear testing, disarmament, Berlin, Vietnam, and the struggle between Russia and China are nothing comparable to the Elizabeth Taylor story.'

Cleopatra was budgeted at $2 million but cost over $35 million. The epic movie was career-ending for the president of Fox, Spyros Skouras, the producer Walter Wanger, and the director Joseph L. Mankiewicz. But for Richard and Elizabeth, not only did they make millions, they came to represent the age of *la dolce vita*, and where news and pictures of the extravagances of film stars behaving badly when on location became an industry.

Given that Elizabeth Taylor set her price at $1 million, the studio was set against casting her. Instead they would have preferred alternatives such as contract actress Joan Collins, Sophia Loren or Susan Hayward. But for Wanger, Elizabeth was the only woman who possessed 'the necessary youth, power and emotion', to play Cleopatra.

Inspired by the success of *Ben-Hur*, Walter Wanger and the original director Rouben Mamoulian had wanted to use authentic locations, particularly after Carlo Ponti advised Wanger that Rome was the only place to make it. But the 1960 Olympic Games meant the city would be jam-packed and accommodation all booked up. So they moved the huge production to Pinewood Studios near London.

On 31 August 1960, Elizabeth Taylor and husband Eddie Fisher arrived in London to a hive of newsmen and photographers waiting for them at the airport and at the Dorchester hotel. Elizabeth refused to play the game that day and the British reporters threatened to boycott the film, angered at her lack of co-operation. 'I must say she has a lot of courage. There are very few actresses with nerve enough to stand up to the British press,' said Wanger. The *Daily Mail* ran a story that Elizabeth was not appearing in public because she had put on too much weight from indulging in all her favourite foods and couldn't fit into the costumes. So upset over this was Elizabeth that she eventually won a libel case against the paper.

Elizabeth was beset with illness from the start and this combined with the sets and costumes still being constructed caused lengthy delays which resulted in millions being lost without anything having been filmed. By the end of 1960 Fox president Skouras told Wanger: 'You've ruined us by having that girl in the picture. We'll never finish the picture with her. I wish to hell we'd done it with Joanne Woodward or Susan Hayward – we'd be making money now.'

After the New Year, with millions spent and no footage to show for it, Mamoulian was replaced by Joseph L. Mankiewicz, whose *The Barefoot Contessa* had been filmed in Rome in 1954. Elizabeth had been directed to another Oscar nomination by Mankiewicz on *Suddenly Last Summer* and she trusted him to help her create a depiction of a modern, strong, educated woman.

Despite the hopeful new start to the production, on 4 March Elizabeth was struck by double pneumonia and when she collapsed in her suite, unable to breathe, she was rushed to hospital and was given only one hour to live. An emergency tracheotomy was performed and she was placed on a respirator.

Reporters and cameramen from around the world camped outside the clinic, obituaries were prepared and there was a news report she had died. When he heard this, Skouras called Wanger in a panic, 'My God, how did it happen?' Three days later, Elizabeth was almost out of danger and a week later she was sitting up in bed drinking champagne and acting hostess to visitors including Truman Capote.

With this major set-back, it was decided that the production in London should be scrapped, with losses claimed back on insurance. They would start over in Rome, where the warm and balmy climate would be nourishing and allow Elizabeth to recover fully.

Elizabeth was worried at first about the change of location to Rome for the safety of her family – she knew how steadfast and relentless paparazzi could be, and that security could be much more difficult in Italy. On 1 September 1961 Elizabeth and Eddie made their much-awaited arrival in the city to great fanfare, with dozens of police drafted in to protect them from the most aggressive photographers in the world.

A Roman princess who now earned money working in real estate was set the tricky task of finding a place for the Fishers to live. Their request was for a large, luxury space with plentiful bathrooms, and those with palazzos were unwilling to rent because of the sheer number of children and animals that the Fishers brought with them. There was Michael and Christopher, her two sons with Michael Wilding, Liza, her daughter with Mike Todd, along with a cornucopia of cats, dogs, rabbits and other creatures.

Finally they secured the ranch-like Villa Pappa, just off Via Appia Antica and only ten minutes' drive from Cinecittà, for $3,000 a month. It was set in 8 acres of gardens and had a swimming pool surrounded by trees, seven bedrooms, six bathrooms, a huge living room, a salon, and a dining room.

Before Elizabeth had even moved into the villa, photos of its bathrooms and bedrooms had appeared in the papers. The staff in the villas, despite careful screening, were bribed by reporters for any slivers of information. The high trees around the villa at first made it appear private, but when the paparazzi staked out the property, they realised the heavily foliaged trees around the swimming pool offered vantage points and they climbed up into their branches, decorating the trees with their long-lens cameras. Wanger complained that 'every time I turn around there are grinning, leering, shouting photographers – the paparazzi. They are everything and everywhere. They are like the cats of Rome, hiding on rafters, hiding under bed, always screaming for a morsel.'

No sooner had they arrived, the Fisher's immediately went on a cruise on Sam Spiegel's yacht. Elizabeth was so impressed with a Greek chef who was working on board the yacht that she insisted he be brought to Rome to cook for her. Elizabeth had a Cadillac and Rolls-Royce on twenty-four-hour standby, ready to whisk her to the studio or to restaurants and nightclubs. She was exacting about how her household was run, with the beds made up every day with clean sheets, and full place settings at the dining table. Mankiewicz said she expected 'the best of everything – the best linens, the best wines, the best champagnes'. As one of the most famous women in the world, she was used to getting what she wanted – always the star in the room, always desired, always deferred to. When she felt the urge for baked salmon she called Linny's, a Beverly Hills delicatessen. They would carefully wrap the salmon and pack it with dry ice to send by air freight to Rome, along with a few corned beef sandwiches made 'the way Eddie likes them'. Sometimes she wanted her favourite chilli from celebrity restaurant Chasen's in Los Angeles, and it would be delivered to her in the same way.

In Rome, not only did she shop in Christian Dior, but Elizabeth discovered Bulgari's on Via Condotti, where proprietor Gianni Bulgari would take her into the VIP area. 'My home away from home is the House of Dior,' she said, 'and my favorite hobby is collecting real jewels.'

For Elizabeth's dressing room at Cinecittà, an entire building was redesigned for her. It included wardrobe and make-up room, bath, salon and an office for Eddie. 'Isn't this a bit much?' she said, with a trace of humility.

It was the late producer Mike Todd, her third husband, who showed her a life of private planes, yachts, tours around the world. 'She drinks champagne at breakfast every morning', he said proudly. He sparked her jewel fetish with a $30,000 friendship ring, a $92,000 engagement ring and a diamond tiara, which she enjoyed wearing while swimming laps in the pool outside of Monte Carlo. And even though she was spoiled, he was strong enough to stand up to her:

I will get away with murder if I can. I used to try, out of my perversity, sometimes to drive Mike mad. I'd be late, deliberately just fiddle around and be late, and I loved it when he would lose his temper and dominate me. I would start to purr because he had won.

In the lead up to the new Rome date, the vast sets were frantically being constructed and the 20,000 costumes required for the cast and extras were still to be created. By the start date of 25 September only one of the sixty sets had been completed and Mankiewicz was surviving on a supply of amphetamines to power him for writing and rewriting the script.

As she recovered from double pneumonia and worked to build up her strength, Elizabeth indulged in large breakfasts of hash browns, eggs and waffles, and dinners of steaks and pizza. When it came to the fittings with new costume designer Irene Sharaff, Elizabeth realised she had put on more weight than she had intended to, and so went on a crash diet to ensure she could wear those costumes skintight. Elizabeth and Irene Sharaff got on well and they worked together to update the traditional costuming for a modish 1960s style. 'I think Egyptian dress and make up are very becoming to a woman,' Elizabeth told the press. 'We're doing things with eye makeup that are more accentuated, more colourful, more fantasy-like than ever before—to give a catlike look.'

> On being told that Richard Burton was now her co-star, Elizabeth said she was 'naturally very excited'.

A deal was struck with Prince Borghese to rent his private beach at Anzio, where the Allies had landed during the war. But the production hadn't counted on the mines still buried in the sand and which would have to be cleared. A replica of Alexandria was built up on the cliff tops, and the schooners and Cleopatra's royal barge were all constructed here.

The *Cleopatra* production resembled something like a huge thousand-man circus coming to town. The cast and crew took over Cinecittà, with legions of extras dressed in colourful Roman clothing filling the commissary at lunchtime, and with athletes practicing their pole-vaulting, sword-fighting and archery. Dance legend Hermes Pan rehearsed for months for the sequence where Cleopatra arrives in Rome. The sheer number of staff resulted in labour disputes, on one occasion over the skimpiness of the costumes worn by the handmaidens and slave girls. Italian cats also added thousands to the budget. Rome's stray cats were well-known to visitors to Rome. They prowled the streets looking for scraps of food, and on the set at Cinecittà they found resting places under the sets and in the rafters.

The doors of dressing rooms were always open, and an intimacy between the technicians, the crew and the actors was built up during filming, with gossip and arguments taking place behind the scenes. There were 90 Americans, 350 Italians and 16 Britons hired on the crew. Mankiewicz reminded the Americans and British to be respectful that they were in Italy and not to expect that the local crew should necessarily speak English.

When production moved from Pinewood to Cinecittà, Peter Finch and Stephen Boyd had been replaced by Rex Harrison as Caesar and Richard Burton as Marc Antony. On being told that Richard Burton was now her co-star, Elizabeth said she was 'naturally very excited'.

Charming, rugged Burton was making waves in *Camelot* on Broadway, where after each show his dressing room filled up with fans and well-wishers who he greeted in his affable, dynamic manner. He was incredibly well-read, could recite Shakespeare and Keats and Dylan Thomas at the drop of a hat. One evening in June 1961, Walter Wanger paid him a visit to his dressing room and noted that a chorus girl, Pat Tunder, who was his unofficial girlfriend, stayed on after the guests drifted away and joined them for dinner at 21. Wanger recalled that 'Burton entered the restaurant like a football hero at a college prom with the prettiest cheerleader at school on his arm. He exuded confidence, personality and sex appeal.'

Burton and Elizabeth had first met in 1953 at a pool party at Stewart Granger's home, the year after she had married Michael Wilding. There was beer on ice and bronzed movie people on sun-loungers by the pool, one of whom was Elizabeth, nonchalantly reading a book. She briefly glanced over to the rugged Welshman holding court and concluded he was full of himself. 'She was so extraordinarily beautiful that I nearly laughed out loud,' he said. 'She was, in short, too bloody much, and not only that, she was totally ignoring me.' They met a couple more times – at a Manhattan cocktail party hosted by Tyrone

Power, at a restaurant in Los Angeles and during a 20th Century Fox luncheon with Soviet leader Nikita Khrushchev.

Burton had been married to loyal, elfin-pretty Sybil Williams since 1949, after acting together in *The Last Days of Dolwyn* (1949), and they had two daughters, Kate and Jessica, who was diagnosed with autism. But he freely indulged in extra-marital affairs and was accustomed to sleeping with all his leading ladies.

Richard Burton, Sybil and their two daughters were furnished with a villa complete with household staff, and which they shared with Roddy McDowall, who played Octavian, and his companion and lover John Valva, who was given a small role in the film. McDowall was one of Elizabeth's oldest friends, having both been child stars at MGM and co-stars in *Lassie*.

Rex Harrison chose to stay at the Hotel Excelsior with Rachel Roberts, a Welsh actress whom he would marry in Genoa in 1962. Both heavy drinkers, their relationship often descended into mayhem with boozy, and at times violent, arguments where Rachel would seek solace with Sybil Burton. Rex Harrison complained about the amount of attention lavished on Elizabeth in the first weeks of production. 'Just because Elizabeth's tits are bigger than mine doesn't entitle her to be driven around in a mile-long limo, while you restrict me to the backseat of a two-bit Fiat sedan,' he complained to Wanger.

Cleopatra was finally on track on a hot day in Rome, 25 September 1961. As reported in the *Los Angeles Times*: 'Elizabeth Taylor, lightly veiled in a cool slate-blue silk tunic with plunging neckline, was described as "healthy and radiantly happy". In her first scene she made an offering to the Egyptian god Isis.'

On that first day on set, Richard Burton watched Elizabeth with fascination. He had made a comment with typical bluster that he could easily bed Elizabeth, but when he saw her in her plunging gown, he was quite taken with her. Burton was dressed in a short Roman tunic that just skimmed the top of his thighs, an outfit he had been reluctant to wear, but which he was tanned and muscular enough to pull off. 'You're much too fat, but you do have a pretty little face,' he said as way of introduction as she was seated in the make-up chair. Elizabeth laughed at his nerve, a genuine peal which he found beguiling, but to demonstrate that she was already someone's wife, she girlishly planted herself on Eddie's lap.

Elizabeth proved herself to be the star attraction of Rome, now dethroning Anita Ekberg as the symbol of *la dolce vita*, when she created pandemonium at the Italian 'Oscars' held at the Sistine Theater on 28 September. Elizabeth, who was awarded the Silver Mask for her role in *Suddenly Last Summer*, made a dramatic arrival on Eddie's arm, dressed in a plunging silver gown. Hundreds of flashbulbs popped, the crowd of 2,000 went wild for her and dozens of policemen had to hold back the paparazzi racing to the stage to take her photo.

Newspapers and magazines from around the world clamored for any news angle from the set of *Cleopatra*. At the end of September, the Communist daily, *L'Unita*, ran an article about on-set segregation between the white dancers and those of colour, where they had to dine and dress separately. While the story was denied instantly, the issue was raised in the Italian parliament and blame was heaped on Elizabeth. The story was retracted after dancers signed a joint letter to state the inaccuracy. A ticket to the *Cleopatra* set was the most sought after in town, with a troupe of US Congressman and their wives being brought to the set in the hope of meeting Taylor, and the President of Indonesia preferring a visit to Cinecittà over meeting the Pope.

While Burton had justly earned his reputation as a lady's man, Eddie Fisher was initially unthreatened by him. Burton appeared to arrive on set most mornings looking hungover, dirty and unkempt, with his acne scars covered in make-up. Fisher couldn't imagine that Elizabeth would find him attractive, particularly when she made jokes about his dirty fingernails. Burton at first thought Elizabeth had no technique, but when he saw the rushes he realised her quiet impact on screen.

Richard and Elizabeth were first drawn together with their shared humour. Like Mike Todd, Burton was a raconteur always at the centre of any social gathering. Burton's dressing room was known as 'Burton's Bar' where cast and crew could have lunch and drinks with him and where Elizabeth would laugh at his salty jokes.

Elizabeth brought her own vodka and tomato juice to her dressing room so she could mix Bloody Marys in the mornings. She and her co-stars would break up filming with long lunches with bottles of wine, coming back to set a little drunk, and expecting the crew to wait for her. They joked it should be called Waiting for Elizabeth. But she was the most powerful actress in the world, the first to get $1 million, and she could bend the rules whichever way she wanted.

Eddie Fisher tried to encourage Elizabeth to switch boozing for early nights. Considering that she had come very close to death earlier in the year, he was anxious about her health, and he tried to water down her drinks when she wasn't looking. Elizabeth referred to her 'hollow leg,' where she could drink anyone under the table. Despite his concerns for her drinking, she would leave the set at 6 p.m. every evening for dinner with her family and learnt her lines perfectly for the next day.

Rome in autumn 1962 seemed to be full of movie people. Tony Martin arrived in Rome and had dinner with Liz and Eddie. He and Eddie started singing, and when the diners applauded, they went round tables with a plate to collect tips to give the waiters. Eddie was also captured in paparazzi photos serenading his wife in the back of a car with Elizabeth on their way home from dining on the Via Veneto. He mugged it up for the cameras as he sang along with a violinist standing beside the car.

The Fishers held a party for Kirk Douglas on 14 October at the Grand Hotel to celebrate the anniversary of *Spartacus*. Guests included Jack Lemon, Cyd Charisse, Joan Collins and Gina Lollobrigida. Elizabeth was having a wonderful time sitting next to Richard, and while Eddie, her caretaker, wanted to leave at 9 p.m. and refused her another glass of champagne, Richard kept on topping up her glass when Eddie wasn't looking. While she was captured in a photo looking hostile as Eddie adjusted the flower brooch on her pale Valentino chiffon gown, she was full of laughter as she sat next to Richard. 'I absolutely started to adore this man,' she recalled thinking.

With Burton's reputation as a ladies' man, and with Elizabeth onto marriage number four, columnists were dying for them to have an affair. Looking for different angles in the *Cleopatra* story in the meantime, Eddie was painted as a 'handmaiden' to Elizabeth. *Il Giorno* reported: 'Miss Taylor must have her children and husband around her every free moment she has. She treats Eddie like a slave but acts madly in love with him.' Some people joked that Fisher was only of third importance in Elizabeth's entourage, after her hairdresser, Alexandre de Paris, and her agent, Kurt Frings.

Elizabeth, despite her command, saw her main role as being wife – she was Mrs. Michael Wilding, Mrs. Mike Todd, Mrs. Eddie Fisher – but by the time she was in Rome Elizabeth began to realise that Eddie was not strong enough for her. Maybe she had been too quick to marry him, but she had been so devastated when Todd was killed, and Fisher, Todd's best friend, was her way of staying connected to the memory of her late husband. Eddie was married to sweet girl-next-door Debbie Reynolds, with two young children, but he and Elizabeth's mutual devastation led to the bedroom and then a wedding in May 1959. When the Liz, Eddie and Debbie story broke, it became the biggest celebrity story of the year. Instead of being considered a bereaved widow, Elizabeth was now a man-hungry marriage wrecker.

Her thoughts during these first few months in Rome were conflicted. She confided in her director Mankiewicz: 'I somehow believed I could keep Mike's memory alive through Eddie. Instead, I now find that all I have is Mike's ghost. How can I be his wife, when I am still married to a ghost?' Elizabeth placed Mike Todd's photos on display in Villa Pappa and she kept Todd's twisted, blackened wedding ring on her finger. It was Richard who helped to bring her out of mourning – telling her on a visit to the villa that it was ghoulish to see these photos of Mike.

Elizabeth proclaimed Christmas 1961 as 'the best I've ever had'. She and Eddie ordered in a 30lb roast turkey and two Virginia hams from Chasen's by air express to enjoy in their villa with Roddy McDowell. The Burtons and the Fishers held a New Year's Eve party at Bricktop's on the Via Veneto to welcome in 1962, and it was attended by many of the *Cleopatra* cast and crew. Hedda Hopper, who had been invited, reported that 'All the years I've known Liz I've never seen her this happy, contented and congenial. She looks absolutely radiant …

everyone seems completely confident and extremely happy about *Cleo* and the way it's going.' The party continued on to Villa Pappa, and when Fisher observed his wife giggling to Burton on the sofa, he tried to catch her attention by crooning to her.

The first weeks of 1962 began strongly for Liz and Eddie as their adoption of a little girl, Maria, was made official. After having her three children by Caesarian operation, and with a painful, dangerous delivery of third child Liza, Mike Todd had allowed doctors to perform a tubal ligation, something that was absolutely devastating to Elizabeth when she awoke from the surgery. Because she couldn't have more children, she decided to adopt, because, as Wanger said, 'Liz sees herself as a mother-goddess figure. Part of her function, in her mind, is to bear a child by the man she loves.'

But as they welcomed their new addition to the family, on 15 January a column by Louella Parsons made waves around the world when she reported that the Fishers were to get a divorce – a prophetic article that indicated how the year would go. The studio issued a denial that nothing could be further from the truth and the Fishers kept up a united front. Richard and Elizabeth hadn't acted in a scene together as yet, but on 22 January their first one was scheduled, where the attraction between Marc Antony and Cleopatra becomes obvious during a meeting with the senators in Cleopatra's villa in Rome.

Richard, nervous about this scene with Elizabeth, got drunk the night before. When he came onto the set he had the bleary eyes and shaking hands of a man with a severe hangover. Elizabeth, in a stunning yellow silk dress, helped him to drink a cup of coffee, by steadying his trembling hands. He was vulnerable and sweet in this state, and when he fluffed his lines, she was further endeared.

Between filming of these scenes, Wanger noticed Liz and Richard Burton sitting together, intent in conversation, she in her plunging Cleopatra gown and he in his knee-length toga. When called to take their places and the camera began shooting, it was as if 'the current was literally turned on' and they became 'the characters they play'.

They began meeting privately, for long lunches in Burton's dressing room, likely to be the location where they first sealed their affair, or in the back of a Cadillac, as Richard bragged. They would hide out for afternoons in her personal manager Dick Hanley's apartment, which was near to Villa Pappa. When they filmed their first screen kiss, each take seemed to last longer than before. For Taylor the movie magic of *Cleopatra* crossed over into her real life. Just as the queen of Egypt had her love, Caesar, ripped from her, Elizabeth had lost Mike Todd so devastatingly. And just as masculine, commanding Marc Antony stepped into the void left by Caesar, so did Burton. Burton referred to her 'breasts jutting out from that half-asleep languid lingering body, the remote eyes, the parted lip'. They were both hooked.

The *Cleopatra* grapevine provided cast and crew gossip to dine out for days on the stories they heard. Both the film and the affair were the talk around café tables at the Via Veneto. Irene Sharaff had her own unrivalled intelligence from her seamstresses and wardrobe girls who had the latest on what Elizabeth was up to and it was impossible for nuggets of gossip not to be spread around Rome.

At the end of January Countess Volpi, the widow of Mussolini's Minister of Finance, held a party at the Volpi palace. The ballroom was dressed to look like a modern nightclub, and a guest list of actresses, models, ambassadors and nobility were all gossiping about *Cleopatra* as they took to the dancefloor to do the twist. The extravagance of the *Cleopatra* production had become transfixing to everyone in Rome. The city, as it had been during the days of the Roman empire and the fifteenth century Borgia court, was a hive of gossip and whispers about the scandal, where thousands of artisans, technicians and extras got a chance to be part of it themselves.

'Tell me the truth. Is there something going on between you and Burton?' She confessed that, yes, she was in love with him.

By the end of January Mankiewicz, who had observed the chemistry from his two stars, felt he had been 'sitting on a volcano all alone for too long', and he confided in Wanger that 'Liz and Burton are not just playing Antony and Cleopatra.' Mankiewicz didn't protest too much about their affair – he thought it would be good for her to learn discipline from theatre-trained Burton on learning her lines. Wanger's primary concern was that Elizabeth, who could be emotionally unpredictable, would be unable to work if the affair ended badly.

At the beginning of February the Fishers went to Paris for the weekend, while Burton took the chance to escape to Naples with his older brother. He needed a sounding board to explain the truth behind the gossip and talk over his conflicting feelings. Burton was wrought with guilt over Sybil, he did not want to break up his family and he was also concerned about the damage being done to his career. Back at Cinecittà, Burton asked Wanger, 'am I fired, chief?' He nobly offered to quit the film, so as not to ruin the picture.

Eddie, well aware of the rumours, didn't want to risk losing his wife. Eventually Eddie confronted Elizabeth when they were in bed one night. 'Tell me the truth. Is there something going on between you and Burton?' She confessed that, yes, she was in love with him. Eddie packed his bags and drove to a friend's villa, but Mankiewicz told him he needed to get back to his wife, otherwise she would have grounds for divorce by desertion.

Eddie went to Gstaad to clear his head at their recently purchased villa, Chalet Ariel. But before he left he put in a call to Sybil Burton, telling her of the affair. As far as she was concerned, she had known about it, but believed Richard was playing along for the sake of the film. Roddy McDowall, sharing a villa with the Burtons, arrived on set to alert them that Sybil was about to turn up to raise hell after her concerning conversation with Eddie. Richard made it clear to Elizabeth that this was just an affair and that she should stay with Eddie. She was so distraught that she didn't come in for work the next day.

Wanger and Mankiewicz, having heard that there had been a disturbance with Elizabeth, went to the villa to see how she was. When they arrived at 11.30 a.m., she was in her upstairs bedroom being treated by a doctor. Wanger and Mankiewicz were offered a coffee and they waited in the living room with her entourage, including Dick Hanley and her hairdresser Zavits.

Elizabeth eventually emerged looking pale and sad, but still every inch the glamorous star in a blue-grey Dior nightgown. Mike Todd had been the love of her life, she said, and while she loved Eddie, it was Richard who she was drawn to. He called her 'Ocean', and it must have been irresistible to find a man who appreciated her depths. Her heart, she said, 'feels as though it is haemorrhaging'.

When Wanger and Zavits went to check on her again with some sandwiches and milk, they noticed she had taken a number of sleeping pills, and immediately called an ambulance. The paparazzi were waiting for her as she arrived at the Salvatore Mundi hospital, and rumours circulated that it was an attempted suicide. In response to all the press calls, Wanger tried to reassure them her illness was only down to the bully beef they had eaten at lunchtime. Eddie instantly returned to Rome when he heard what happened, further fuelling the gossip on her suicide attempt. 'Why did you tell Sybil?' she asked him when she saw him again. 'Because I love you and would do anything to keep you,' he replied.

On 19 February Burton returned from a trip to Paris, telling the paparazzi who greeted him that 'it's all bloody nonsense,' and released a statement on the 'uncontrolled rumors' and a 'series of coincidences [that] has lent plausibility to a situation which has become damaging to Elizabeth'. He said he and Elizabeth had been 'close friends for over twelve years' he had known her as a child star 'and would certainly never do anything to hurt her personally or professionally'.

This statement only validated the rumours, planting their affair firmly on the front pages. Press releases relating to anything other than *Cleopatra* was of no interest – all that was wanted was information on Liz and Burton. According to Associated Press. It was the biggest story ever handled in Rome, only of slightly less interest than the death of the Pope. Two priests knocked on the door of Burton's villa asking for a donation, and after suspicious household staff questioned them, it turned out they were two paparazzi. One employee in the publicity department was even discovered to have hidden a mini-camera in her beehive hair, having been bribed by the press.

On 27 February, Eddie Fisher threw a party for Elizabeth's 30th birthday at Rome's Borgia Room. The Dom Perignon was flowing, the guests danced, and Eddie presented her with a huge diamond ring and an antique mirror to convince the world they were in love. But for Elizabeth, it was 'the most miserable day of my life'.

Not only was she disappointed Burton had not bought her a gift for her birthday, but she couldn't understand why he appeared so cheerful on set, drinking beer as he bantered with the cast. He had become famous overnight, with offers flooding in and a sudden increase in salary. Pat Tunder, the blonde from New York, was also buzzing around the set vying for Burton's attention – adding a further complication to his life. He spent St David's Day boozing on a Rome pub crawl with Pat, arriving on set still drunk and proceeding to fall asleep in his dressing room. Elizabeth, jealous at the sight of Pat trailing beside him, berated Burton for being late and for keeping everyone waiting. He offered to pay for the delay as Wales' national day was an important celebration for him.

Pat would often turn up on the set, watching intently as Elizabeth and Richard performed for the camera, until Wanger had to ask her to leave. Pat returned to New York not long after, turning down all money offers from newspapers and photographers to dish the dirt. With Pat gone, Elizabeth and Richard's relationship became more intense.

A story appeared in the papers that Burton had no intention of leaving Sybil, coincidentally on the same day Elizabeth was to act out the scene where Marc Antony deserts Cleopatra. She stabs all his clothes and their bed, and then breaks down in tears. Elizabeth went so wild and frenzied while acting out this scene that the doctor was called and she was admitted to hospital for an X-ray of her hand to make sure it wasn't fractured.

Wanger arrived at Villa Pappa one day after having bought a book for Elizabeth from the Lion bookshop on the Via Veneto. He was shown to her luxury bedroom where he found Elizabeth and Eddie giving out an impression of marital bliss as they sat in bed reading, surrounded by a scattering of newspapers.If Richard had no intention of leaving Sybil, then she was going to give her marriage a try, at least, for the sake of appearances.

Fisher tried to convince himself that Burton was only interested in Liz's fame, and would go back to Sybil when filming was over. But on the evening of 18 March, Elizabeth and Richard had dinner together at an intimate restaurant, and she didn't come home until sunrise. It was too much for Eddie, and he packed his bags and left for New York. 'If you leave you'll never see me again,' she said, and in fact they didn't see each other for two years.

Elizabeth was in shock that he had really gone, and had a restless night without sleep, feeling lost and alone in her villa. She called in sick to work the next day, with the excuse that while wiping away her make-up she had cut her eye with one of the many glass sparkles painstakingly applied to her eyelids.

With Eddie away in New York, Elizabeth and Burton lost all sense of discretion. *Gente*, a Milan news weekly, published the first long-lens photo of Liz and Burton kissing on set, both dressed in bathrobes, and the photo, taken by Elio Sorci, was splashed around the world.

Back in New York, Eddie drank heavily to mask his pain and he visited Dr Max Jacobson, known as Dr Feelgood for his famed injections of uppers and downers. He ended up in a New York hospital after a breakdown, although his publicist insisted it was flu. Eddie appeared on TV show *What's My Line?* looking thin and tired, and publicising Cleopatra cosmetics marketed by the studio. 'Are you married to a very beautiful girl?' he was asked. 'I'm here on some *Cleopatra* business,' her replied, and predicted that 'Elizabeth Taylor Fisher will win the Academy Award for it.' A few days later Eddie held a press conference at the Hotel Pierre, telling media that rumours of a break-up were 'preposterous, ridiculous and absolutely false'. He left the room to call Rome with the hopes of putting Elizabeth on the phone. However she refused to take the call, and he was humiliated in front of a gathering of media. 'You know, you can ask a woman to do something and she doesn't always do it,' he said.

The same day, Richard and Elizabeth decided to turn the tables on the paparazzi for a night on the Via Veneto smiling and holding hands – the first time their affair was publicly sealed. Elizabeth was dressed in a striking leopard-print coat and cloche hat, still with her Cleopatra make-up on, and with this photo '*Le Scandale*', the media story of the century, was created. A photographer caught them at

3.30 a.m. at the exit of Bricktop's, where they had spent two hours. They smiled and appeared almost willing to pose. Then they dashed for their car and roared away, losing pursuing photographers on the road to Ostia Antica. 'I just got fed up with everyone telling us to be discreet,' Burton told Jack Brodsky. 'I said to Elizabeth, 'Fuck it! Let's go out to fucking Alfredo's and have some fucking fettuccine.'

The next day, after their night on the Via Veneto, they were on set filming the Bacchus tribute scene. Elizabeth was dressed in a low-cut green gown, while they enjoy a feast surrounded by hundreds of dancing slave girls. Marc Antony was to be drunk and intoxicated by the wine and the beauty of Cleopatra.

In order to control the damage, Elizabeth put out the statement that she and Fisher had mutually agreed to part and divorce proceedings would soon begin. Fisher had abandoned his family for Elizabeth, and now it was he who was being abandoned. Burton sent a reassuring telegram to Sybil, who was in London, with a message in Welsh that everything was fine. Thinking he was the only one who could understand Welsh, he was surprised when his note had been translated and hit the headlines.

Elizabeth turned from the wreckage of her shattered marriage with singer Eddie Fisher to a hectic round of dating with Burton. They brazenly flaunted their affair in the restaurants and bars of Rome, captured outside Tre Scalini in Piazza Navona, and in the Taverna Flavia just off Via Venti Settembre, and by this time Elizabeth didn't care what the gossips said. She was sick of the constant hounding of paparazzi. Burton was scolded by Wanger to stop flaunting his private life by going to 'the Via Veneto and those cheap joints'. Burton furiously replied, 'Those places are not cheap, they are very expensive.'

There was some distraction from the Liz and Dick story when on 28 March Rex Harrison went to the airport to pick up his new wife, Rachel Roberts, having recently married her in Genoa. She was asked by Rome airport security to open her handbag for inspection by customs. Incensed, she shouted xenophobic insults aimed at the Italians. She was lucky to avoid jail for the night as Rex Harrison apologised in court and the case was dismissed.

In America, Richard and Elizabeth were condemned for their immoral behaviour. Elizabeth was also denounced by a letter published in the *Vatican Weekly*, calling her a 'capricious princess', and criticising her marriages and adoption of children: 'If nature does not allow you any more children, you at least should not go around asking for them.' Like many other publications, it was she, the woman, who was being blamed for the affair. Wanger wrote: 'These are hypocritical times, when men are permitted to have more than one love at a time and women are castigated for the same kind of behavior.'

The same day this letter was published, Elizabeth went with Richard for dinner at the Grand Hotel. She was dressed proudly in a black silk ballerina dress and they enjoyed cheese soufflé and steak. They were later joined by director Mike Nichols, whom she had been spending time with in Rome. That evening they continued to a nightclub, but the booze brought emotions to the surface, and when she thought she could hear people whispering about her, she broke down in tears. They were chased by paparazzi as soon as they left the club.

When Elizabeth received a letter at her villa threatening her death unless she stopped dating Burton, police were assigned to escort her to Cinecittà and a car was stationed in front of her villa. The only safe space seemed to be the sound stage, where she was protected by the crew who rallied around her.

The most ambitious scene in the film was Cleopatra's entrance into the Roman Forum, sitting on top of a black Sphinx drawn by 300 slaves. Leading up to the scene, it played on Elizabeth's mind that the 7,000 Roman extras may have read the Vatican letter and condemned her as a force against morality. She was tense before the scene was shot, worried about the reaction she would receive, but when the director called action and the Sphinx was drawn through the crowd, thousands of voices called out 'Liz! *Bacci, Bacci*'! She felt the pressure drop away from her as she was greeted by thousands of loving voices. Elizabeth, like Cleopatra, was considered a woman who followed her own path, who was true to her own heart, and this drama and excitement was what made her one of the most celebrated in the world.

On 8 April, Richard flew into Paris with Sybil and was photographed going for dinner together at Maxim's, only a week after Elizabeth had announced her divorce. Burton was greeted at Orly by a swarm of newsmen and photographers, he pleasantly parried their chorus of questions over whether he planned on marrying Miss Taylor with the persistent reply: 'I am married. I am married.' Sybil returned to London to settle their daughter in school, and when Richard arrived back in Rome he and Elizabeth took up where they had left off. They lunched together at a gourmet restaurant outside the city and then went back to her luxurious villa on the Appian Way. On nights like these they were herded into a car, with paparazzi on scooters and in cars following them at high speed.

In their darkened mind, she told him she would kill herself for him, returning with pills in her hand.

Over the Easter weekend in April, Richard and Elizabeth escaped to Porto Santo Stefano in a little Fiat 500 in the early hours of the morning without telling anyone where they were going. Two hours from Rome, and on a mountainous poplar-covered peninsula linked by a causeway from the town of Orbetello, it felt completely private and discreet. The ice cream-coloured homes of the Porto Santo Stefano, on a majestic harbour, wind their way up the steep mountain-sides, and Elizabeth and Richard stayed in a pink villa in a quiet, aquamarine cove one bay beyond the harbour.

The town was quiet because of the Easter holiday and they enjoyed café latte and cognac in a deserted bar, without their security in tow. He wrote in his diaries: 'All the worlds' press were searching for us. We thought we had got clean away.' They were disheartened to encounter a lone local newspaper reporter covering the arrival of a Dutch royal figure, and so they escaped to the sanctity of their villa, where they could explore the beach and rocky coastline. As they scrambled on the rocks, they discovered that paparazzo were hiding in the bushes and had captured them kissing and sharing oranges.

Trapped in their villa, they drank to the point of 'stupefaction and idiocy', had desperate sex and played gin rummie. In a darkened state of mind, she told him she would kill herself for him, returning with pills in her hand. 'The sad truth is I can't live without you anyway, so if it's as over as you said it was back in Rome then I may as well do myself in.' 'Don't be ridiculous,' he said. 'I left a perfectly good woman to be with a lunatic.' She was tormented further, and as she tried to open the tub of pills, he made a grab for it and they tussled.

Later he found her unconscious on the bed, and, realising she had taken the pills, there was a hair-raising drive to Rome with her chauffeur and she was checked into hospital with a black eye and bruised nose. She said her chauffeur stopped the car suddenly and she hit her face, but there were concerns that she and Richard had had a fight before he had hurried off and left her.

Sybil had seen the pictures and read the story of Porto Santo Stefano in the *Sunday Times*. This was a respected newspaper, not a tabloid rag, and she felt she needed to take this affair seriously. She arrived back in Rome on Easter Sunday, and Burton returned to the villa (named Beautiful Solitude) to face his wife, all the while waiting for news on Elizabeth's recovery. On 3 May, Burton agreed to have a meeting with columnist Sheilah Graham to reassure and protect Sybil, and replied with a firm no when asked if he was going to marry Elizabeth. Sheilah wrote: 'he was casual and unconcerned about it in his debonair British way, admitting frankly that he is enjoying all the publicity.'

The production arrived on the island of Ischia in the Bay of Naples on 13 June to shoot the Battle of Actium scenes. The sun was shining, the water was sparkling blue and it was the height of the tourist season. Burton and Taylor arrived by helicopter and then escaped on a hired yacht. The paparazzi waited it out with long lenses focused on their boat ready to capture any movement. It was photographer Marcello Geppetti who took the picture of them kissing on the bow of the yacht and was published by Italian newspaper *Oggi*. They were lying on the decking of the yacht, which was docked by the pier, Elizabeth in a one-piece swimsuit, their packets of cigarettes scattered around them. The shot was the precursor to the intrusive, grainy paparazzi shots that we have become so accustomed to – the ones that remind us of holidaying royals, like Princess Diana, in a private moment made public.

While the stars of the show were taking the opportunity to enjoy the location, production was so pushed to get the scenes finished at Ischia, that Italian crew working around the clock had taken to sleeping in their clothes near the set. They eventually demanded, and were given, a day off.

Elizabeth filmed her last scene in *Cleopatra* on 23 June, although production continued to Alexandria, Egypt, for some final scenes. 'After my last shot,' Elizabeth said, 'there was a curiously sad sort of aching, empty feeling. but such astronomical relief. It was finally over. It was like a disease, shooting that film – an illness one had a very difficult time recuperating from.'

While the ultimate cost of *Cleopatra* came in at $37 million, advance tickets guaranteed $11.5 million, the largest in history. Burton was made a very big star, with a salary almost tripled on the back of *Cleopatra*. Mankiewicz, who never made another film, blamed the end of his career on Elizabeth and Richard. But Elizabeth said of *Cleopatra*, 'It wasn't a flop for me,' as she made $7 million from it in all.

The huge furore around *Cleopatra* had inspired Italian fashion collections in spring and summer 1962, with Elizabeth Taylor-style heavy eye make-up and hairstyles popular, and when the film was released in 1963 Elizabeth's look sparked a global trend. Andy Warhol noticed that girls 'in Brooklyn looked really great. It was the summer of the Liz-Taylor-in-*Cleopatra*-look – long, straight, dark, shiny hair with bangs and Egyptian-looking eye makeup.'

As Elizabeth returned to Chalet Ariel in Gstaad with her mother and children, she packed up sixty of the Irene Sharaff gowns as they would make 'fabulous evening gowns,' and would be a reminder of her time in Rome. It felt lonely in this quiet Alpine location without Burton, the colour and liveliness on the Via Veneto with him beside her, the thrill of dodging paparazzi in high-speed car chases. Eddie was now out of her life, and Richard had returned to his wife, although the Burtons were also staying at their home in Lake Geneva. They tried to stay away from each other. 'But it is a hard thing to do, to run away from your fate,' said Elizabeth. 'When you are in love and lust like that, you just grab it with both hands and ride out the storm.'

They arranged to meet for lunch at Château de Chillon, a twelfth-century fairytale castle resting on Lake Geneva. Elizabeth was with her parents, and suffering from what felt like first date nerves. 'Richard and I arrived at exactly the same moment,' recalled Elizabeth. 'The top of his car was down, he was terribly suntanned and his hair was cut very short. I hadn't seen him since *Cleopatra*. He looked nervous, not happy, but so marvellous.'

Their affair had been the biggest Roman shocker since Ingrid Bergman and Roberto Rossellini in 1949. Taylor readily admitted her affair, and unlike Bergman, her career didn't suffer – in fact she and Burton would make millions from it, including their next film together, *The VIPs*. Elizabeth and Richard's continued relationship heralded the sixties sexual liberation, a symbol of relaxing morals. They were the new era of celebrity – her looks, his style, there excessiveness and glamour and passion all played out on the front pages around the world.

'I behaved indiscreetly,' said Elizabeth, of that season in Rome. 'I can't try to justify myself, and I can't expect the whole world to understand. The people directly involved understand, and I hope my friends understand.'

16

BRIGITTE

Almost as soon as the 1960 Olympics were over, the foundation stone was laid for the controversial new Hilton Hotel at Monte Mario, the highest of the city's seven hills. The hotel opened in 1963 and was hailed as a symbol of the economic ties between Italy and the US, evoking the European Recovery Programme of the late 1940s, where America provided funding to Italy to help rebuild the country. Its brutalist style, characteristic of early 1960s architecture, was not considered attractive, and many in Rome didn't approve of the building of the hotel, including writer Carlo Levi. 'These Hiltons seem to be colonial hotels, hotels that are about more than business, hotels that have to do with prestige and the cold war.'

With the arrival of the Hilton, Rome seemed even more like the tainted playground of Fellini's films, of *Boccaccio '70* where Anita Ekberg is a giant billboard come to life. *8½* was Fellini's autobiographical depiction of the creative process, where he wanted 'to tell the story of a director who no longer knows what film he wants to make.'

La Dolce Vita, on its release in 1961, had created the image of Rome as the glamour capital, while *Cleopatra* had been transfixing to those watching the movie stars behaving with complete indiscretion while on holiday. Inspired by the movies, the girls in Rome wore their make-up like that of Audrey Hepburn and Sophia Loren, becoming known as the Alberto de Rossi look. The make-up artist was credited with creating the heavily-kohled, winged eye makeup, while his wife always did Audrey's hair. But in 1963 it was Brigitte Bardot whose image inspired complete idolatry. As she travelled on a speedboat off the island of Capri, she looked cool and remote behind her sunglasses, with her blonde crown of backcombed hair on top of the white shirt and full skirt. Amongst the limestone cliffs and Mediterranean shrub that hummed with cicadas, photographers hid behind rocks and trees, their long-lens cameras focused on Brigitte as she performed a scene in a bikini 100m below.

Perhaps there was no star of the late fifties and sixties who suffered so much from the relentless pursuit of photographers. Her life was analogised in Louis Malle's *A Very Private Affair*, filmed in June 1961, using some of her own experiences with the paparazzi. She played Jill, a model and actress who becomes a film star, but is hounded by the press. In the final scene Jill is hiding on a rooftop when she is startled by a photographer's flash and falls to her death.

When production moved from Geneva to Spoleto in Italy, Brigitte felt instantly on edge. Her car would frequently be surrounded by crowds of people, as if she was a trapped animal in the zoo. Brigitte stayed in a three-floor house in the town, sharing the building with Malle. But the paparazzi were so relentless she couldn't leave her home unless she was prepared to be met with thousands of flashbulbs. She locked herself in her apartment while the other cast members went to a trattoria for dinner. Real-life paparazzo Marcello Geppetti was assigned to record images of Bardot and his photos captured her surrounded by watchful fans and photographers, in sunglasses and Capri pants, as if she was unaware of the camera. These images created the sense of voyeurism and of the camera as predator to reflect the themes of the film.

Brigitte Bardot, born into a bourgeois Paris family, would be torn by the respectable image of her parents, the poise of her ballet training, and the bad girl identity shaped by Svengali Roger Vadim. Vadim indoctrinated the teenage Bardot into his bohemian Parisian life, introducing her to Colette, Juliette Greco, Cocteau, and she even met Marlon Brando, who was staying in Vadim's apartment building. She turned 18 on 28 September 1952, and married Vadim in December of that year in Paris.

Her breakthrough role was in Vadim's 1956 controversial film *And God Created Woman*, in which she did the cha-cha-cha on tables and sunbathed naked. It was really Vadim who pushed her to be sexy, which created conflict between a rebellious side and her bourgeois upbringing. She came to represent European sex appeal and was sought-after by the American press from November 1957, when the film was released there.

Bardot had first become a target of photographers during her visit to the Cannes Film Festival in April 1953, when she was photographed on the beach in a bikini. She arrived in Rome in the spring of 1954 to play a slave to the Spartan queen in *Helen of Troy*, sharing an apartment with Ursula Andress. She returned to Rome to work in a film called *Mio figlio Nerone*, or *Nero's Weekend*, playing one of Nero's mistresses opposite Gloria Swanson as Agrippina, Nero's mother, and Vittorio De Sica is Seneca.

She and Vadim divorced in December 1957. It ended on good terms, but Vadim was heartbroken, and would try to recreate the blonde sex kitten with Catherine Deneuve and Jane Fonda.

Summer 1958 was swept with 'Bardolâtrie'. She appeared in *Life* magazine highlighting the 'Bardot Boom', and in July 1958 *Match* headlined with 'BB: Vacation for a Tracked Animal'. The article highlighted the assaults by photographers on the Côte d'Azur, in which photographers disguised themselves as fishermen to emerge from the sea to take pictures of her, looking sad and suspicious, trapped in a seemingly never-ending holiday in Saint Tropez.

Making an appearance at the Venice Film Festival in September 1958 she was chased by photographers every time she took a gondola, or a walk across the bridges over canals. Brigitte, who was sensitive to the press intrusion and found it difficult to adjust to being a star, tried to kill herself on several occasions, using the gas oven and taking pills in her attempts.

When expecting a baby in 1960 with French actor Jacques Charrier, she felt completely under siege. She was locked in her apartment, unable to leave to go to the doctor. She felt like she was having a breakdown from the stress of the crowds of photographers and onlookers outside her home, with reporters dressed as deliverymen, photographers disguised as nuns.

Brigitte was in Italy in May 1963 to star in Jean-Luc Godard's *Le Mépris* (*Contempt*), based on an Alberto Moravia novel she had enjoyed, and with scenes again drawn from her own life and the intrusion of photographers. Her co-stars included Fritz Lang as a film director, Michel Piccoli as her screenwriter husband, and Jack Palance as an American producer.

Rome was the main paparazzi haunt, and when her parents visited, it seemed impossible to leave the hotel to go for dinner. At first Brigitte's mother didn't believe how bad the situation was for her, and to demonstrate, Brigitte placed one of her wigs on a stick and lifted it up to a window. Instantaneously they were hit with flashes of light and a symphony of camera clicks, and they ended up crawling on their hands and knees to avoid being photographed. Eventually Brigitte asked a friend to don a wig and sunglasses and to drive off in her Mercedes, acting as decoy so they could get out of the apartment and go for dinner.

'They insult me in the street, and the people I'm with are forced to react.'

Production moved to the Island of Capri, where filming took place at a villa situated in an isolated, rocky area on the south east side of the island which was only accessible by boat. At the time it was almost impossible to reach the area without permission from the police. However locals were so excited to catch a glimpse of the most photographed woman in the world that families piled into boats to try to glimpse her. Godard had to ask them over speakerphone if they could leave the area, so they could continue filming.

The paparazzi had followed Brigitte from Rome to Capri, and with their 300mm lens they could hide in the cliffs and photograph someone standing 100m away, as long as they were patient.

On 25 May they were filming scenes of Bardot in a bikini, but Godard was irritated by the constant spying of paparazzi hiding in the rocks. He went up with security to speak to them directly. The photographers told him, 'we are just trying to make some money, trying to earn something,' and even when they were sent away, they vowed that they would get a picture of her that night.

They spoke to a couple of local journalists, recounting that they had been assaulted, and the day after the newspapers published the story with the headlines 'No one in Capri is doing advertising for BB. Not even the paparazzi. They risk getting beaten up for a photo of La Bardot.'

'They insult me in the street, and the people I'm with are forced to react. And then (the paparazzi) complain about it, saying that they got beaten up,' Brigitte said at the time – adding sarcastically, 'oh the poor things.'

A couple of these photographers spoke in a documentary called *Paparazzi* about their experience stalking Brigitte in Capri. 'We were very angry with Brigitte,' they said. 'We wanted the public to know what she was like. Why do you never let us take any pictures?'

They said that the most valuable images would be of Brigitte in a swimming costume, but:

If we could take a picture with a little dog, all the big papers would love to publish that picture. But it is impossible because she is always surrounded by police. They just prevent us from taking any pictures. Despite trying to convince the sergeant that we need to eat … we were hoping for much more, but we can't work like this. We climb mountains to take two pictures from 100 meters and we are risking falling down a cliff.

It wasn't quite so simple to say that all the paparazzi were despised by their subjects; they would often form mutually beneficial relationships. There were in fact a number of 'official' paparazzi on the set of *Le Mépris* who had been commissioned to capture candid images of Brigitte. Tazio Secchiaroli took unguarded shots of the star in black bobbed wig. He preferred action shots where the photo comes to life, and, true to his paparazzo background, imbued them with a sense of voyeurism.

Elio Sorci was also trusted to take official photos of stars. He later captured Brigitte with her hand in the Mouth of Truth, Raquel Welsh dancing on a table while filming a scene with Marcello Mastroianni in *Shoot Loud, Louder ... I Don't Understand* and became a good friend to Italian actresses Claudia Cardinale and Gina Lollobrigida. Sorci had grown up in the Rome suburbs, beginning his career as a photographer in the 1940s, after being inspired by Rome photojournalist Ivo Meldolesi. 'A paparazzo,' Sorci once said, 'is a young, carefree, happy man who earns his daily bread by putting other people into difficulty and doesn't mind the risks.'

For Ava Gardner, after breaking up with Walter Chiari there was no permanent man in her life and no responsibilities. Her MGM contract had ended in 1958, and while she had been nervous about being freelance, the first movie she negotiated herself was impressive – Stanley Kramer's *On the Beach*, filmed in Melbourne.

Ava was fearful of the press, who hounded her relentlessly, always trying to get the bad angle, the unflattering photo that would make her look old, and the juciest stories of her bad behaviour. Supposedly banned from the Ritz for urinating the lobby, it was said that her haughty, imperialistic manner brought dread to the restaurants she would frequent. Hedda Hopper generously commented in a column in 1963: 'She's still without pretence, but success has brought many phobias – the candid camera heads the list.'

On 5 November 1962, Reuters reported that Ava has been dropped from *The Pink Panther*, to be filmed in Rome, because of her excessive demands. Producer Martin Jurow had wooed Ava for the film by having her to Madrid for a whirlwind of nightlife and flamenco bars while negotiating a deal. As well as a high salary, she wanted 'a large personal staff around her', a villa on the Via Appia Antica, a twenty-four-hour limousine, personal secretary and hairdresser.

Blake Edwards refused to change the location to Madrid from Rome, but it was agreed Yves Saint Laurent would provide a fabulous wardrobe. She flew to Paris for fittings with the designer, but after being greeted by a crowd of photographers and reporters at the airport in Paris, she threw a tantrum, swore and lashed out at those around her. Jurow, having seen this loss of temper for himself, didn't want the diva behaviour to happen when they were only two weeks from filming, and so left a note for her at the hotel that she was cancelled from the film.

She was replaced by the relatively unknown Capucine, a model who was good friends with Audrey Hepburn. Peter Ustinov, originally signed as Clouseau, dropped out because he didn't want to act opposite an unknown model, and so Peter Sellers replaced him. A classic of the swinging sixties was created all because of Ava's temper tantrums, diva behaviour and fear of the press.

'Fame ain't what it's cracked up to be,' Ava reflected. 'It's a pain in the ass if you ask me.' While Ava was scared of the photographers, Elizabeth Taylor was much more confident and knew how to handle them. 'Elizabeth was a darling because she took a lot off my shoulders,' Ava recounted, of their time in Puerto Vallarta filming *The Night of the Iguana* for ten weeks from September 1963:

> I'm not very good with the press. I'm frightened of them. So I tend to be shy in their presence. And they were all there because of all the situations and relationships. And we were cornered, day and night. Elizabeth was marvellous because she was around the whole time and she was very good with them. Very brave, wonderful, and strong.

She considered John Huston her absolute favourite director, particularly after such a good response to *The Night of the Iguana*, and so she agreed to play Sarah, the mother of the Jews, his new film *The Bible*, produced by Dino De Laurentiis. It was to have been made using five directors for a film of twelve hours, but when it was reduced to just Huston as director, he chose the most well-known elements of the Bible – the creation, Adam and Eve, Cain and Abel, Noah's Ark, Sarah and Abraham, the Tower of Babel, Sodom and Gomorrah.

'The script John gave me had all these archaic words in it. "I want thee to go forth", "Thou art blah blah blah",' she said. 'What the hell was that? I wasn't the right gal for that. But John, being John, just used that soothing voice of his and convinced me to go along. "Sure you can do it, honey. Sure you can." Well, welcome to my new nightmare.'

The film was of epic proportions, and the sets near Rome included a 200ft-long Noah's Ark populated with exotic animals, and the Tower of Babel with thousands of extras carrying baskets of bricks. A blonde Swedish actress, Ulla Bergyrd, was cast as Eve and as she walked around the set just with her long hair covering her, paparazzi jumped out from the trees to take her photo.

By the time Dino De Laurentiis's *The Bible* was being made, the battle between celebrity and paparazzi in Rome had reached fever pitch. Calabrian-born photographer Saverio (Rino) Barillari enjoyed showing the scar from when Peter O'Toole caught him with his ring outside the Pipistrello nightclub in 1964, or demonstrating where Ava Gardner had once kicked him in the groin. In one famously candid shot, he was captured in a photograph with Yugoslavian actress Sonia Romanoff planting an ice cream cone onto his forehead as he clutched his camera.

However, Rino later noted that *The Bible* marked a decline in the photographers' fortunes. But by 1966 he said that the Via Veneto had changed. *The Bible* was the perfect situation for paparazzi who could photograph the many actors employed for the epic, but after the film finished, he said, 'The picture buyers stopped believing us. They said we created every picture. The public got a little tired I guess, and so did the big movie stars. They began going elsewhere.'

It wasn't just the press that Ava was worried about. She arrived in Rome mid summer 1964 to film her segments of *The Bible* and checked into the Grand Hotel for the duration. Playing her husband Abraham was George C. Scott, a man who would for many years later make her shake with fear whenever she saw the film on the television. He was 6ft tall, broad-shouldered and with a broken nose. But Scott was known as a violent drunk, with the nickname 'the wild man of Broadway' gained after he punched a mirror during an argument with a cast member on a stage production. He fell madly in love with Ava, but his heavy drinking brought on jealous, possessive rages.

Ava had experience of men with tempers from the rows with Frank Sinatra and Walter Chiari, and had to defend herself from Howard Hughes, but when George C. drank, his violent outbursts were terrifying. 'Me, I'm a happy drunk. I laugh, I dance. I certainly don't break bottles and threaten to kill,' she said.

She was first introduced to George by Huston one evening before the start of shooting and she liked him immediately. They chatted and exchanged pleasantries, and as they went their directions to their hotel rooms, he called after her and asked her to dinner the following night. They fell for each other quickly, with Ava considering George 'highly intelligent and civilised, very gentle but with a slightly sardonic sense of humour', but when he drank his personality changed.

George had a wife, Colleen Dewhurst, and a baby, staying with him in a villa in Rome, but after only a short time he fell madly in love with Ava. He was an alcoholic who had a past history of attacking women, twice attempting to kill a lover who was pregnant with his child. If she so much as mentioned Frank, he would be driven into a jealous rage. Once, while filming a scene he was angered by the director and tore off his costume and stormed off set.

Location shooting moved to the inland city of Avezzano, set in the Abruzzi mountains, where the cast stayed in a small hotel. They went out for dinner one night and returned to his room for more drinks. But his mood quickly changed. He tightened and clenched in rage and threw a punch right in Ava's face. Next thing he came down on her, pounding on her with his fists, and she was trapped in the room. The following day the make-up man was taken aback by the bruises he saw on her and couldn't hide them all with make-up. Huston was furious, and hired some security to keep an eye on the situation.

George apologised profusely the next day, and promised that it would never happen again. Ava kept up appearances for the sake of the film, and when production moved to Sicily she went for dinner at a hilltop restaurant in beautiful, rugged Taormina with George and her maid Reenie. The burley security guards were sitting discreetly at another table After drinks, George started to get angry, and Ava, sensing this, rushed to get the bill. Outside, in the warm night air, the restaurant lights illuminating them, George was volatile, but the three security guys stepped beside him, took him by the arm and escorted him into a waiting car. He was locked up in a jail cell until he had calmed down.

In September 1964, with a long weekend off from filming in Sicily, Ava flew to Rome to visit Frank Sinatra who was in the city while filming on location for *Von Ryan's Express*. He was staying in an eighteen-room villa, heavily protected and with a heliport so he could fly to the shooting location at Cortina d'Ampezza each day. She enjoyed her time relaxing by the pool with an endless supply of cocktails. Here she could feel completely safe – until George found out somehow where she was, arrived drunk one night and gained access to the terrace. He found Ava in her room and began throwing items around and hitting Ava once more. He made such a commotion that he woke the caretaker, and Frank's security arrived to usher him off the premises.

When filming of *The Bible* wrapped up, he followed Ava to London and Beverly Hills, subjecting her to drunken rows and violence. He insisted he wanted to marry her. He divorced Coleen Dewhurst, and told friends he would 'move heaven and earth to marry Ava'. She managed to loosen his grip on her, but the memories would remain terrifying.

After decades of a transient lifestyle in Europe, Ava Gardner settled into an apartment in Kensington, London, where she would remain for the rest of her life. It had been the paparazzi that had driven her away from Rome. 'If I can feel happy and protected and secure everything can be all right but, you see, they never leave you alone,' Ava said in the 1970s, on how much she disliked the paparazzi:

The last time I was in Rome, I went there to have a dress made for my Godchild's graduation. I went there on the spur of the moment, false names and everything, just Renee and me, and it was so great for three or four days. Just to walk in the park and see the little puppet shows and to drive around and watch the fountains and go buy my clothes for a very special occasion … then the paparazzi caught up with me. I was trapped in a hotel and I had to stay there until they could smuggle me away.

17

SOPHIA

Sophia Loren's connection to food, from her fame as the pizza girl in *Gold of Naples* to her penchant for spaghetti, was evident in how she was described. She was said to have honey-coloured eyes and caramel skin. Noël Coward thought she should have been 'sculpted in chocolate truffles so the world could devour her.' Peter O'Toole, who played Don Quixote to her Dulcinea in *Man of La Mancha* in 1972, described her as 'edible' and she was named Macaroni Woman of the Year by American macaroni manufacturers, as the perfect example of women who ate their product. The Rolling Stones wrote a song for her, 'Pass the Wine (Sophia Loren)', on the remastered version of *Exile on Main St*, placing her in the heart of pop culture.

Having experienced starvation during the war, food was of importance to her. 'If I ever have to lose a couple of pounds, I simply skip dinner,' she said:

> I've always loved pasta and eaten it by the ton. When I first came to Rome I couldn't leave anything on the plate – no matter how much I didn't want it – because, after a few years of starvation in the war, it was still a sin to throw food away. Besides, for a while, I needed more weight and spaghetti was cheap.

By the mid 1960s Sophia had created her own myth around her image, with her screen persona as strong as that of Marlene Dietrich, Greta Garbo or Elizabeth Taylor. In 1964 she was paid a million dollars for *The Fall of the Roman Empire*, matching Elizabeth for *Cleopatra*. By the end of 1965, Sophia Loren had the third highest annual income in Rome at 350 million lire (about $580,000).

She had returned to Rome from Hollywood in July 1959 to film interiors for *A Breath of Scandal* at Titanus Studios. Photographers had gathered in front of her apartment on quiet, leafy Via di Villa Ada, near the Catacombs of Priscilla, in anticipation of her return, following the controversy of her supposedly illegal marriage to Ponti. She was pleased to be back in her home country, away from the Hollywood that stereotyped her as the statuesque 'Italian'. 'They had me eating spaghetti for breakfast, lunch and dinner – I eat spaghetti sometimes, everybody does,' she said in an interview in 1961.

Sophia's life had been transformed by the wealth and trappings of fame and the jewellery she enjoyed collecting was a reminder of how far she had come. She may have had the Rome apartments, the home in Switzerland, the jewels, a successful career, but one thing that eluded her was the security of legitimate marriage. 'I am a woman', was her reply when asked if she wanted a family, and she was willing to give up her career to have children. But the bigamy charges were hanging over both Carlo and Sophia, and their life in Rome could be considered atypical.

'We were constantly under surveillance and we had to invent an absurd existence in order to avoid being clapped in jail as public sinners,' she said. 'Our life was an exercise in studied confusion. Some nights we stayed in my mother's apartment. We regularly changed the apartments we rented, often renting them under assumed names. Sometimes we stayed overnight with friends. When we were invited to dinner, we always arrived and left separately, or with a group of guests. Of course, we never appeared together in public. It was a silly and strenuous way of life, but I must confess that the cops-and-robbers aspect of it made it rather exciting.'

Carlo Ponti had bought the rights to *Two Women*, a harrowing novel by Alberto Moravia depicting a mother's struggle to protect her daughter during the Second World War, and he planned to make the film with Paramount Pictures. Anna Magnani had been the obvious choice to play the mother, with Sophia as her daughter and George Cukor as director. However Magnani told the producers of *Two Women* that while the role of the mother was perfect, she could not play the part if Sophia was to be the daughter – Sophia was too tall and bosomy. Anna told them, 'Sophia is a fine actress but I honestly feel she is physically too strong and self-sufficient looking to make mother-daughter relationship convincing ... I must reluctantly decline play mother. I beg all concerned to believe that my decision has nothing to do with relative size of parts.'

Her decision caused a ruckus back in Hollywood, where the movie was being planned. Power agent Swifty Lazar felt it could be 'overcome by performance and makeup', and he couldn't see the role played by anyone but Magnani. However he held out hope that it was just Magnani being temperamental: 'I do not know the case history of Magnani and her various enterprises, but I suppose they always start with refusals, counter offers and a lot of shenanigans.'

For George Cukor, working with Magnani on *Wild is the Wind* had been an exciting and deeply satisfying experience, and he told her so in the hope that she would reconsider. But her answer was clear – if Sophia was to play the daughter then she would not do the part, and if Magnani was not going to play the mother, then Cukor would drop out too.

After Cukor left the project, Carlo Ponti withdrew Paramount's rights, and Vittorio De Sica was signed as director instead. When De Sica tried to lure Magnani once more, it was she who suggested Loren play the mother. At the Roman premiere of *Black Orchid*, Sophia had been seated next to Anna Magnani, who had made such an impression on her when she was a little girl. When the lights went back on after the film had ended, Magnani heaped praise on her. 'Brava, Sophia, I really liked it!' It had been a proud moment, and while Magnani had not felt Sophia was right to play her daughter, she had faith Sophia could be the mother. Magnani instead would take on the similarly challenging role of whore and mother in *Mamma Roma* in 1961, considered her finest part.

Vittorio De Sica, who had noticed something special in the 15-year-old Sophia at Cinecittà, also believed she could play the mother. So the part was adapted from a 50-year-old mother with a teenage daughter, to that of a younger woman with a younger daughter.

To prepare for the part Sophia remembered moments from her own childhood. She thought of hiding in the railway tunnel as bombs rained down, of being tired and hungry and scared, of the drunk Moroccan soldiers who were camped downstairs from their home, of the American GI enjoying music and cherry brandy in their apartment.

Sophia thought of her mother most of all – of how Romilda would do anything to clothe and feed her daughters.

During filming she would be up at 5 a.m. to get to the location for 7 a.m., and tirelessly worked throughout the day to hone her performance. De Sica observed that 'her capacity to rebound, her resistance to fatigue, make her the most tireless worker of all the actresses in the world. And she has such an appetite, especially at seven in the morning. She's afraid of putting on weight, but her compelling youth makes her eat thick slices of bread with peppers, prosciutto and mozzarella.'

The film arrived in Italian cinemas just before Christmas 1961, and it brought praise from across the political spectrum, with comparisons made with Soviet cinema and its courageous, battle-worn characters. Sophia said she had been nervous and scared ahead of its premiere in Rome. 'It is very important to me. It is a very good picture. I care very much about it.'

As well as in Italy, the film struck a chord in the United States and Sophia found out at the start of 1962 that she had been nominated for an Academy Award. The ceremony for the Oscars took place on 9 April 1962; Sophia was too nervous to attend. She stayed in Rome in their new apartment at Piazza d'Aracoeli where she received phone calls from well-wishers throughout the evening who told her they were sure she would win. She was up against Audrey Hepburn for *Breakfast at Tiffany's*, Natalie Wood for *Splendor in the Grass*, Geraldine Page for *Summer and Smoke*, and Piper Laurie for *The Hustler*.

The ceremony was not transmitted on Italian television, so Sophia and Carlo listened to music, drank wine and smoked cigarettes on their terrace in the spring night air. She had cups of chamomile to try to keep calm, and as the anxiety became too much she went into her kitchen and began making her tomato sauce. It was while she was heating the sauce on the stove that a call came through at 6 a.m. from Cary Grant in Los Angeles early in the morning, with his smooth clipped voice. 'Darling, have you heard? You won the Oscar!' As soon as she hung up, she began jumping around the living room, until the exhaustion kicked in. She remembered the sauce on the stove and raced back into the kitchen to stop it burning. Following her win, the Ponti home was packed with journalists, friends, family, telegrams, and flowers. Carlo and Sophia were photographed that morning in their bathrobes with Vittorio De Sica, who had arrived at some point to wish them well. Sophia was embracing her director while Ponti popped open a bottle of champagne. One of the bouquets that arrived was sent by Elizabeth Taylor, in Rome filming *Cleopatra*.

De Sica 'wanted me to do a striptease so sexy, so arousing, so provocative it would make a man howl'.

'I would never have won the Oscar if I'd stayed in Hollywood,' said Sophia. 'I knew that there, in Italy, I could really show what I had inside, what came from my background.' While Magnani was the first Italian actress to win an Academy Award, Sophia was the first actress to win an Oscar for a foreign-language film. It also changed the perception of Sophia in Italy as purely a comedy actress, and she could fully finally express the drama of her Neapolitan blood. She would shift from the American roles to becoming an icon of Italian cinema, guided by Vittorio De Sica.

Shortly after the news of her Academy Award nomination, the Italian courts announced that Carlo was to be charged with bigamy. Her press agents, Matteo Spinola and Enrico Lucherini, had worked hard during the filming of *Two Women* to reconstruct Sophia's image as a mother, with photos released of her playing with children, with hints that she might be expecting a child when she fainted on set. While this theme was being played up, Sophia continued to struggle to conceive. When she was in Switzerland she would often visit Audrey Hepburn, who had gave birth to a boy, Sean, on 17 July 1960. Sophia fussed over baby Sean and they shared pasta suppers together in the warmth of their homes, surrounded by the beautiful alpine scenery.

After the success of *Two Women* she further worked with Vittorio De Sica throughout the sixties. *Yesterday, Today and Tomorrow*, consisting of three short comedies, was a portrait of Italy during the economic boom and was set in Naples, Rome and Milan. For the Rome sequence, where she played a kind-hearted call girl called Mara, De Sica 'wanted me to do a striptease so sexy, so arousing, so provocative it would make a man howl'. The choreographer of the Crazy Horse Saloon was brought in to teach her some moves, and she was so nervous for a week in the lead-up to that now classic scene that she asked for the set to be cleared.

For the Adelina episode, set in Naples, Sophia played a black-market cigarette seller who keeps on having children so that she won't go to jail. It was when she was filming this sequence that she suspected she might be pregnant herself. A doctor from Rome came to examine her and to do the frog pregnancy test, where a frog was injected with the urine of the woman. It was said that if the frog died it meant that the woman was pregnant. In Sophia's case the frog appeared to be dizzy and confused, but did not die, and so the doctor was uncommitted, telling her that she *might* be pregnant. She was desperate to have a baby, particularly as she was going to be 30 soon. That age felt like a huge turning point for her, and the Mother Earth inside her was 'fiercely unsatisfied'. So when the tests came back to confirm the news, she was ecstatic.

When the crew arrived in Milan to shoot the final segment, the first night in the city she felt sharp pains in her abdomen, and after being rushed to hospital she was told the news that she had miscarried. Despite her devastation, the complete feeling of emptiness and aloneness, all she could do was return to work as she didn't want to keep the crew waiting. The making of the film may have had traumatic moments, but it was nominated for the Academy Award for Best Foreign Film, and proved hugely popular.

Three years after winning her Oscar, Sophia was nominated again, for *Marriage, Italian Style*, directed by Vittorio De Sica, and based on the well-loved play *Filumena Marturano* by Eduardo De Filippo. Sophia played one of Italy's best-loved characters, Filumena, a prostitute from Naples desperate for a commitment from her long-term client and lover, played by Marcello Mastroianni.

Mastroianni had become friendly with photographer Tazio Secchiaroli during *La Dolce Vita*, and during the making of *Marriage, Italian Style*, the actor recommended Tazio to Sophia Loren as a personal photographer. During the filming of the movie he captured her behind the scenes, using his paparazzi training for unguarded, naturalistic images. Tazio said:

> She was fed up with the stagey stills that made her look like a statue posing. It's not that easy on the film set to capture motion with a still camera. But instead of just glorifying a beautiful actress – beauty for beauty's sake – I felt something more going on and I found myself groping for the real woman with my camera.

When he personally delivered the photos to her home, Sophia personally called Tazio, telling him they were marvellous. Tazio became one of Sophia's most trusted figures in her entourage. Now as a legitimate photographer, his paparazzi background crossed over into the industry he had watched and infiltrated. But Sophia had never been one who took part in the salacious escapades of the era. She said in 1973 of her and Carlo, 'Neither of us has time for *la dolce vita*. We don't do strange things and we don't give strange parties to strange people.'

Sophia's sister Maria was more inclined to mix with the Roman café society. When she fell in love with Romano Mussolini, the jazz musician and dictator's son, after meeting at a jazz festival, Sophia begged her not to marry him. Sophia felt he wasn't strong enough for her, and too interested in his own life, But Maria loved his mother Rachele

Mussolini – her Forli farmhouse smelled of just-baked cake, fettuccine hung up to dry by the fire, and the elderly lady was wise and passionate and kind. Maria, who had struggled with the shame of illegitimacy, was also overwhelmed that a man could give her his name.

Maria's wedding in 1961 had turned into a circus, with the church in Predappio surrounded by paparazzi and with thousands of people trying to cram into it. Sophia had to force her way through the crowds to get to the car, and decided to go back to Rome rather than risk the ceremony. As her chauffeur pulled out from the church, the car hit a man on a Vespa, and he was killed instantly. 'It took me a long time to recover from the terrible effects of that day,' she said. Maria would have two children, but the marriage didn't last much longer after that. He was 'a married bachelor. Most Italian men are,' said Sophia.

In terms of Sophia's own marriage, *Life* magazine in 1965 referred to it as 'Bigamy, Italian Style', 'a real-life drama', saying 'Italian lawyers have been working on the script of this one for seven years now, and all they have proved so far is that lawyers are lousy script-writers.' The article continued, 'Nobody knows whether Sophia and Carlo are married, unmarried or bigamous. If they are the latter, they're subject to one to five years in jail.'

the buxom figure, winged eye make-up, her pale lips contrasting with her deep tan.

By 1965 the courts had voided the Mexican marriage, meaning there had been no bigamy, but Ponti struggled to annul his first marriage to Giuliana Fiastri. Sophia was hurting that she was being denied a husband and family, 'sometimes I am afraid; it seems that I have to expiate sins that I don't know anything about or that I don't remember.'

In Italy where divorce was still illegal, it was believed at least 3 million people, including Vittorio De Sica, loved openly in 'established concubinage', with a partner outside of marriage. Fiastri, an independent attorney, also wanted her freedom from all the negative publicity, and so she agreed to become a French citizen along with Ponti, in order for their divorce to go through.

Once Ponti got the French divorce, he could have the French marriage to Sophia. The low-key ceremony took place in April 1966 in Sevres town hall, Paris, with only a few guests present. Sophia had taken a break from filming *Arabesque*, directed by Stanley Donan, to attend her own wedding.

The year before their French wedding, Sophia and Carlo had finally moved into their magnificent villa in Marino, in the Alban Hills, called Villa Sara, and which required a good deal of expensive restoration work. Ponti had owned it since the 1950s but they hadn't made the move, partly because of the drama around their marriage. The red-coloured villa dated to the seventh century when it was built for a cardinal. They later changed its name to Villa Ponti, and while it was architecturally protected they modernised and updated it, creating a rococo interior of wooden-ceilings, eighteenth-century frescoes, Louis XVI furniture and gold taps in the bathroom. Ponti brought in a sixteenth-century marble fountain from Sorrento to decorate one of their living rooms. When they began work on a poolside guesthouse, builders discovered a pre-Roman cave, and so they opened it with stone steps leading down, and a lift for those not wanting to take the steps.

> ... marriage and children were hugely important to Sophia and she felt as if she had to fight for both.

Villa Sara had 18 acres of beautiful grounds where olive trees were entwined with roses. There was a family farm with fawns, pheasants, storks and rabbits, a riding stable, an aquaduct, tennis courts, a sauna and a pool. There were also paparazzi hidden in the hills, staking out her home with long-lens cameras. She later complained: 'if I'm in old clothes with my hair not combed, the caption says that people criticise me for this. What people?'

Cinderella, Italian Style, directed by Francesco Rosi, was set in the Neapolitan countryside at the time of Bourbon rule. It was a 1960s version of the story and defined the Rome style of that era – the buxom figure, winged eye make-up, her pale lips contrasting with her deep tan. During filming Sophia discovered she was pregnant again, but despite bed rest, had another miscarriage.

As a southern Italian woman of the fifties and sixties, marriage and children were hugely important to Sophia and she felt as if she had to fight for both. After the trauma of two miscarriages, she saw a number of specialists to determine what was going wrong. She was diagnosed with low oestrogen and was given doses of hormones, and when she became pregnant a third time she was advised to rest in bed for the duration.

Sophia took a room on the eighteenth floor of the Intercontinental Hotel, Lake Geneva until her baby was born. She was checked into the hotel under great secrecy – the press had an idea why she had disappeared from Rome, but were unable to locate her, despite keeping a watch on her mother and sister, and phoning her friends to find out where she was.

It was her mother's maid who sold the information to an Italian journalist, and the world's press arrived in Geneva, crowding into the hotel lobby, or trying to send up room service. But Sophia was doing her own cooking in her suite – 'Very plain and low in salt or fat. Spaghetti every once in a while but not in a rich sauce. Sometimes I had a little craving for ice-cream.' She watched television, read Chekhov, replied to her fan mail, all the while trying not to think too much about the baby. The public were completely invested in Sophia's pregnancy – as an actress so aligned with playing mothers and daughters her own struggles for motherhood struck a chord. An American woman in Rome in 1969 said, 'From just following the papers, I know more about Sophia's Fallopian tubes than I know about my own.'

Carlo Ponti Junior, nicknamed Cipi, was born on 29 December 1968. They held a press conference in the hospital's amphitheatre to announce his birth, with Sophia wheeled in her hospital bed, holding her son. It was a time of student protests against Charles de Gaulle in Paris, when the Vietnam War raged, and the year Robert F. Kennedy and Martin Luther King were assassinated, but Sophia's pregnancy was a major cover story for magazines throughout 1968. She was a representative of blissful new motherhood, the Italian icon with child, and all those who called her a marriage wrecker now held her in high esteem as a role model for the country. Four years later her second son, Eduardo Ponti,was born on 6 January 1973.

Despite her bubble of riches and happiness, Sophia wasn't oblivious to the changes happening in the world. In July 1969 in Rome, at a press conference, she issued a statement supporting women's liberation. 'The issue of war and peace will be radically different the day when women are able to influence humanity's destinies to the same extent men do. Mothers and wives have only one response to this issue: peace,' she said.

18

RICHARD

By the time Elizabeth and Richard arrived back in Rome, four years after *Cleopatra*, they had been through so much together. In the spring of 1963, Burton had made the decision he would leave Sybil. After a two year affair, involving global travel and million dollar salaries for the film *The VIPs*, Elizabeth and Richard married on 15 March 1964 at a hotel in Montreal. She wore a yellow Irene Sharaff gown based on the one she wore in her first scene opposite Burton in *Cleopatra*.

To avoid tax, they could only stay in countries for three months, moving between their chalet in Gstaad, hotels in New York, Paris and London, and for longer stays when filming at Cinecittà, expensive villas in Rome. It was a whirlwind of luxury where they were treated with complete reverence wherever they went, and travelled with a large entourage, including bodyguard Bobby LaSalle, Elizabeth's makeup artist Ron Berkeley, Burton's valet Bob Wilson, Dick Hanley and his partner John Lee, a chauffeur, a tutor and a governess.

Between 1962 and 1966 they appeared in seven films which grossed over $200 million, but they still felt the bruises of Le Scandale in Rome in 1962, with two marriages broken up, and careers lost as a result of the production disaster. In the two years after *Cleopatra* they had been shunned by friends. Richard recalled in his diary, somewhat bitterly, that Marie Helene and Guy Rothschild were almost the only society people who would speak to them. He said that Audrey Hepburn:

> supposedly a long time friend of E's, was unobtainable on the phone and refused to acknowledge flowers that were sent for her birthday. David Niven was toffee-nosed too, though he has apologized since. Grace (Kelly) wouldn't have been seen dead in our company, though I'm sure that Rainier didn't give a bugger.

After signing up to Franco Zefferelli's *The Taming of the Shrew*, with Burton as Petruchio and Elizabeth as Kate, the 'shrew' of the play, they arrived back in Rome in March 1966 for an extended stay in the city. For Richard, it was returning to his classic roots, to prove he was more than the headlines.

> Richard and Elizabeth were having a row, 'one of those magnificent rows that made them so alarmingly electric'

Forty-three-year-old Zefferelli had a particular vision, used in his operas, stage shows and films, which captured the spirit of the Italian Renaissance. Described by a journalist as 'a mixture of classic Shakespeare, the Marx Brothers and a Renaissance painting', the bawdy, colourful adaptation of *The Taming of the Shrew*, with its flouncing costumes and overflowing bosoms, used slapstick comedy to play on the Burtons' fights and battling reputation during an era where the sanctity of marriage was shifting, as divorce, extra-marital affairs and casual sex were becoming more acceptable.

The Burtons first met with Zefferelli in Dublin, where Richard was filming *The Spy Who Came in from the Cold*. After being shown to their suite at the Gresham Hotel, the director arrived to find a whirl of chaos. A little bushbaby they had recently acquired had ripped up the soft furnishings and was now fearfully clinging onto the hot-water pipes in the bathroom. Richard and Elizabeth were having a row, 'one of those magnificent rows that made them so alarmingly electric', while she was trying to coax the animal down. Elizabeth cried out from the bathroom, 'Forget about this Shakespeare and give me a hand!' The director managed to step in to rescue the bushbaby and handed it over to Elizabeth. It was only once the situation had been calmed that they were able to discuss the project.

Instead of flying from Rome to Switzerland to begin production, the Burtons decided on a road trip, travelling to Rome in an Oldsmobile sports car through the Alps while their chauffeur-driven Rolls Royce, loaded with luggage, followed behind. The Burtons posed for photographs in Stresa, Italy, on the terrace of their hotel at Lake Maggiore. The clear mountain air was a contrast to arriving in the city. By the mid 1960s, the traffic and exhaust fumes were choking up Rome, and Burton observed that 'Rome is now, on certain windless days as smog-ridden as any of the really big cities. That deadly miasma is slowly creeping all over this earth.'

They were given a villa on the Via Appia Antica to stay with their family of four children and menagerie of dogs, cats, a rabbit, tortoises and goldfish, and at the studio they were lavished with huge white-carpeted dressing rooms complete with kitchens and offices and wardrobe rooms. Once they arrived Elizabeth checked into a fashionable Rome clinic for a twenty-four-hour check-up ahead of what was expected to be a very physical performance.

Four soundstages at the Dino De Laurentiis Studios, outside of Rome, were transformed into sixteenth-century Padua. The first day of production took place on Monday 21 March and the Burtons travelled to the studio with their children and nurse, to chat over drinks with the cast and the crew. He was feeling 'edgy and cantankerous' which was usual for just before starting a new film. When the cast and crew attended a press conference, Richard was particularly annoyed at 'the usual stupid answers to the inevitable stupid questions. What a bore they are,' he said of the reporters.

When they arrived in Rome, they were still waiting for *Who's Afraid of Virginia Woolf?* to come out and they were nervous about its reception. They needn't have worried, as when it was released in June, it received critical acclaim.

Michael York, whose film debut was *The Taming of the Shrew*, recalled 'there was an overwhelming sense of glamour about them, intensified by the way they lived, you know, with their dressing rooms with dazzling white carpets and all of their butlers and maids and so on … the Rolls-Royces, the jewels. They behaved like movie stars; old-fashioned movie stars. But I also found them to be enormously kind. There was also a sense of family.'

This time in Rome, they partied less than they had before. Instead of spending their nights at Rome's hot spots, they rehearsed together in the evenings, with Elizabeth conscientious but nervous about how her first Shakespearean performance would be received. Burton bought detective stories from the Lion bookshop on the Via Veneto, and they spent the evening reading passages to each other over dinner together. They were following Wales in the rugby but trying to deny themselves alcohol in favour of going to bed early.

Burton was feeling in a content state of melancholy during this time. He was annoyed at himself for sleeping in to 11 a.m. when he wanted to be up at 6 a.m., which he blamed on his boozing and his age, and he worried about their finances and of being poor again, having sunk a lot of money into the production in the hopes of it making a profit. 'I worry enormously about the fact that we have no money. I worry that I will not be able to look after my wife and my children after I'm dead – nobody else will.'

The cast halted production for long lunches every day from 1 p.m. to 4 p.m., where the free flowing wine in the sunshine took a toll on afternoon performances. They enjoyed having lunch at La Strega, a restaurant in the village of Practica di Mare, where on one occasion Elizabeth ordered for the entire table the restaurant's famous spaghetti with whiskey sauce, followed by crepes with lemon cream. Sometimes they enjoyed a glass of brandy with the owner, looking out onto the surrounding fields dotted with cows:

In the evening one night, we learned lines, read books, learned a little Italian (me) in the bedroom suite, had dinner, both of us ravenous, of roast chicken, potatoes, salad, cheese, and fruit all washed down, in my case with water – I don't fancy drink at the moment – in Snapshot's case with a Vin Rose.

One of his nicknames for Elizabeth was Snapshot, perhaps because she was always having her photograph taken. The press attention was less frenzied than before – although they would call Richard 'Mr Taylor No. 5', a comment designed to annoy him. On a break from filming they took a trip to Positano, which they hoped would be a peaceful getaway, but when Burton went for a walk with one of their dogs, his presence shut down traffic. After a dinner at Hotel Ranieri, near Piazza d'Espagna, with Zefferelli and other guests, they were chased home by the paparazzi, a hair-raising moment as their chauffeur-driven car tried to outrun them, 'the butterflies of the gutter,' as Richard called them.

On 24 March they saw Rudolph Nureyev perform a ballet at the Teatro Sistina a grand. Elizabeth underwent several fittings for her dress the day before, and while they were enjoying the performance, the paparazzi managed to get inside the theatre to take photos, despite the attempts of the management to control it. After the performance they went for drinks at the Little Bar jazz club on Via Gregoriana, managing to dodge the photographers, who had been 'behaving like lunatics'.

The next day Richard took Elizabeth and their daughter Liza for lunch in Ostia at a restaurant overlooking the sea. Their peace was interrupted when 'an enormous and terrible lady journalist appeared and asked us questions. I sent her off in a burst of fury.'

Despite the unwelcome attention, the Burtons' five months in Rome was idyllic, with many trips to Bulgari's to buy the exclusive pieces kept for the very special patrons. When Zefferelli admired her diamond earrings one day, Elizabeth let

> Her large chest and short legs didn't fit with the Twiggy-like style sweeping from Milan into Rome.

him know they were from a director and that she expected all her directors to buy her a gift. 'There's a little shop called Bulgari on the Via Condotti,' she informed him. He took the hint and bought her a bracelet that had once belonged to Napoleon's sister.

Zefferelli planned a Sunday excursion for the production to the spectacular sixteenth-century Villa D'Este fountains in Tivoli, on a day when it would be closed to tourists. Elizabeth wanted to make an event of it by ordering in hamburgers and hot dogs to serve up at their villa. After enjoying an afternoon barbeque washed down with cold beers, actor Cyril Cusack suffered a mild heart attack, and so the bus trip was cancelled and the shoot was postponed for two days.

On the first weekend of April, Richard and their driver Mario took the children to see the floral tributes on the Spanish Steps. Every spring the steps were ritually covered in potted pink azaleas, with more and more added onto the steps as the days got warmer, until they represented a colourful, blooming flower market that contrasted with the white of the marble.

They lunched and drank in the afternoon, and back at home Richard reminisced with Mario about the 'frightful weekend in Porto Santo Stefano four years ago. It depressed me profoundly and I stared a lot and slept at last.' That weekend seemed to haunt Richard – the struggle to get Elizabeth back to Rome in time after she had taken an overdose, the bruises on her face after a drunken, violent argument. This Easter weekend was very different. Instead of being hauled up in a hideaway in Porto Santo Stefano, they enjoyed Easter egg hunts in the sunny garden and armfuls of presents that could match Christmas.

Richard and Elizabeth hosted a lunch at their villa with Vittorio De Sica and his wife and two boys, but one of the children was strumming a guitar. Richard found it excruciating as he hated that 'horrible instrument', and that 'the Beatles have a lot to pay for.' Richard was a man still in the 1950s, who struggled with the modernity of popular culture, with mod fashion and music. Elizabeth was more aware of trends, but her figure was difficult to dress in sixties fashions like mini skirts. Her large chest and short legs didn't fit with the Twiggy-like style sweeping from Milan into Rome.

> Burton wrote in his diary. 'I wish Farrow would put on 15lb and grow her hair.'

Even Via Margutta, the cobbled, ivy-decorated street of old coach houses which had housed artists' studios for decades was being restyled as a 'Carnaby Street' inspired hang-out. The street was more accustomed to being a place for existentialists and Italian beatniks, but to capture the mood of Swinging London a number of boutiques opened to sell mod fashions such as Lord John and Mary Quant. 'The beatniks are expected to be greatly outnumbered by the mod youth who come from the growing middle and upper economic classes of Rome,' wrote the *New York Times* in 1967.

The Burtons' friend Mike Nichols, who had just directed them in *Who's Afraid of Virginia Woolf?* was one person who was hip and switched on to the counterculture. By 1966 Nichols was considered the It director of Broadway, having won a Tony Award for his 1963 *Barefoot in the Park*. He followed it with *Luv* and *The Odd Couple*, and picked up an Oscar for his direction of *The Graduate*.

Mike Nichols arrived from New York on 5 April 1966, with his latest girlfriend Mia Farrow, the hippie girl who had dramatically cut her long blonde hair into a short, boyish crop. She was taking a break from Frank Sinatra, who she would marry only a few months later.

'That M Nichols really gets the girls,' Burton wrote in his diary. 'I wish Farrow would put on 15lb and grow her hair.' The couple, who had registered in their hotel as Mr and Mrs Nichols, spent time with Elizabeth while Richard was on set doing his scenes. Mia Farrow, with her wispy voice and flower-power, seemed almost too simpering for Richard, and it was another reason why he was cantankerous about the hippie era. He wrote of Farrow: 'I remember her at lunch forever apologising, with eyes as round as her fist, for her silly little ability not to know anybody in theatre or films before her time.'

To make matters worse, Elizabeth's eldest son, 13-year-old Michael Wilding Junior, arrived from boarding school with an ear stud and a nose ring. On one visit Michael complained that the beach was too sandy, that he didn't know how to order Coca-Cola in Italian and that the bathing costumes were not 'bitchen', which, according to Richard was 'the new and horrible word for "up-to-date"'. Michael would grow his hair long and marry at the age of 17, moving to a commune in Wales, with Richard and Elizabeth having to admit their son was indeed a hippie.

While the initial rushes for *Taming of the Shrew* were looking good, by the end of April, relations appeared to break down on set. With a lot of money invested in the film, Richard was concerned they were falling behind schedule, and blamed Zefferelli for his slowness and of taking too many unnecessary shots.

Richard had to get his hair permed for the role, which he called a 'ghastly business'. He hated the fussing over hair and costumes, and was irritated when Zefferelli wanted to change his costume to make it heavier and more imposing. Irene Sharaff was angered by Zefferelli for making her change the costumes, particularly when she considered that they resembled '1930's opera'. Elizabeth took Irene to lunch with Richard to try and pacify her, but Richard, fed up with the griping, snapped at Elizabeth and stormed off, taking their Pekinese E-en So for a walk. Burton found Irene Sharaff 'bone lazy, inflexible, faintly condescending to most people, an intellectual snob and a crashing bore'. However Richard warned Zefferelli to keep Irene sweet, as the designer and Elizabeth were trusted allies, and that if Elizabeth lost affection for Zefferelli, that would be the end of her performance. Burton warned the director that if there were any more hold-ups and costume problems, he would have to go. 'We had invested $2 million in this venture and I didn't want another *Cleopatra*.'

By the end of the month, the on-set fighting appeared to have calmed down, and while the rushes had looked good, some of Elizabeth's scenes were reshot so that she could appear more animalistic and violent, a snarling, wild beast. Sons Michael and Christopher were invited to be extras on set one day, and after being given period costume, they threw vegetables as Richard rode a horse through the crowds, dressed in his new imposing costume. On 29 April they filmed a scene where Richard was to pick Elizabeth up in the artificial rain and place her on a donkey, and it took a tiring, long day to get the scene right.

There was more tension when Zefferelli purposely did not invite Cyril and Maureen Cusack to a cast and crew party at Cinecittà restaurant on Sunday 1 May because he had felt Cyril had insulted him. The Burtons, having slept all day after a late night, enjoyed a cooked English breakfast before getting ready for the evening. Cyril came along anyway, and proceeded to get drunk, threatening to shoot

Elizabeth when she tried to calm him down from the fights with his wife and others at the party. He had to be taken home.

Early May was beautiful and warm, with the fields close to their home bursting with poppies, daisies and buttercups. Some of the days filming could be tough in terms of physicality where they 'waded through wool, ran through bats, swung on trapezes, threw each other around'. Elizabeth was particularly exhausted after filming the whipping scene with Natasha Payne. Driving home that evening she got the urge to stop for wine at a rustic roadside trattoria, invitingly wrapped with vines. They drank glasses of wine and snacked on kidney beans, cheese and baskets of bread, watching the other patrons with fascination, and for this one evening it was as if they were a normal couple on holiday without the trappings of their fame. As the sun began to set music from the mass at the Church of the Madonna of the Divine Love began to drift over them like mist. They stopped eating to listen, and they were driven home feeling content and at peace, with the moon bright in the sky. It was this simplicity of life where they could feel happy.

One evening they went to see the newly released *The Bible* in the cinema, which Ava Gardner had filmed in Rome the year before. It was not as boring as Richard had thought it would be, but it didn't elicit much emotional response either. But he hoped it would do well all the same. They met tall, dark Gore Vidal just before the performance, and went on for dinner at Fontanella Borghese for meals of battered turkey, and tripe, finished with frascati and sambucca and stopping for another drink at L'Escargot. On another evening they watched Anna Magnani perform in *La Lupa*. While they were impressed by her performance in an otherwise monotonous play, they were received backstage by Magnani afterwards. Richard wrote: 'She turned out, when we met her afterwards, to be a charming woman but forthright and not easy.' They had only planned to say quick hellos to the star, but inevitably ended up in a restaurant once the awkwardness and shyness subsided and found they got on well.

They borrowed a friend's apartment at Corsetti's, Tor Vaianica, for a weekend at the beach with their children. But when they saw two paparazzi observing them and their family on the shoreline, they left in a hurry to go back to Rome. So quickly, indeed, that they left their new white Pekinese, Oh Fie, behind. The dog was found hiding under the bed in the beach apartment all along, and was brought back to them, where Elizabeth kissed and fussed over the dog, while Richard shouted in relief.

Richard began old habits again by drinking all day on set, which he felt guilty about. But he excused it because the character of Petruchio in this version was supposed to be a little sozzled. The wedding reception scene was filmed on 1 June, and Richard drank beer throughout the day.

The 5 June marked the 7,601st day since war ended. It was the equaliser day – the exact number of days between when the First World War ended and the Second World War began – and for Richard, after reading this in the *Sunday Times*, it signified that every day could now be a blessing of peace and counted as a bonus. Rome was getting hotter, and they spent the weekends sunbathing and swimming in their refreshingly cold pool, dozing in the sun, strolling through the fields around their house dotted with neat haystacks and then enjoying southern fried chicken. Elizabeth and Richard 'agreed solemnly that we never want to work again but simply loll our lives away in a sort of eternal Sunday'. Sometimes it could be difficult to sleep with the sunburn and the mosquitoes buzzing in their villa at night-time.

In June, the Burtons and Zefferelli were invited to the home of Princess Luciana Pignatelli, to meet Senator Robert Kennedy and his wife Ethel. They had dinner followed by a visit to a nightclub. When they returned to the Hotel Eden, Burton and Bobby Kennedy battled with lines of Shakespearean poetry, competing as to who could recite the most sonnets.

Towards the end of July, Elizabeth received a phone call from Roddy McDowell in New York that her closest friend Montgomery Clift had been found dead from a heart attack, exacerbated by his addictions. Despite her devastation, she held it together on set as much as she could. but she couldn't break from the shooting schedule to go to his funeral. Clift had been scheduled to star opposite her in the John Huston-directed *Reflections in a Golden Eye*, also to be filmed at the De Laurentiis Studios in October 1966, and Marlon Brando was chosen to replace him.

At the same time, Dino De Laurentiis loaned Richard his Rome studios to make the film version of *Doctor Faustus*, in which he had invested $1 million, and which continued their stay in Rome.

To escape from the heavy traffic and noise of Rome, and the petrol smells which made them feel ill, the Burtons stayed at Corsetti's at Tor Vaianica for a month while he continued filming *Faustus*. Now that she had finished the heavy schedule of *The Taming of the Shrew* she had some time off before beginning *Reflections*, and turned heavily to booze again. A favourite drink was Campari with vodka and soda, and which they named 'Goop'.

Elizabeth practised cooking on the barbeque that Richard would light, turning out hot dogs, hamburgers and her first ever steaks with intense concentration and grabbing of implements. Richard added to their domestic set-up by cleaning a little and preparing salads. 'E's delight in cooking is lovely and I think she has a natural gift for it. So far she's done everything right. And has her own pet condiments and sauces,' he wrote.

They would go down to the beach when it was quiet, except for the fishermen on the beach, and it was a relief not to be overwhelmed by the crowds and the paparazzi. 'Apart from people staring and the occasional autograph we are not much bothered. One fat young girl last weekend asked me to autograph her behind – only barely covered by a bikini. I declined and signed her arm instead.'

Sybil, after their divorce, had moved to New York and opened a nightclub, finding a new lease of life with the cool Manhattan crowd. But she refused to speak to Richard, not even sending commiserations on the death of his sister Edie. His elder daughter Kate came to visit them in Italy, and they kept her for two weeks longer than Sybil had agreed, until she was well tanned and entrenched in the relaxed lifestyle.

On Tuesday 4 October, the Burtons returned to Rome to accept Silver Masks, five years on from when Elizabeth arrived with Eddie Fisher. At this ceremony all of Italy's great performers were out for the evening – Alberto Sordi, Marcello Mastroianni, Vittorio Gassman, Monica Vita, Franco Zefferelli, who Elizabeth sentimentally hoped could direct them in another film. The experience of *The Taming of the Shrew* on reflection had turned out to be better than they had thought.

However, as Richard recounted, 'the award evening was monstrous. For about three quarters hour endless hard faced breastless models paraded before our bored eyes an extraordinary tasteless concourse of fashions.' After the awards they went back to the Hassler Hotel and drank with Zefferelli and Sheila Pickles in the little bar off the side of the lobby. Elizabeth was giving a history of her illnesses and operations when Sheila projectile vomited over the carpet, swiftly clearing out the bar. The next day they were so hung-over that Richard couldn't face going into the studio.

Faustus finished filming on Thursday 13 October, and the next day, relieved that the work was over, they woke early, with hot toddies to cure their colds and travelled to Positano, on the Amalfi Coast. They checked into the Hotel Sirenuse, located up a short, steep hill from the town square. From their balcony they could observe the town below, with the noise of car horns and engines, the sounds of surf, the church bells and giggles of children playing on the beach forming a background to the beautiful views over to the sea.

Strolling around sun-filled Positano, the well-dressed, well-heeled visitors offered glances of admiration at the celebrity couple as they shopped at Pucci or Dior, and drank negronis in their hotel bar. The crowds in Positano were one step behind the mini-skirts and long hair of Rome, with women in full dress and gentlemen in suits. But the photographers and the fans were as intense as in the city.

They enjoyed a lunch of zuppa di Vongole, crepes al formaggio, with their molten cheese and prosciutto – but their experience was ruined by the persistence of their fans and a female photographer. One woman ran alongside them, saying 'if only she takes off her glasses for me to see those beautiful eyes'. When Richard took E'en So for a walk up the hill, he literally stopped traffic and had to turn back. 'Let's hope it's the weekend crowds otherwise we'll have to move on or back. Why do they do it? I never gaped at anybody in my life,' he wrote.

So tired was Richard of the harassment that when an actor named Tony Britton said hello to him as he was walking up to the hotel he dismissed him, although he regretted it later and would enjoy drinking beer and sambucas with him Tony while Elizabeth went shopping with his wife.

They went for lunch at La Minervetta in Sorrento, a huge restaurant over two floors, where the food was mediocre, but they drank sambucas, bickered and drove back to Positano in silence. Sometimes they enjoyed caffe lattes, rolls with jam or cream puffs for breakfast at a café on the beach or socialised with sambucas and negronis with their small group of friends in town.

In preparation for the beginning of *Reflections*, Elizabeth was fitted for her costumes by Dorothy Jeakins, who travelled down to Positano especially. They travelled back to Rome on Monday 24 October to begin filming, as Marlon Brando and John Huston had already arrived in the city.

For Richard's 41st birthday, Elizabeth bought him a movie camera, a briefcase, a rare book, a sweater and cardigan – modest purchases compared to what they would buy in the next year, in May 1967, the super-yacht that would become their aquatic playground, and which they named *Kalizma* in honour of their daughters Kate, Liza and Maria. They travelled to Portofino on their yacht, sunning themselves on board in order to avoid the American and German tourists who swarmed around them, but the paparazzi were never too far away, watching from the road above the shoreline, with their long lenses focused on them.

They would come into town so that Elizabeth could pay a visit to Pucci, where she wanted to buy almost every item. Rustic organic-looking Pitosforo restaurant by the harbour would be one of their favourite hangouts, where they would drink Tom Collins and enjoy cheese and salami boards, steaks and crepes suzettes. On the days when the sky was grey, and the boat rocked from the swelling harbour, they settled on board and read through the scripts sent to them, including a new Tennessee Williams script called *Boom!*

At the end of May, Rex Harrison and Rachel Roberts were back in town as indicated by the flag raised on the pole in the garden of their home. The week spent with the heavy-drinking Harrisons proved to be an ordeal, particularly with Rachel going manic when she drank too much. The Burtons spent Monday 29 May at La Gritta American Bar in Portofino having drinks with Rachel and Rex, before meeting Tennessee Williams at Pitosforo restaurant with his partner Bill and friends. Tennessee was sloshed, talking loudly, and Elizabeth had to shush him as he was being embarrassing. The next day the group came on board the Burtons' yacht, and after drinks were served in the sunshine, Rachel began to get more and more drunk as she threw insults around. Tennessee and the others had to leave in disgust, after, as Richard described it, 'she insulted Rex sexually, morally and physically in every way. She lay on the floor of the bar and barked like a dog, and at one point masturbated her basset hound.'

The Burtons were convinced Rex and Rachel were avoiding them because of what had happened on board until they saw them a few days later in the American bar, already drunk at 2 p.m. On another occasion Rachel was wrecked on gin, and began stripping off to the cheers of passersby – until Richard stepped in and prevented her from going too far. Rex was reaching breaking point with her behaviour, and the Burtons, who enjoyed their drinks, looked modest in comparison.

After travelling the Mediterranean in the *Kalizma*, they were back in Rome for Richard to film *Candy* in November 1967, staying at the Grand Hotel. Elizabeth would go for shopping sprees in the boutiques of Pucci, Valentino and Bulgari. Richard didn't relish the city anymore. He believed that 'all the bad things that have happened to me have almost always happened in Rome. Something to do with its elevation perhaps. It is too near sea-level.'

The paparazzi in Rome were preferable to the English press, whom Richard described as 'so smirky and sneaky and smug and provincial. They are not honestly scandalous with the awful dirty pornographic glee of the Italians.' An article in the *Daily Mirror* written by Tommy Thompson had angered them by describing Elizabeth as 38, rather than her real age of 36, and claiming that she was thickening around her waist, she was going grey (which was true), and that they were only concerned with money. All these writers do the same, thought Richard. 'The rich couple, living their lives in a fishbowl glare of publicity, unable to take an ordinary walk in an ordinary city street, mobbed wherever we go, protected by a huge entourage.'

Looking back, years later, Elizabeth would say:

When I think about the sixties, I'm glad that I knew the wildness, glamour and excitement when I was in my prime: the parties, the yachts, and the private jets and the jewellery. It was a great time to be young, alive and attractive and to have all those goodies. I enjoyed it.

19

JANE

A new kind of excess came to Rome in 1967, with the arrival of the hippie jet set. They pushed the hedonism further by indulging in weed and LSD, and peppering their language and their thoughts with eastern spiritualism. Psychedelia spread across the United States to Europe and made a huge cultural impact as it merged with eastern philosophy, rock n roll and art. It was in August 1967 that the Beatles would first meet the Maharishi Mahesh Yogi and studied Transcendental Meditation, and when they went to the ashram in Northern India, along with actress Mia Farrow, Brian Jones, Mick Jagger and Marianne Faithful, it infiltrated their direction on the White Album.

Psychedelia and the avant garde also reached into Rome. While Elizabeth Taylor was buying out Pucci's kaleidoscope prints in Positano, this new, younger crowd arriving in Rome were looser and more eclectic in the way they dressed and lived. They were scruffier, with long-hair and a drop-out attitude, and somehow the image of *La Dolce Vita* of the early 1960s seemed old fashioned. With the studio system and censorship codes having crumbled, directors experimented with avant-garde European styles, and pushed the boundaries of sex and violence. Carlo Ponti had recently produced the counter-culture era *Blow-Up* directed by Michelangelo Antonioni in 1966, depicting a fashion photographer in Swinging London.

In 1967 Jane Fonda arrived in Rome with her husband Roger Vadim to film camp sci-fi movie *Barbarella*, based on the French comic book by Jean-Claude Forest. Dino De Laurentiis bought the movie rights, signed up Roger Vadim as director. There was an extensive search to find the right actress to play the blonde intergalactic heroine, with Sophia Loren and Brigitte Bardot considered, before Vadim's wife Jane Fonda was chosen.

At the end of July 1968 the *Los Angeles Times* announced that 'the sexiest girl of the year AD 40,000 arrived at Rome's Fiumicino Airport, looking very much like Jane Fonda, accompanied by her husband, director Roger Vadim, four scriptwriters and a wardrobe of 20 intricate space gowns weighing ten pounds. She is settled for a long summer in Rome.'

Jane, daughter of Henry Fonda, had been raised in the rarified environs of Hollywood, although her childhood had been tumultuous following her mother's suicide and her father's numerous marriages. She came from old Hollywood, a childhood surrounded by famous faces, where her father's friends were John Wayne, John Ford and James Stewart. 'They used to come to the house and sit around playing cards and talking cowboy talk. It was all pretty fakey, but it was fun for me and my brother Peter,' she said.

She may have come from old Hollywood, but Fonda represented new cinema. It was Vadim who created Fonda's image in the same way he created Brigitte Bardot, with the just-out-of-bed blonde hair, the long limbs on display, the artful kitten-ish makeup. *Barbarella* was a film that explored the permissive late sixties, escapist and pleasure-seeking with an 'orgasmatron' as a plot point, and acted as an alternative to the horrors of the Vietnam War.

Fonda was in perfect shape, having honed her figure through taking ballet lessons every day, and would wake at dawn to attend a class in Rome. She travelled to the film studio every day from their rented home on the Via Appia Antica in her light blue Ferrari, weaving through Rome's busy traffic.

The $500,000 sets were built at Dino Di Laurentiis's crumbling studio just outside of Rome, which he had named 'Dinocittà' in the hopes of being able to rival Cinecittà. The fantasy planet Lython and an intergalactic space ship were recreated, with complicated design and special effects which didn't always work the way they were supposed to. For one scene, 2,000 'killer' wrens were blown into a cage with Jane, where they were supposed to peck off her clothes. But even though Vadim poured birdseed into her costumes and fired guns to scare them, the birds refused to do what they were supposed to. Eventually, after three days of trauma of being in a birdcage, she was taken to hospital to be treated for nausea, and the scene was reshot with lovebirds.

Their rambling fifteenth-century stone castle, Complesso di Santa Maria Nova, was set in an area of the Appia Antica sometimes referred to as 'millionaires' row', in an isolated spot at the end of the road, and surrounded by Cyprus and pine trees and ancient stone piles. It had no heat, a lack of hot water after the tank exploded, intermittent lighting and an elevator that got stuck between floors. There was also the odd sighting of rats.

> 'I'd heard about orgies, acid, a lot of drugs. I was never invited. I wanted to be.'

Fonda and Vadim shared the home with fourteen other guests. They included Jane's younger brother Peter Fonda; co-star John Phillip Law; Fonda's ex-boyfriend Andreas Voutsinas, hired as dialogue coach; Jean-Claude Forest and his wife; and cameraman Claude Renoir. Also staying at the villa were Vadim's two children, 9-year-old Nathalie and 3-year-old Christian, and their young Scottish nanny.

To look after the household, Jane had assistance from a cook, maid and butler, but it was a lot to take on and organise, particularly with the number of bodies coming and going. It was Jane who ensured the guest bedrooms were in order, with the right selection of books and magazines by their bed, and organised the packing when Vadim and his children and ex-wives came and went.

Their salon, where drinks were served, was a plush, exotic space of red silk sofas, blue velvet chairs, marble columns, gilded cherubs and wreaths, a huge fireplace and giant candelabra with a dozen candles on its limbs. It was a home that suited the exotic, eclectic style of the hippie-deluxe.

Over lunch one day, a visiting journalist noted the chaos – the food arriving two hours late, the children entertaining themselves by throwing bread pellets at guests, to their irritation. Jane looked at Vadim adoringly when he arrived late. Asking what the croquettes were made of, Jane replied that it was veal. He replied, 'why have veal when you know I like chicken?' The others were embarrassed enough to pretend not to hear, but it was clear that there would be chicken next time.

Members of the Rolling Stones dropped by, as did Brigitte Bardot, who was still on good terms with her ex-husband. There were many rumours that the home was a hotbed of drug-fused orgies. It came to represent something of a commune, particularly with Peter Fonda and his weed-smoking friends. Buck Henry, the screenwriter for *Catch-22*, to be directed by Mike Nichols, came by one evening. 'I'd heard about orgies, acid, a lot of drugs. I was never invited. I wanted to be.'

It may, of course, all have been conjecture. Fonda was disciplined, with her ballet lessons every morning, and she was described by the visiting journalist as, 'a nice girl – decent, friendly, polite, kind, generous, thoughtful, loyal'. They also had children present, which might have impinged upon the parties. Jane, however, was eager to please her new husband, whom she was desperately in love with. She adopted his philosophy and way of life, one where he declared he wished to 'eliminate all sense of guilt about the human body and all erotic complexes'. Jane Fonda was said to lack bitchiness and to have humility. As she explained in her memoirs, she would be a chameleon to the men in her life. 'I don't basically like marriage,' she said. 'But I think it would have been just as square to go on being an old unmarried couple. I belong to him, whether I'm married or not. Marriage is a commitment, the one step further. I think Vadim felt he needed to make that extra step.'

British photographer Paul Joyce was hired as set photographer for *Barbarella*. He said: 'The goings on there were an eye-opener … naked women appearing from behind balcony curtains chased by rock musicians with upraised members, cries and moans of pleasure and (I assumed) pain echoing around the Roman artifacts, all this and more.'

He recalled that The Rolling Stones visited the set with Anita Pallenberg, where the 'musty smell of marijuana hung over their colourful clothes'. Enigmatic Pallenberg, cast as the Great Tyrant, was considered a muse of the Rolling Stones, and a woman whose life could be chaotic and contagious. She had dated Brian Jones, but was now with Keith Richards, whom she would later have a child with. Anita had been born in Rome in 1942, and turned 18 in 1960 – just the right time to enjoy *la dolce vita* when it was in full swing. She hung out in fashionable, arty circles, where she met Federico Fellini and Luchino Visconti. In 1963 she went to New York, where she modelled and became immersed in Andy Warhol's factory in New York.

Keith Richards and Mick Jagger had been busted for drugs following a raid in London in February 1967. They were found guilty and sent to jail, but following an outcry were released at the end of July. Keith arrived in Rome to see Anita shortly after. Richards was said to have metamorphosed in style through Anita's influence, wearing scarves, applying kohl under his eyes, his hair worn in the multi-layered cuts with trinkets tied into it.

Anita was staying at a hotel at the top of the Spanish Steps, and they spent their time making hash brownies at Spaghetti-western actor Billy Berger's place, or hanging out with Italian pop artist Mario Schifano and political director Pier Paolo Pasolini. Keith recalled in his biography, *Life*, that:

> Anita's Roman world centered around the Living Theatre, the famous anarchist-pacifist troupe run by Judith Malina and Julian Beck, which had been around for years but was coming into its own in this period of activism and street demos. The Living Theatre was particularly insane, hard-core, its players often getting arrested on indecency charges.

He said it was an 'avant-garde elite drawn together by a taste for drugs'.

Anita ended up in prison in Rome for one night, after being pulled over for drugs when she was with the Living Theatre members. After swallowing a lump of hash to hide it from the police, she spent the night in jail extremely high, until she was bailed out in the morning.

Also cast in *Barbarella*, in a small role as a sultry revolutionary, was model and socialite Talitha Getty. If Jane Fonda represented the new Hollywood coming to Rome, a counterculture daughter of classic cinema, Talitha was considered a leading member of Rome's exclusive hippie jet-set. Talitha, with her golden red hair and dark eyes, was a sixties boho fashion icon who lived an enviable lifestyle which was regularly featured in *Vogue*. 'Talitha Getty is the stuff fashion is made of these days,' wrote the *Los Angeles Times*. 'She follows all the right unwritten rules. She doesn't want to look like anyone else. She dresses in bits and pieces from Italy, England, Saudi Arabia. Thailand or wherever.' She combined dresses from Ozzie Clark's London boutique with pieces she designed herself and items picked up on her travels – a silver cuff bracelet from Persia, good luck charms given to her by Nepalese children, a leather bracelet from a Syrian water carrier and luxury robes. Of course, one of her personal friends was jewellery designer Verdura, whom she could borrow expensive pieces from.

Talitha was born in Bali to Dutch artist Villen Pol, and was the step-daughter of British portrait painter Augustus John. She met John Paul Getty Junior, son of the billionaire oil baron, at a London party in 1965, where she had been living. He divorced his first wife Gail, with whom he had four children, the following year, and he and Talitha were married on 10 December 1966 in a simple civil wedding at Rome's City Hall, with the bride wearing a mink-trimmed miniskirt.

John Paul Getty Jr loved the *dolce vita* lifestyle of 1960s Rome, where he managed his father's oil interests in Italy, but spent boozy nights living like a Fitzgerald character with friends like writer Gore Vidal. He and Talitha travelled around the world on psychedelic benders, which horrified his conservative father when he read of their expolits in the papers. Talitha and Getty were sought-after for exclusive magazine spreads, posing all in white in their labyrinthine, candle-lit home in Marrakech for the *New York Times* magazine, appearing in *Vogue* and *Harper's Bazaar*, and photographed by Patrick Lichfield on the rooftop of their Moroccan home in their harem pants, kaftans and flowing robes.

The *Los Angeles Times* in 1969 visited their ten-room apartment in an old palazzo, up four double flights of stone steps and with a number of terraces to relax on. They lived with their young son, his nanny, a Persian cat, and a cook who visits daily. Their huge bathroom featured a mauve marble bath mounted on a dais, and was furnished with a potted palm, upholstered chairs and a large birdcage.

They had two living rooms which they would use for different guests. 'When we're entertaining square people,' Talitha said, they used the room furnished with bamboo, a rug from the Crystal Palace in London and pieces of modern art. For their friends, they entertained them in their living space, where there were two elephant chairs from India, silk tankas from Tibet and a shrine to Buddha with burning incense that filled the whole apartment with scent. Carved gold doors from a temple in Thailand opened into the bedroom.

In 1968 Getty Jr and Talitha had a son whom they named Tara Gabriel Galaxy Gramophone, but like many in their circle, they had descended into heroin addiction and in July 1971 the party came to an abrupt end when 31-year-old Talitha was found unconscious in her home, just across the road from the city hall where she had married almost five years before. She died shortly after in hospital; it was a heroin overdose. Her death occurred in the same period as those of Jim Morrison, Janis Joplin and Jimi Hendrix. At the time she was living apart from her husband. Paul Jr was devastated, and moved to London where he gave up the hedonistic lifestyle, instead becoming a recluse. They came to represent the glamorous underbelly of the sixties.

20

AUDREY

In the mid sixties the Ferrers moved from Bürgenstock to the village of Tolochenaz-sur-Morges on Lake Geneva, where Audrey bought an idyllic eighteenth-century stone farmhouse, La Paisible, fairy-book perfect with its blue shutters and clad in weeping ivy. Pregnant again in 1965, she pottered around their farmhouse and tended the garden as she prepared for the new baby. But she suffered another miscarriage and fell into great sadness. Sophia Loren had also lost a baby at the same time, and they wrote letters of consolation to each other.

Two for the Road and *Wait Until Dark*, released in 1967, would mark the end of her film career until the mid seventies. Motherhood was vital to her life and she enjoyed nothing more than waking up early in the morning, taking Sean to school and picking him up again. 'Success isn't so important for a woman,' said Audrey. 'And with the baby I felt I had everything a wife could wish for. But it's not enough for a man. It was not enough for Mel, He couldn't live with himself, just being Audrey Hepburn's husband.'

Mel and Audrey announced their separation in September 1967, and to lift her from the slump she was feeling at the end of a marriage she had thought was for life, she threw herself into the Rome social scene, relaxing with the European jet set. Her hair had been cut into a short, angular haircut by her hairdresser and friend Alberto De Rossi, and she looked fresh and sophisticated, suiting the geometric style of the mod fashions. Rome was not quite as fashionable as Milan, still catching up with Swinging London, but Audrey was one of the first of her aristocratic crowd to wear Mary Quant mini-dresses, her legs looking more slender than ever as she struggled with her happiness following her separation. She was photographed in a modish mini-dress with tennis stripes around the neckline, sleeves and pockets, with her large sunglasses on, as she wandered through Piazza di Spagna with her good friend Lorian Franchetti Gaetani, before climbing into a little Fiat.

Audrey spent much of her time in Rome with Lorian, also known as Contessa Lovatelli, wife of Count Lofreddo Lovatelli and sister of Afdera Franchetti. Afdera had married actor Henry Fonda in 1957, after being introduced by Audrey and Mel on the set of *War and Peace*. They had divorced in 1961, but Afdera remained very much part of the *la dolce vita* café society of the 1960s. Now that Audrey was single again, Afdera set her up on dates with figures from Rome's faded nobility, including Prince Alfonso de Bourbon. Audrey continued to go to some of Italy's film events. In 1968 she attended the Teatro Sistina for the Maschere d'Argento award presentations, where she met with Claudia Cardinale and Valentina Cortese.

Audrey was a guest at Lorian's house, the sixteenth-century Palazzo Lovatelli on Piazza Campitelli, for eight months during her divorce. Count Lofreddo felt protective of her, and like an Italian father, he tried to feed her spaghetti so she could put on weight.

Lorian organised dinner parties to introduce Audrey to European aristocratic figures, including the recently exiled King Constantine of Greece to Rome, and to Princess Olimpia Torlonia and her husband, French industrialist Paul-Annik Weiller. The Weillers adored Audrey so much that they invited her to join them on their yacht for a cruise around the Greek islands. Also on board was Dr Andrea Dotti, the 30-year-old son of Count and Countess Domenico Dotti, and a wealthy psychiatric assistant and Roman playboy. Audrey was attracted to the doctor and they spent their days chatting and swimming in the

Mediterranean Sea. They fell in love 'somewhere between Ephesus and Athens,' as Andrea recounted. 'We were playmates on a cruise ship with other friends, and slowly, day by day, our relationship grew into what it is.' After the cruise, Audrey invited him as her guest to the Lovatellis' Tuscany home on the Isola del Giglio, where she spent the rest of the summer of 1968.

Audrey was nine years older than Andrea, and while she was a little concerned about the age gap, she thought that he was just as mature as she was, that she was a youthful 39 and that age shouldn't be a limit to love. It may have been disconcerting that Andrea claimed to have met Audrey when he was 14 – she was filming *Roman Holiday* and he was a boy in the crowd who came up to her to shake her hand – but he had long admired her as an actress and beauty.

After a glorious, romantic summer, Andrea was busy with work during the week, but their weekends were spent together in Rome. Audrey enjoyed spending time with the large, colourful Dotti family, and his mother taught her Italian cooking in the Dotti's townhouse in Via della Barchetta, in Rome's old quarter. Audrey and Andrea were often photographed outside the heavy doors of the building as they waited to get in.

Dotti may have been dedicated to his career but he also liked to unwind at nightclubs, and found the glamour of her celebrity exciting. Audrey didn't really enjoy spending too long at nightspots, but to keep him company she attended his favourite clubs, pictured with her hair short and wavy, wearing a flower choker, and smoking a cigarette at a table filled with glasses and bottles of champagne.

Six months after their Greek island hopping, they spent Christmas 1968 together in Rome where Andrea presented her with a ruby engagement ring and a large solitaire diamond ring from Bulgari. Not wanting to have a long engagement, they married on 18 January 1969 in Morges town hall, just six weeks after the divorce from Mel came through.

The newly-weds spent a week together in Tolochenaz before continuing their honeymoon in Rome, while they searched for a terraced apartment. They found an historic penthouse just 500m away from Dotti's mother's home, and close to Ponte Vittorio, which 400 years before had been the home of a mistress of a cardinal. Their large, light and bright rooms overlooked the Tiber and Castel Sant' Angelo. Audrey painted the interiors in white and pale yellows with soft, billowing curtains, to provide an airy backdrop to their antiques and paintings – quite different to the normally heavy, ornate appearance of Rome apartments. All those other apartments looked like lasagna by comparison,' her friend Audrey Wilder once said.

Audrey simply wanted to be known as Signora Dotti, and to live an uncomplicated life as an Italian housewife, without any thought to returning to work. 'I don't have a secretary, I don't have attack dogs, I don't go to parties or official functions, and I answer my own phone,' she said. Yet life in Rome didn't always run smoothly, sometimes with no tap water coming into the house. 'From June to November I had no hot water,' she said. 'I had to bathe at my husband's office.'

She integrated herself into the Roman community by walking the streets hand in hand with Andrea, or taking Sean to his new school in Rome, the French Lycée Chateaubriand, and picking him up from the gates most days. She would shop on Via Frattina and Via Condotti, where she would experiment by visiting hip boutiques rather than solely wearing Givenchy. When she was looking for suggestions for a good Italian designer, Lorian recommended Valentino. Sergio Russo, a former assistant to Alexandre, the famous parisian stylist, became Audrey's Italian hairdresser.

From the late sixties into the early seventies, Audrey's style really adapted with the times. She was snapped in 1969 on the Via Borgognona with her good friend Doris Brynner, looking particularly fashionable in a mini shift dress and patterned tights. She mixed Givenchy with boho Valentino dresses with romantic ruffles, or a mini-dress with high-neck collars and sleeves, showcasing her preference for wearing Italian while in Rome. Her tweed jackets were made at a men's tailor, Cifonelli, and her favourite shoe designer had been Florentine San Ferragamo ever since she had met him in 1954.

Four months after their wedding, Audrey discovered she was expecting. Audrey relaxed into her pregnancy at the Gambrinus Beach

Club in Ostia for the first few months, but on orders from her doctor she retreated to La Paisible, her haven of peace and solitude. Dotti stayed on in Rome, and even while awaiting the birth of their child he continued to visit nightclubs, often accompanied by beautiful young women. It was difficult to hide from this, as he was often captured by the paparazzi coming out of clubs in the early hours, with the photos appearing in newspapers and magazines.

Audrey gave birth to her second son, Luca, on 8 February 1970 in Lausanne. The Dottis returned to Rome, where she devoted herself exclusively to being mother and wife, taking care of their apartment. 'Now Mia Farrow will get my parts,' she said, with no regrets at giving up her career to stay at her husband's side:

> It's sad if people think that's a dull world. But 'keeping house' is in a very real sense just that. You have to be there to contribute. You can't just buy an apartment and furnish it and walk away. It's the flowers you choose, the music you play, the smile you have waiting. I want it to be gay and cheerful, a haven in this troubled world. I don't want my husband and children to come home and find a rattled woman.

After having Luca, she enjoyed her motherhood in the city – she was spotted pushing the pram through Rome streets and she loved cooking Italian meals at home. Her favourite was *spaghetti alla puttanesca*, or 'slut's spaghetti', so named because the tomato, olive and anchovy sauce could easily be whipped up in brothels between clients.

There were lunches with friends at Trattoria Bolognese in Piazza del Popolo, dinners at La Fontanella Borghese, Romolo and La Casina Valadier, and she hosted supper parties in her penthouse for friends visiting Rome, like the Weillers and Gregory Peck, where her Sardinian cook Giovanna made traditional dishes for the guests, or cheesy *pasta al forno* for lively children's party.

Audrey had a small but close circle of good friends including Lorian Franchetti Gaetani and Laura Alberti who lived in Piazza Navona. One of her best friends, Doris Brynner, recalled that she wasn't a social person, and found the most joy in being home with her children:

That was where she wanted to be most. She was a great cook and loved her food. Yul (Brynner) didn't like pasta, so whenever he went on trips, Audrey would come to my house and we'd have pasta and vanilla ice cream and fudge sauce. That was our great treat.

Sunday's often involved the family escaping from the city to visit the beach at Fregene, where she had visited as a little girl, to Arcinazzo Romano, a quiet village and resort 50km from Rome or to Hadrian's Villa in Tivoli. Audrey enjoyed relaxing at Gambrinus Beach club in Ostia, where painted huts lining the beach were perfect for enjoying the sea views in comfort.

Her sanctuary was Switzerland, allowing an escape from the noise and pollution of Rome, but with Dotti's reluctance to give up his career in Rome, she sacrificed the safety of Switzerland for the city. When in Rome she would wake up early for Andrea to get off to his clinic by 7.30 a.m., and because he didn't return until 9 p.m. they ate dinner at 10 p.m. As someone who had to have sleep, she would take afternoon naps to make up for late nights. Audrey and Andrea moved from their big Via Del Consolato apartment, which could be hot and muggy in the summer, to a cooler apartment home at Via San Valentino 21, which caught the breeze from its elevated position north of the Villa Borghese.

> 'With the paparazzi in Rome, there is no privacy.'

Audrey was often photographed by the paparazzi as she walked through Rome – outside her husband's office on Via Crescenzio in a headscarf, sheepskin maxi coat and large sunglasses, shopping on Via Belsiana with crowds onlookers, carrying bags of pastries with the help of her driver Franco, or buying flowers from the florist in the Piazza di Spagna.

While she accepted the photographers as part of her life, it could be distressing when chased through Rome with her children, particularly with a toddler. 'I could take him nowhere, not to a park, not down the street, not put him on a terrace without paparazzi.' She said it was infuriating, 'to have photographers jump out from behind trees and he would be howling because he was so startled'. Sean remembers:

I would go out with my friends in my stepfather's Mercedes Convertible 220 xl which he had inherited and he would go out to the mountains for the weekends. I remember sitting in the back seat of the car with my friends and the paparazzi would chase us around in these Fiat 500s. My friends thought it was exciting being chased through the streets.

Sean recalled that there would be photographers sometimes at the gates of his *lycée*, and where his friends, from all walks of life, would at first be startled, but would soon get used to how normal their family life really was.

'The cities are not a place for you if you are famous,' Audrey said. 'With the paparazzi in Rome, there is no privacy.' She would escape to La Paisible when she could in order to avoid the intrusion, and where she felt she could truly be herself. Andrea, left to his own devices in Rome, continued to spend time in nightclubs. Even when she was in Rome he stayed out late while Audrey was at home looking after the children. Andrea's favorite clubs were Bella Blue, Rome's most chic private nightclub, and Jackie 0, nearby, where he would socialise with celebrities like Olivia de Havilland and Ringo Starr. He tried to shield himself as photographer Tony Menicucci captured photos of him leaving nightclubs at 2 a.m. in the company of Lorian's daughter, Coritelli Lovatelli, and Daniela Ripetti, model and star of *fotoromanzi* magazines. Daniela was infamous for interrupting a Beatles press conference in Milan, for spending a brief time in jail on drugs charges and for being engaged to Brian Jones of the Rolling Stones at one time.

One evening Andrea was coming out of a nightclub with Dalila di Lazzaro, when he spotted Menicucci as the flash went off. Andrea yelled at him, 'Don't you ever go to sleep? I don't want pictures!' Menicucci recounted that with Dalila particularly, he went mad, running to his car to hide her.

'Andrea's an extrovert. I'm an introvert. He needs people and parties, while I love being by myself, love being outdoors, love taking a long walk with my dogs and looking at trees, flowers, the sky,' Audrey excused. But it was deeply painful to her to know that the man she loved was philandering. Despite her humiliation Andrea defended himself, arguing that it was just what Italian husbands were like – never faithful.

Andrea's circle was the cream of European society and in the summer of 1972 they were all having a great time appearing in *Andy Warhol's Frankenstein*, directed by Paul Morrissey and filmed in Rome. People like Warhol, Franco Zefferelli and Roman Polanski were renting villas, and the new wave in-crowd spent time in the exclusive Parioli area, as they went out all night and slept during the day. Andrea's friends may have considered Audrey a bit of a drag and a square – she wasn't a gossip and she preferred an early night so that she could wake up early in the morning. Many of Audrey's friends were worried for Audrey and were concerned that Andrea was taking advantage of her love and her good nature, and that she turned down many film roles in order to look after him.

It was a very painful time for Audrey in Rome, and apart from the joy brought by her children, it was quite different from the blissful days in the city during the filming of *Roman Holiday* and *War and Peace*. The maids in her home, including chef and good friend Giovanna, tried to protect her by hiding the newspaper articles which featured photos of Andrea with other women. But Andrea even brought his 'girlfriends' back to their apartment on a couple of occasions.

'I think she knew soon enough that she had married a wonderful man, but that he was not reliable,' says her son Sean:

He was a typical Italian male of the era. They'd go for dinner, and she would be tired and want to go home to sleep, but he would want to go and have a few drinks with friends and he would be out all night. She found out from family, the maids, they told her what they knew, he was not very discreet, and two times he brought them to the house. The maids made breakfast for the girlfriends. It's not a very delicate thing to do. And so I think, the marriage lasted very short time, maybe three years, four years, at which point I was off to boarding school. She tried to keep things together for her little boy, my half brother.

Audrey also began to be fearful of kidnapping, particularly as it became more prolific with news of the kidnapping of John Paul Getty III. He was the teenage son of John Paul Getty, at boarding school in England while his father and stepmother Talitha lived their life of exotic hedonism. After being expelled from school in 1971 when he took inspiration from Charles Manson to paint the hallways, he came to Rome to be with his father. But the death by heroin overdose of Talitha had a devastating effect, and he was left to live alone in the city when his father returned to England. After being snatched by a mafia organisation, his ear was cut off and delivered to his family to push for his billionaire grandfather to pay the ransom. Eventually he was released by his kidnappers, but it was a distressing time in Rome, with persistent rumours of tourists being kidnapped for $50, with car thefts and apartment break-ins.

'Two years ago, the joy of Rome was to walk around in the streets at night,' Audrey said in 1974. 'Not anymore. The whole world has changed.'

21

ELIZABETH

The Via Veneto, once considered the most glittering street in Italy, had by 1973 become a parody. It was now filled with tourists who were too late to the party, who instead of mingling with Anita Ekberg or Federico Fellini or Michelangelo Antonioni, could only observe the prostitutes and hustlers that prowled the street. The street was once packed with crowds of people until dawn, but by the 1970s the sidewalk cafés during the winter were cordoned in with sheets of glass, where the wealthy watched the action of the street through a screen – as if it was no longer tangible.

By 1973, business owners on the Via Veneto announced a campaign of protest against the dirt, prostitution and neglect which they saw as destroying the attraction of this once elegant street. The Via Veneto Merchants' Association called on the police to tackle what they considered to be the increasingly brazen male and female prostitutes.

The decline of the street was evident in the lack of the paparazzi present, with most of those original photographers said to have found steady jobs and had all but given up the excitement of the street. Elio Sorci retired in the early seventies to spend time with his family. Felice Quinto, injured by Anita Ekberg's bow and arrow, moved to the United States in 1963, working for the Associated Press and then as a photographer for Studio 54. Ivan Kroscenko was a Russian photographer who arrived in Rome in the mid 1950s, having been a Russian soldier who defected to the West after the Second World War. He was one of the top paparazzo during the 1960s, and spoke to a journalist at the Café de Paris, saying, 'the stars are finished. The values have shifted. There is a lot of confusion. Everybody's a celebrity but nobody's a celebrity. Scandal has become mundane. Perhaps readers are too sophisticated.'

The 1970s were a politically fraught time for Rome, particularly for the wealthy who lived in fear of kidnappings. The period from the late 1960s until the early 1980s became known as the Years of Lead, defined by political and social unrest and terrorism. When President Richard Nixon visited Rome in summer 1970 there were waves of protests from Roman youths, acting out against capitalism and America as its symbol, and the horrors of the Vietnam War. Protesters broke the windows of the American Express office in the Piazza di Spagna, while others threw a rock through the window of Harry's Bar on the Via Veneto, a symbol of the decadence of the jet-set. The Secret Service locked down the American Embassy and took extra precautions against the threat of kidnapping of the president.

The Red Brigades, a guerilla movement founded in 1970 by two students at the University of Trento, aimed to break down the state by creating fear and terror. They began by sabotaging the Siemens, Pirelli and Fiat factories in the North of Italy and after expanding in numbers, spread to Rome in 1974 and where they evolved into bank robberies, kidnappings and arms trafficking.

After John Paul Getty III's kidnap, Audrey Hepburn was worried about the safety of her sons, and she began to think that Sean and Luca were being followed. Andrea refused to give up his clinic and teaching in Rome, and one day he was attacked outside his clinic by four men in ski masks who jumped out of a Mercedes and he believed, tried to bundle him into their car. His struggles caught the attention of guards at the Egyptian embassy, but he was hit on the head with the gun and his attackers fled. Andrea was taken to hospital for seven stitches in his head. Sean Ferrer remembers:

My mother was terrified for me. If I was kidnapped it would be something that would mark me for the rest of my life. They had a conversation, I heard her talking about it all night long with her husband, and the next morning she said, 'look, it's going to be one of two ways, either you go to boarding school in Switzerland or you will have to go around with a bodyguard. Which do you prefer?' She was very democratic that way. 'I said what do you prefer?' And she said 'well honesty, even though I won't see you as much you will have a better quality of life in a place where you don't have to hang around with a bodyguard.' So I went, and within a couple of weeks I was in school.

However, the attack wasn't quite was it had initially seemed. Sean recalls: 'It emerged later on that this was not an attempted kidnapping, but my stepfather's infidelities with a married woman, and the husband had hired two thugs to teach him a lesson. So his infidelities caused me to lose four years of my family life.'

Audrey had put her career on hold for husband and family, but in 1975 when she was offered a part in *Robin and Marian*, with location shooting in Spain, it appealed enough to her to accept it. Audrey returned to Rome at weekends, but while she was away Andrea would continue to be photographed by paparazzi in nightclubs with other women. She explained:

> He's done it all his life. It's not as if all of a sudden he's breaking out at the age of thirty-seven to go to nightclubs. It's his way of relaxing, and I think it's important for him to feel free. I don't expect him to sit in front of the TV when I'm not there. It's much more dangerous for a man to be bored.

To try to preserve the marriage she accepted that perhaps they could have an open relationship. 'It's inevitable, when the man is younger,' she said. However, her husband's infidelities became too much, and after Sean went to boarding school in 1975, Audrey moved to another apartment with Luca at Via Ceracchi 4, after buying it off her close friend and press relations manager Arabella Ungaro. Sean adds that

Audrey 'decided to stay in Rome as my little brother loved being in Rome and seeing his dad a little bit. But he was not very reliable as a husband, and not very reliable as a father either.' They finally divorced in September 1980 and Audrey moved to her permanent home in Switzerland with Robert Wolder, her final partner until her death in 1992.

One weekend after her separation, Audrey took 18-year-old Sean to the Spoleto Festival in Tuscany, and her son, with a beard, looked older than his age. When the paparazzi took a few shots, it was splashed in the papers the next day with the caption that Audrey was pictured with her new love. 'Well apart from the 'new', for once they got something right,' she said.

〰〰〰〰〰〰

Sophia Loren was also feeling threatened in Rome, as the safety of the city shifted. But it wasn't just Rome that felt dangerous. In October 1970, Sophia was staying at the Hampshire House in New York when she was robbed by three armed, masked men who held a gun to her head and took away a million dollars worth of jewellery. 'When I held Cipi in my arms again, I was taught the biggest lesson in my life,' she said. 'Believe me, I have deleted the word jewelry from my vocabulary. To own something which could make people resort to murder and kidnapping is a threat not a possession.'

The Ponti's 50-room home in Marino, the 'most beautiful house in the world', was beginning to feel less secure. It was in an isolated place, and attracted petty thieves and even fans with mental issues. One incident involved a man who had escaped from a psychiatric institution and after having crept into their garden, yelled that Cipi was his son and had come to take him away. He escaped from the psychiatric hospital on several occasions and sent strange letters, and while they kept an eye on where he was, a certain uneasiness crept into their lives – especially with the kidnappings that marked that period. Carlo, on his way home from his office, was driving down the Appia Antica when a car swerved in front of him, cutting him off. Another car blocked the road from behind, and a man with a covered face, and holding a rifle, jumped out and ran in his direction. Carlo slammed down on the accelerator, dodged the car that blocking his way, and ducked down as shots were fired. When he got home he saw his Alfa Romeo had been sprayed with bullets. It happened a second time on the Appia Antica, when a car tried to run him off the road, and hidden in the bushes was a van with its engine running and with ropes, chloroform, tape He was saved by the police security that arrived on the scene.

With deep concerns around crime in Rome, Sophia and Carlo moved permanently into their triplex penthouse on Avenue George V in Paris. Carlo was still working during the week in Rome, but flew back to Paris for the weekends where they spent evenings in bathrobes, watching television hand in hand. They would lament 'siamo senza terra', of not having a safe place that was their own home, and missing Italy and their villa and their family.

While she was in Rome, Sophia had slowed down her career for her two sons, but when she took on the role in *The Voyage* in 1973 it would be the eighth and last time she would be directed by Vittorio De Sica, her mentor, father figure and champion. There seemed to be a feeling of death hanging over the film. De Sica was old and tired and would soon be diagnosed with lung cancer. Sensing it was his final film, she asked him for a signed autograph, which he presented to her, reminiscing about their first meeting at Cinecittà when she was just 15. It was the last time she saw him. Co-starring with Sophia in *The Voyage* was Richard Burton, who was invited to stay in the guesthouse of Sophia's villa while he was going through a separation from Elizabeth.

Throughout 1969 the Burtons argued and griped, drinking too much and coming close to breaking up. Richard reflected heavily on the choice he made between his daughter Kate and Elizabeth. He wrote in his diary that even though he loved them both, 'perhaps I shall never forgive myself' for choosing Elizabeth. Elizabeth took pills to ease her chronic back pain, and regularly began the day with vodka and orange for breakfast, a ritual that she had picked up from Richard. She felt mistrustful of her husband, worried that he could cheat on her with one of his beautiful co-stars.

They had lived through all the headlines – the stories of their time on Via Veneto, bathing on the sun-kissed decks of their yachts off Capri – yet they retained a certain old-fashioned glamour. In Portofino in August 1970 they tried desperately to evade the crowds of gawkers, but their yacht was surrounded from morning until night by pedalos, swimmers, motorboats and even cruise ships, while the paparazzi, hiding in the bushes above their anchor point, held their long lenses on them.

On 13 August 1971, on one of their Mediterranean cruises, they returned to Porto Santo Stefano and visited the café by the harbour where they had stopped for cognacs and coffee during the Easter Weekend in 1962. They reminisced about that near-fatal trip, where they had violently fought and she had taken sleeping pills. He grimly thought, 'By god, what if she'd died. Worse what if she'd lived with an impaired brain?'

Elizabeth later watched *Cleopatra* on board the *Kalizma* as they stopped at Capri, and on reflection it wasn't so bad – quite a spectacle of filming, she thought. They moored off Ischia, opposite the Isabella Regina hotel, 'where we used to live in sin while locating for *Cleopatra*. We went ashore to the pizzeria which we used to do then.' They attempted to do shopping but were forced back to the yacht when the crowds swelled around them.

'Maybe we loved each other too much – I never believed such a thing was possible.'

In November 1971 they returned to Rome and visited Valentino's for lunch, on Via del Babuino, as the still-novice designer was making Elizabeth's gown for the Rothschild's ball at Ferrieres, which would be attended by Grace of Monaco and the Duchess of Windsor. They stayed at the Grand Hotel, and noted the streams of traffic along the Via Veneto, the sirens and horns blasting 'Everyday here seems to be a day of demonstrations,' Richard noted:

Yesterday it was something to do with the Coca-Cola factories which, presumably in despair with the endless strikes, have closed down entirely. This morning there was a tremendous hullaballoo about 'no repression schools' which I don't understand and, since the local papers never or hardly ever mention the demonstrations I don't know what the protest marches are about. Italian friends confess to being equally baffled though we can hardly expect couturiers like Valentino and Tiziani to be much interested in social disputes. They only deal with the very rich.

Angered by Richard's flirting while filming *Bluebeard* in 1972, Elizabeth flew to Rome to meet Aristotle Onassis for dinner. Photographer Kroscenko was part of a group of paparazzi who staged a siege on the Hostaria dell' Orso to get past security and capture a shot of Elizabeth Taylor dining with Onassis. It was one of his final spectacular images of that era. On 4 July 1973 Elizabeth released a statement confirming that she and Burton were separating. 'Maybe we loved each other too much – I never believed such a thing was possible.'

Richard wanted to get into shape and stopped drinking in preparation for his role in *The Voyage*, and staying at the Ponti villa allowed him to escape from the paparazzi that gathered around Rome's major hotels. He arrived at Villa Ponti with his entourage, including a doctor, as he tried to stay away from drink.

Richard found he could think of no one else but Elizabeth, and as he sat on the terrace eating lunch with Sophia and her children, she listened to him patiently. He was nervous and on edge from his detox but was still charming, intelligent, and had a genuine connection with children. He played around the pool with Cipi and the two bonded – an odd but charming pair.

Elizabeth also arrived in Rome to film *The Driver's Seat*, and was keen to see Richard, even though they were going through divorce proceedings. She arrived on 20 July at Fiumicino airport, looking vibrant and healthy in jeans and an orange t-shirt, with the huge diamond ring on her finger commanding attention. She was met by Richard in his Rolls Royce, and after kissing passionately for the benefit of the excited paparazzi they were driven away at high-speed, their car protected by a security procession as a chain of motorbikes followed them.

Sophia had extended the invitation to Elizabeth to also to stay at their villa, but the Burtons began arguing before they had even arrived. Elizabeth left Richard to sort out the luggage from the car while she went ahead and climbed up the steps to the villa. Sophia was reading a book on the terrace, and they greeted warmly, Sophia telling her how gorgeous she looked. Despite the compliments, Elizabeth harboured jealousy when it came to her hostess, who Richard would describe in gushing terms of her body like an 'erotic dream' and her 'vulpine, satanic face'.

Over the week at the Pontis, Elizabeth accused Richard of flirting with Sophia, and of having an affair with his Milanese co-star of *The Voyage*, Annabella Incontrera. Sophia's maternal instincts meant she tried to soothe the warring couple and she warned Elizabeth, after hearing the grumbles and the accusations, that all this suspicion was not a good sign of a marriage that could last.

Elizabeth left the Ponti villa after a week and checked into a seven-room suite at the Grand Hotel, the day before she was to begin filming *The Driver's Seat*. That night she ordered drinks from room service, and the next day didn't turn up to the set until 5 p.m. Knowing that her marriage was now over, she felt as devastated and as raw as when Mike Todd died.

While staying at the Grand Hotel she began dating Henry Wynberg, who would take her out dancing and partying. He was more fun than Richard, who was trying to give up drinking and preferred to avoid Rome's night spots. As she was photographed around the Via Veneto with Henry, she fully played up to the paparazzi.

Richard and Elizabeth reunited in Rome for New Year celebrations, and while they tried to make their marriage work, they announced once again, in April 1974, they were getting a divorce.

Elizabeth, Sophia wrote, was 'a rogue wave, a loose electron, an arrow aimed straight for his ailing heart'; they couldn't stay away from one another. They married again in October 1975, but all their jealousies and arguments and drinking problems came to the surface, and they divorced once more. Richard went on to marry glamorous blonde Sally Hunt, while Elizabeth would briefly find herself as a politician's wife, when she married John Warner.

'Wrinkles on your face are bearable, you know. Especially if you've enjoyed yourself enough while you still didn't have them. But wrinkles in the brain, what a horror!' Anna Magnani once said. She hadn't minded getting older, but had hoped her mind would always remain sharp. However, she began feeling unwell and was diagnosed with pancreatic cancer. Magnani and Roberto Rossellini may not have talked for many years, but when he heard that she was seriously ill he sent flowers to her hospital, and after she asked if he would come to visit her, he visited her regularly until she passed away in 1973. She was only 65 years old. For her funeral, huge crowds gathered in the streets of Rome and around the church, watching the procession as Rossellini, a loyal friend at the end, followed the coffin. 'She was so loved by the Italian people,' said Ingrid Bergman. 'So many people that couldn't all get into the church. And when the coffin was carried out they applauded. I think that's so moving. You could only do that in Italy.' Because Magnani didn't have her own plot in the graveyard, Roberto brought her to their family grave.

Rossellini's life had been cursed with court battles and custody disputes, money worries and bad publicity around his relationships. He had suffered a lack of recognition for his arthouse films, despite his ground-breaking neorealist works, and that had been wounding to him. He died from a sudden heart attack four years after Magnani, in 1977.

1993 saw the loss of Federico Fellini, the director responsible for the term 'paparazzi'. After his death, it seemed ironic, or possibly quite fitting, that a paparazzo bribed his way into the Rome hospital and photographed his dead body.

That joyful, aggressive, hedonistic celebrity culture in Rome may have faded, but the Trevi Fountain still whispered memories of Anita Ekberg splashing in the water, as tourists to the city hoped they could feel some of that magic amongst the baroque marble.

INDEX